Follow the Money

Follow the Money

How Foundation Dollars Change
Public School Politics

SARAH RECKHOW

OXFORD
UNIVERSITY PRESS

OXFORD
UNIVERSITY PRESS

Oxford University Press is a department of the University of Oxford.
It furthers the University's objective of excellence in research, scholarship,
and education by publishing worldwide.

Oxford   New York
Auckland   Cape Town   Dar es Salaam   Hong Kong   Karachi
Kuala Lumpur   Madrid   Melbourne   Mexico City   Nairobi
New Delhi   Shanghai   Taipei   Toronto

With offices in
Argentina   Austria   Brazil   Chile   Czech Republic   France   Greece
Guatemala   Hungary   Italy   Japan   Poland   Portugal   Singapore
South Korea   Switzerland   Thailand   Turkey   Ukraine   Vietnam

Oxford is a registered trade mark of Oxford University Press
in the UK and certain other countries.

Published in the United States of America by
Oxford University Press
198 Madison Avenue, New York, NY 10016

Library of Congress Cataloging-in-Publication Data
Reckhow, Sarah.
Follow the money : how foundation dollars change public school politics / Sarah Reckhow.
    p. cm. –(Oxford studies in postwar American political development)
Includes bibliographical references and index.
ISBN 978–0–19–993773–8 (hardcover); 978–0–19–022734–0 (paperback)
1. Public schools—United States—Finance.   2. Privatization in education—
United States.   I. Title.
LB2825.R394 2013
379.1'3—dc23
2012018098

To Matt and Norah

CONTENTS

ACKNOWLEDGMENTS

I had valuable support and guidance on this project from colleagues, friends, and family. I could not have completed this book without the input and encouragement I received at Berkeley and Michigan State and from dozens of informants and experts in New York City and Los Angeles. This project began while I was at Berkeley, where my mentor, Margaret Weir, supported my work in countless ways. I thank her for her encouragement, thoughtful guidance, and the opportunities she has offered me to develop as a scholar. Cynthia Coburn contributed much needed expertise on education policy and the workings of school districts. Taeku Lee offered support and helpful insights that strengthened my analysis. Without Chris Ansell, I may never have started this research. Chris brought me in as a research assistant for a project on Oakland school reform, which opened my eyes to the important role of major foundations in urban school districts, and he taught me how to do social network analysis. I had many long and helpful conversations with colleagues at Berkeley, including Veronica Herrera, Margaret Boittin, Miguel de Figueiredo, Crystal Chang, Danielle Lussier, John Hanley, Peter Hanson, Dave Hopkins, Amanda Hollis-Brusky, Andrew Kelly, Jennifer Bussell, Thad Dunning, and Lee Drutman. I am grateful to the National Science Foundation for funding that supported my research.

At Michigan State, my colleagues have read chapters, critiqued methods, and offered their support. I am grateful to Ric Hula, Laura Reese, Cynthia Jackson-Elmoore, Sandy Schneider, Josh Sapotichne, Cory Smidt, Eric Juenke, Ani Sarkissian, Jeff Conroy-Krutz, Dan Lee, Cristina Bodea, Ryan Black, Mark Axelrod, Zachary Neal, Rebecca Jacobsen, and Jeff Snyder. I also benefited from invaluable assistance in preparing the manuscript from Benjamin Evans and Megan Johnson.

My work on this project was also guided by input from a broader network of scholars who study urban politics, education policy, social networks, and philanthropy. In particular, I would like to thank Jeff Henig for his interest in this project and valuable feedback. Many others have offered their time, resources, guidance, and support as I completed this book, including Clarence Stone, John Mollenkopf, Rick Hess, Katy Bulkley, Constancia Warren, Diane Ravitch, Priscilla Wohlstetter, Jennifer Jennings, Norm Fruchter, Richard Arum, Jeannie Oakes, Michael Heaney, David Cohen, Megan Tompkins-Stange, and Shayna Klopott. I am also incredibly grateful to dozens of people in New York City and Los Angeles who took the time to speak with me about their involvement in education policy.

During the transition from manuscript to publication, I received essential assistance and feedback from Steven Teles, the series editor. He showed an interest in this project early on, and I am grateful for his support. I would also like to thank my editor at Oxford, David McBride, and two anonymous reviewers.

I am living proof that the apple does not fall far from the tree. My mom, Ellen Reckhow, has served as a county commissioner in Durham, North Carolina, since 1988. Local politics frequently dominated our dinner table conversations. In 1992, my mom voted with the majority on her board to merge the predominantly black Durham City school system with the predominantly white Durham County school system. This decision, which was highly controversial at the time, sparked my interest in education politics at a young age. My mom's passion for public service and her particular dedication to education and youth have motivated me to focus on public education in my own career. My dad, Ken Reckhow, is a scientist and academic. With my dad, I never know when a question about a book he is reading will lead to an hour-long discussion about the particulars of scientific research applied to tough public policy issues. These discussions taught me a great deal about the complex relationship between research and the world of politics. My brother, Michael, is always a source of good conversation and tough questions. For all these reasons and many more, I thank my family for their guidance, support, and love.

I owe a very large thank you to Matt Grossmann, my loving husband. He has endured hours of debate and discussion on the findings contained in these pages. His insights often push me to ask new questions or pursue directions I thought were unfeasible or unnecessary. Very often, this leads me to valuable new findings. I thank him for challenging me, for supporting me, and for his unconditional love. Last, I would like to thank my daughter, Norah, who adds joy and wonder to my life every day.

Follow the Money

Introduction: The Boardroom Progressives

The bully pulpit for promoting new ideas in American public education has moved out West. In November 2008, after a hard-fought presidential election, the leading national figures in education did not gather in Washington, D.C., to hear an address from President-elect Barack Obama. Instead, urban school district superintendents, current and former governors, the secretary of education, presidents of both national teachers' unions, and leaders in the education nonprofit world convened in Seattle, Washington, to hear Bill Gates and Melinda Gates speak about the new education priorities of the Bill and Melinda Gates Foundation.

A gathering of national education leaders at the home of the world's largest private foundation, rather than the seat of the national government, is emblematic of a new education reform movement driven largely by private actors. A new cohort of "Boardroom Progressives"—officers in major national foundations, leaders of education nonprofits, charter school founders, and nontraditional urban superintendents—are leading a charge to reform public education. Due to national press coverage, leaders of education nonprofits such as Geoffrey Canada of the Harlem Children's Zone, charter school organization founders such as Steve Barr of Green Dot Public Schools, celebrity school district leaders such as Michelle Rhee and Joel Klein, and foundation heads such as Bill Gates and Eli Broad have been the public faces of this movement. Many of these figures were featured in the 2010 documentary film *Waiting for "Superman,"* a call to arms for education reform that was heavily supported by the Gates Foundation.

Recalling the Progressives of the early 20th century, many Boardroom Progressives represent elite segments of society.[1] They also share a suspicious view of the role of politics and special interests in education policy, as well as a common sense of idealism. Both sets of Progressives have focused on the nation's large urban areas, regarding cities as the places most in need of radical reform.[2] Yet the Boardroom Progressives are driven by a new set of expectations in public education. A century ago, many Progressive reformers asserted that public schools ought to sort students into "appropriate" roles in the emerging industrial economy, from corporate titans to workers on the assembly line.[3] The terrible consequences of this approach, particularly for African American children, have been well documented.[4] Today, the public-school-as-sorting-machine model has been turned on its head, and the new standard is clearly spelled out as No Child Left Behind.[5] All children can learn, and all children must have an opportunity for an excellent education.

The policy agenda of the Boardroom Progressives has largely been drawn from the two dominant streams of policy ideas in education reform since the 1990s: accountability and markets. The pursuit of accountability involves close tracking of student achievement on standardized tests with new data systems, censuring or closing schools that fail to demonstrate improved test scores and graduation rates, and evaluating teachers based on value-added assessments of student achievement to distribute rewards, such as merit pay.[6] A testing agenda was also touted by the early-20th-century Progressives, though the purpose was sorting students, rather than evaluating teachers, schools, and districts.[7] The use of markets involves opening up public schools to private and nonprofit service providers, increasing public school choice, and creating scores of new charter schools.[8] This set of reforms is a clear break from the hierarchical school bureaucracy idealized by many early-20th-century Progressives.[9] Boardroom Progressives are impatient with public bureaucracies and have focused their efforts on creating a broad network of private and nonprofit alternatives for developing and running schools.[10]

The early-20th-century Progressive reformers did more than change education policy; their activities also had far-reaching consequences for education politics, particularly in large cities. Their reforms included efforts to depoliticize education by planning school board elections in off years and giving unelected administrative professionals control over school operations.[11] Instead of removing politics from education, these changes fostered a particularly insulated form of politics in urban education, dominated by education bureaucrats and a limited set of interest groups.[12] The Boardroom Progressives are also deeply skeptical about the role of politics in education, but the political strategies of the Boardroom Progressives differ in key ways. Early-20th-century Progressives regarded mayors as corrupt machine politicians who should be kept far away from education. Boardroom Progressives want mayors to take on a greater role in urban schools. Early-20th-century Progressives sought to build a strong centralized bureaucracy to govern and operate schools. Boardroom Progressives are working to streamline or even dismantle these bureaucracies by supporting competition and allowing private-sector organizations to run schools. The original Progressive reforms shaped urban education politics for much of the 20th century. What are the consequences of the Boardroom Progressive reforms for urban education politics today?

The Boardroom Progressive movement involves a diverse set of actors—charter school leaders, urban superintendents, and nonprofit founders. Yet private wealth has been an essential resource for supporting many of these leaders and their initiatives. Major foundations, such as the Gates Foundation, Broad Foundation, Carnegie Corporation, and Walton Family Foundation, have financed the development of a new organizational infrastructure in education policy, including charter schools, advocacy organizations, education consulting and research organizations, and countless nonprofits. Without private funding, many of these organizations would not exist. In large urban districts, major foundations distribute grants to promote new policies, implement new programs, create new organizations, and engage in other activities that directly shape the policy direction of the district. Without private funding, urban district leaders would have little reason to divert public funds to risky new initiatives.

Understanding the changing role of philanthropy in urban education is the first step in tracing the political consequences of Boardroom Progressive education reform. The research for this book was motivated by four questions about the relationship between philanthropy and urban education, in order to understand the political consequences of this new education reform movement. First, where and how do major foundations get involved in trying to reform urban education? Second, when foundations become involved in urban education, which local actors stand to gain influence in education policy, and which actors are likely to lose influence? These two questions focus on the basic mechanisms of foundation influence in education—the places where foundations concentrate their resources and the local partners that may benefit from foundation funds. The final two questions move beyond these mechanisms to investigate the political consequences of foundation influence. How do local constituencies respond to foundation-funded policy reforms, and do these reforms foster a supportive political coalition? What are the implications of foundation involvement in urban education for democratic decision making and political accountability in urban school districts?

The Need for Research

Researchers have recently noted the growing importance of major foundations in education policy, but scholars have not systematically examined how foundations influence education politics and policy making or the consequences of their involvement. One important exception to the relative silence in the literature is an edited volume by Frederick Hess of the American Enterprise Institute, which focuses on philanthropic influence in K-12 education. According to Hess, foundations have become more openly political in their efforts to influence education policy:

> When donors are not giving simple gifts to a school or district but are advocating particular policies or models of reform—especially when they dangle large sums contingent upon public officials adopting those proposals—the role of the philanthropist has changed. No longer merely a private citizen making a private contribution, donors are now engaged in an effort to reshape public education, alter public policy, and redirect public expenditures.[13]

Given the increasingly public and political role of foundations, the limited body of research is even more striking. Not only have academics neglected to closely investigate philanthropic activities but also foundations have faced little scrutiny from journalists.[14]

When foundations do receive attention, particularly in the news media, the coverage is largely positive. Hess analyzed coverage in major newspapers of the Annenberg Challenge, Broad Foundation, Gates Foundation, Milken Family Foundation, and Walton Family Foundation. This content analysis of 146 articles revealed that only 5 were critical of the foundations' role in education and 65 were positive; the remaining articles were judged to be either neutral or primarily factual.[15] Meanwhile, academics are well acquainted with foundations as important patrons for their work and are sometimes hired by foundations to evaluate programs. As a result, "researchers have reasons of their own for being cautious when the question is the design or outcomes of philanthropic initiatives."[16] Furthermore, the limited inquiry into foundations by the press and academics may be a consequence of the lack of transparency in the philanthropic sector. Foundations are famously unwilling to disclose grant-making initiatives that they view as "failures."[17] Some foundations report all of their grants on their Web sites or in their annual reports, but many do not. This information does not become publicly available until foundation tax returns are released, often two years after the grants were distributed. Thus, although there may be scholars and journalists who would like to investigate philanthropic activities more closely, foundations are private organizations, which often keep their decision-making processes and evaluations of their work hidden from public view.

In light of the mismatch between significant foundation involvement in education policy and the rather small body of research on foundations, the calls for expanding our knowledge have become stronger. According to Hess, "It is in the interest of both philanthropists and the larger public that skeptical observers step forward and offer gimlet-eyed assessments of philanthropic initiatives."[18]

Echoing this sentiment in her book *The Death and Life of the Great American School System*, Diane Ravitch argues, "This 'conspiracy of silence' makes it all the more imperative that journalists, scholars, and public officials carefully scrutinize the long-term vision and activities of the major foundations, as well as their changes over time."[19] Scholars are beginning to respond to these calls for research to assess the consequences of philanthropy for K-12 education, including the effectiveness of philanthropic initiatives for improving student achievement. The research presented in this book focuses on how philanthropy impacts public policy and politics.

From Foundation Grants to Political Change

This book combines a big picture perspective on foundation grant making in education—using an original data set of more than 2,800 major foundation grants—with a close examination of foundation influence inside the two largest school districts—New York City and Los Angeles. The analytic approach relies on multiple methods of research: large-scale data analysis, detailed case studies, and social network analysis. With the foundation grant data, I assess the relationship between foundation grant making and school district characteristics. The case studies of New York City and Los Angeles involved broad surveys of education policy leaders in each city, as well as 37 in-depth interviews. Using the surveys and interviews, I analyzed attitudes toward policy reforms and the role of foundations in each district. Additionally, I used the surveys to gather data on relationships among leaders in education policy in each city. By applying social network analysis to examine these relationships, I show how foundations are connected to key local actors involved in education policy. This multimethod approach goes beyond a surface-level assessment of foundations and their grants to closely track the influence of foundations and grantees in the complex environment of large urban school districts.

The findings presented in this book offer three major contributions to show how foundations have changed urban education policy and politics. First, I show that foundations have targeted millions of grant dollars to a small group of districts with political features that enable greater foundation influence. Using original data on the 15 largest K-12 education grant makers, I track foundation grants to the 100 largest school districts and show that mayoral or state control of a district has a strong relationship with higher levels of foundation grants. In these districts, the mayor or state officials have replaced or diminished the power of elected school boards. Second, I demonstrate how foundation grant making has shaped and expanded the nonprofit sector in education by empowering new actors at the local level to influence education policy. With the foundation grant data, I explain how foundation funding has shifted away from direct support to public schools toward funding for nonprofits and charter schools. Focusing on New York City and Los Angeles, I use social network analysis to show the influence of specific foundation-supported nonprofit and charter school organizations. In New York City, foundation grantees are closely linked to the school district leadership but insulated from parent groups and advocacy organizations. In Los Angeles, the core of the policy network is more diverse, with foundation grantees such as charter schools sharing policy information with local advocacy groups. I provide additional details about foundation influence and involvement in urban education policy based on my interviews with local education leaders. Third, I argue that foundation-funded reforms in Los Angeles are more sustainable and enjoy broader community support than foundation-supported policies in New York City. Foundations have generally favored districts like New York City that have mayoral control over the schools, but Los Angeles—a district governed by an elected school board—appears to have greater community investment in foundation-funded reforms.

Education reforms in New York City and Los Angeles involve a range of new market-based policies that were promoted and supported by foundations. The most extensive market-based policies in each district were public school choice, involving small schools in New York City and charter schools in Los Angeles. In New York City, the development and implementation of market-oriented policies remained tightly controlled by the mayoral-appointed chancellor and school district administration. The groups that invested time and resources in the new policies were those with close ties to the district administration. In Los Angeles, the development and implementation of market-based policies evolved through a more open, though sometimes chaotic, process. The more open structure of the policy process in Los Angeles engaged a wide range of actors who invested considerable time and resources in the new market-oriented policies.

My comparison between New York City and Los Angeles shows that foundations have mistakenly focused their funding on top-down education reform initiatives, primarily in districts with mayoral or state control. In New York City, centralized political control and the use of private resources have enabled rapid implementation of reform proposals. However, this potent combination of political authority and outside funding also poses serious questions about transparency, responsiveness, and democratic accountability in New York City. Furthermore, the implementation of reforms in New York City has neglected to engage a broad range of stakeholders and garner their investments in policy reforms.

Meanwhile, a slower, but possibly more transformative set of reforms is taking place in Los Angeles. Foundation involvement in Los Angeles is not intentionally oriented to build a grassroots movement; foundations are supporting charter schools in Los Angeles because this conforms to their national priorities, including school choice and competition. Yet charter schools and other market-oriented policies in Los Angeles have enabled some new forms of political involvement and organizing around education, and the elected board in Los Angeles continues to shape the overall policy direction of the district. This combination has built grassroots political momentum and investment in reform policies in Los Angeles that is unmatched in New York City and other districts with mayoral or state control.

Policy Feedback and Civic Capacity

To evaluate the consequences of foundation involvement in education policy in New York City and Los Angeles, I draw on the concept of policy feedback. Policy feedback is a process that begins with policy change. A new policy can reshape political activity and subsequently entrench new policies, limit options for future policy change, or allow policy changes to erode.[20] A widely recognized example of positive policy feedback is Social Security—a policy that enabled senior citizens to increase their political involvement and consequently become highly active proponents of extensions to the policy.[21] Patashnik focuses on several reforms involving market-based policies, such as airline deregulation and emissions trading, showing that these reforms are more likely to last when key constituencies or interest groups make significant investments in the new policy arrangement.[22] Reform that is sustainable in the long term reconfigures the political system, making it unlikely that the policy will be reversed.[23]

Studies of policy feedback demonstrate the link between reform sustainability and the reconfiguration of interest group coalitions. The policy feedback literature has many parallels with the literature on civic capacity, which also draws attention to the coalition dynamics that underpin reform efforts, particularly in urban education reform.[24] Scholars applying civic capacity argue that major education policy reform is unlikely when engagement in education politics is narrowly confined to traditional stakeholders. Instead, civic capacity for reform develops when a broad and diverse set of stakeholders becomes invested in a common reform vision. Although the civic capacity literature does not refer specifically to reconfiguration or policy feedback, these concepts are integral to the process of civic capacity formation. Civic capacity develops when new stakeholders—including groups not traditionally involved in education—become invested and remain engaged in a shared approach to education reform.

Civic capacity is a key feature of reform sustainability. Yet studies of civic capacity have not systematically demonstrated why certain cities develop civic capacity and others do not. There are some factors associated with cities that possess greater civic capacity, such as institutionalization of coalitions through formal organizations and mayoral involvement; however, civic capacity retains an elusive quality that makes it difficult to assess why some cities are fortunate enough to develop broad and sustainable civic coalitions.[25] Policy feedback offers a framework that links policy change to political consequences. Combining the insights of civic capacity and policy feedback, I show how civic capacity can emerge from the development, design, and implementation of policy reforms.

Furthermore, both the policy feedback and civic capacity literatures point to conditions that can lead to the failure of reform coalitions, although they emphasize different challenges. Patashnik's analysis of general-interest reforms and policy feedback highlights the problem of "winnerless reform"—in other words, policy reforms that fail to generate investments or build a coalition of highly engaged supporters.[26] In these cases, the benefits of the policy are often too broad and scattered, so no influential groups recognize a strong interest in maintaining the policy. Coming from a different perspective, the civic capacity literature shows that reform can fail when the policy lacks investment and involvement from a sufficiently diverse set of supporters. According to Stone, "To the extent that civic capacity rests on a narrow foundation of elite cooperation, it is vulnerable to quick collapse."[27] Combined, the findings of policy feedback and civic capacity scholars suggest that major reform efforts are dependent on supportive coalitions that foster deep investments and broad engagement. Philanthropic involvement in reform may increase the challenges to building deep local investment and broad engagement in new policies. Outside funding may substitute for local dollars, and philanthropists may have difficulty developing strong relationships with local partners. In my analysis of New York City and Los Angeles, I assess these challenges and evaluate the vulnerability of reform coalitions in each city.

Both of these theoretical approaches form the basis for the argument of this book. To maintain conceptual clarity, I draw more heavily on policy feedback in the discussion of my findings. Yet I see policy feedback and civic capacity as complementary perspectives. Moreover, both policy feedback and civic capacity draw attention to the greatest political challenge for reformers: the challenge of building a sustaining coalition. My findings offer contributions to both the policy feedback and civic capacity literatures by enhancing our understanding of the circumstances and strategies that can support sustainable policy reform coalitions.

Winning the Sprint, Losing the Marathon

Political leaders and policy advocates often view achieving reform as a race to the finish line. Reforms must be enacted quickly, before opponents can make changes or reverse course. Some institutions can enable this type of rapid change;

in urban education, mayoral or state control of schools can facilitate swift policy enactment and implementation. More commonly, given the divided powers and numerous veto points of most American political institutions, reformers have to move more slowly, incorporating input and responding to criticism as they proceed.

The contrasting political consequences of foundation-funded reforms in New York City and Los Angeles have also been shaped by time horizons. District leaders in New York City moved quickly to develop a comprehensive reform plan for the district and begin implementation supported by private funding. Mayoral control provided the institutional mechanisms to support fast action. Objections or questions about policy changes were often treated as roadblocks, not an opportunity for additional input or deliberation. By 2007, New York City was awarded the Broad Prize in Education, and the district was touted by Broad Foundation founder, Eli Broad, as "a model of successful urban school district reform."[28] By 2011, New York City's reforms were challenged by lawsuits, large protests, contested outcomes, and unclear leadership.

In Los Angeles, an elected board of education, large cumbersome bureaucracy, and sprawling school district have largely served as institutional barriers to swift policy change. Foundation funding facilitated rapid charter school expansion, but school district policy moved forward at its own slower pace. Emerging from different directions and through different processes of engagement, the board of education, the mayor, charter school organizations, and many advocacy organizations have largely converged around an agenda of decentralization and charterlike autonomy for public schools. Los Angeles has not received a Broad Prize, and it has rarely been touted as a model of education reform in recent years. Yet my findings show that education reform in Los Angeles stands on a more solid and diverse coalition of supporters than it does in New York City.

My analysis suggests that foundations have recently prioritized the sprintlike policy victories that are achievable in districts like New York City and underinvested in policy marathons in districts like Los Angeles. Winning the sprint may satisfy the goals of some funders and political leaders, but a sprint victory may be only temporary. For would-be reformers hoping to finish a policy marathon, Los Angeles offers useful lessons.

Plan of the Book

The findings and argument of the book are presented in two parts. The first part, chapters 1 and 2, show how education politics and foundation grant making have changed in the past two decades and how these changes have increased foundation influence in urban education policy. The second part, chapters 3,

4, and 5, show how major foundations have influenced education policy and politics in New York City and Los Angeles. The conclusion assesses the implications of foundation influence for urban education politics and democratic accountability.

In chapter 1, I trace three major trends that have enabled greater foundation influence in urban education policy and increased the prominence of philanthropists as policy entrepreneurs. First, the accountability system mandated by No Child Left Behind has heightened the importance of test-score data as a metric to evaluate student, teacher, and school performance and emphasized the failure to meet annual standards in urban school districts. Second, the largely successful advocacy for market-based reforms in education, such as charter schools, has created new levers for influence in local districts and further undermined the control of traditional school leaders. The third trend is the changing nature of philanthropy and the extraordinary amount of wealth being disbursed by living philanthropists, such as Bill Gates, Warren Buffet, and Eli Broad. A sizable share of this giving has targeted K-12 education. The convergence of hundreds of millions in private dollars, an accountability system that emphasizes the failures of the current system of public schools, and the school choice movement sets the stage for major foundations to exercise substantial influence within urban school districts. In chapter 2, I show that there is systematic variation in the types of districts that receive significant grant dollars and the types that do not. By concentrating their grant dollars in a limited set of districts, foundations are able to achieve greater influence in these places. Using a statistical model to predict grants per student to the 100 largest districts, I show that foundations invest more grant dollars in districts with mayoral or state control and in districts with greater nonprofit capacity and expertise.

In chapter 3, I introduce the two case studies: New York City and Los Angeles. Both cities received Annenberg Challenge grants to reform schools in the 1990s. I discuss the reform approach of the Annenberg Challenge in each city, compare it with current reforms, and show how foundation grant making has increased in the last decade. I explain how a new set of Boardroom Progressive education philanthropies—the Gates Foundation, Broad Foundation, and Walton Family Foundation—have adopted converging grant-making strategies. Compared with the Annenberg Challenge grants, the new grant makers are able to leverage more resources in a more targeted way and empower new sets of actors in local education politics.

In chapters 4 and 5, I examine how foundation grant making has shaped current education politics and policy in New York City and Los Angeles. I also present contrasting social networks of education policy leaders in each city. Chapter 4 focuses on New York City, showing that foundations have amplified top-down coordination and rapid implementation of new policies. Using social network analysis, I demonstrate that foundations are primarily allied with an elite network in New York City, including top district bureaucrats and education nonprofits; advocacy organizations and parent leaders are largely excluded. Furthermore, debates over issues such as school closures and reauthorization of mayoral control have hardened political divisions in the district. In chapter 5, I demonstrate how foundation grant making in Los Angeles, unlike New York City, has engaged a more diverse set of stakeholders. Despite the fragmentation of policy making and leadership in the district, the social network of education policy leaders in Los Angeles shows a closely linked core of diverse organizations involved in education policy. New policies in the district are designed to bring the flexibility of the charter sector into public schools, and stakeholder engagement has remained strong.

In the conclusion, I summarize my findings to show how major foundations have clearly stepped beyond the realm of charity and into the realm of education policy and politics. I also present the implications of my findings for both scholars and practitioners. The strategic targeting of foundation resources and clear policy agenda of the wealthiest foundations has heightened their influence in urban education policy and politics. Furthermore, major foundations and other Boardroom Progressive reformers have increased their focus on national education policy, and their influence is growing more visible under the Obama administration. I argue that scholars should devote greater attention to foundations as political actors, while keeping in mind the characteristics that distinguish foundations from more traditional policy advocates. Finally, I highlight implications for urban school district leaders and foundations, based on the political consequences of foundation involvement in urban education policy. Major foundations, to a large extent, are politically unaccountable. Nonetheless, the reforms that their grant dollars support can be politically vulnerable—particularly in the long term. The resources provided by major funders can facilitate the development and implementation of significant reform policies in urban school districts; however, these resources cannot compensate for a lack of investment or support from local education stakeholders.

CHAPTER 1

Accountability, Markets, and the Philanthropic Agenda

Bill Gates is the most influential individual in U.S. education policy, according to a recent survey of nearly 200 education policy experts.[1] The same group of experts ranked the Gates Foundation as the third most influential institution, falling just short of the U.S. Congress and the U.S. Department of Education.[2] The ranking of a philanthropist and his foundation among the most influential individuals and institutions in U.S. education policy cannot be a product of money alone. The Gates Foundation has more than $30 billion in assets, but the federal government has considerably more funds at its disposal; the U.S. Department of Education spends nearly twice the assets of the Gates Foundation on an annual basis. How does a philanthropist come to rival leaders in the federal government for influence in U.S. education policy?

Three broad trends have played a key role in opening the door for greater philanthropic involvement and influence in K-12 education—particularly in urban school districts. Seeds of these trends began decades ago, but since 2000, all three trends have become increasingly pronounced and influential: (1) the growing role of the federal government in education, (2) the expansion of market-based reforms, and (3) the changing nature of philanthropy. The federal government has become increasingly involved in public education since the passage of No Child Left Behind (NCLB) in 2001, which mandated a new accountability system for schools. Market-based reforms attempt to introduce competition, choice, and privatization into the public school system. The changes in the philanthropic sector have made major U.S. foundations into bigger and bolder institutions. Living philanthropists, such as Bill Gates, Eli Broad, and the Walton family, have accumulated an extraordinary amount of wealth, and they are personally involved in the distribution of these funds. Described as "ambitious," "very impatient," and "hands-on," these grant makers possess billions of dollars and far-reaching goals for reforming education.[3]

During the past decade, a window of opportunity has opened for philanthropists to have greater influence on policy in urban school districts. The combined effects of the increasing federal role in education and the rise of market-based ideas have challenged the legitimacy of traditional urban school leaders and introduced new actors into urban education. Due to NCLB, federal policy tends to emphasize the failures of public schools, most visibly through annual accountability testing and corrective measures required for schools that do not make yearly progress. Meanwhile, market-based reform ideas—including contracting for services, school choice, and charter schools—have gained wider acceptance among district leaders and the public, while offering new ways for private-sector organizations to be involved in public education. These trends make it easier for policy entrepreneurs from outside the school system to influence policy in urban school districts.

Policy entrepreneurs are advocates who invest substantial resources—time, money, and reputation—in promoting a particular policy.[4] Based on his study of federal policy making in health and transportation, Kingdon identified three key characteristics of successful policy entrepreneurs: (1) a claim or reason to be heard in the political sphere (due their expertise, their position as spokesperson for a group, or their role as a decision maker), (2) political connections or negotiating skill, and (3) persistence in promoting their ideas.[5] In other words, successful policy entrepreneurs are willing to act as both policy wonks and political operatives.

Traditionally, philanthropists have not been regarded as policy entrepreneurs. In the eyes of legislators and regulators, philanthropists have sometimes overstepped the line in the sand that limits political advocacy for tax-exempt private charities.[6] Yet philanthropists have not typically engaged directly in politics without the cushion of intermediaries. Scholars have shown that philanthropists act as patrons to policy entrepreneurs by, for example, funding interest group organizations.[7] Others have extended the concept of patronage, demonstrating how foundations have helped to build networks of organizations to promote new political coalitions and social movements.[8] There are many reasons that philanthropists may be ill suited for politics. Philanthropists may claim policy expertise, but they do not claim to speak on behalf of a particular political constituency. The general purpose foundations of the early 20th century, such as Carnegie and Rockefeller, were created to enable open-ended giving, and the nation's largest foundations have typically continued this approach.[9] The goals of philanthropy are often broad social goods—"increasing educational opportunity" or "improving schools"—rather than specific policies.[10] Also, philanthropists have often adopted the role of "disinterested reformers, whose concern is not constricted by any jurisdiction," allowing them to avoid getting involved with localized political conflicts.[11] Despite these tendencies, recent changes in philanthropy are enabling major foundations to become more directly involved in politics. Foundations involved in education are adopting a more strategic and selective approach to grant making, focused on a limited set of school districts where they deploy significant resources. Also, philanthropists are increasingly willing to directly engage with politics, voicing their support for particular political leaders and specific policy proposals. These shifts have allowed some major philanthropists to behave more like policy entrepreneurs, in addition to working as highly engaged patrons.

By tracing the growing federal role in education, the expansion of market-based reforms, and the changing nature of philanthropy, I show why major foundations can have much greater influence in urban school districts than they did in the past. Nonetheless, the trends that exposed urban school districts to greater outside influence have not erased important differences in local context. The diverse governing systems and political characteristics of urban school districts continue to affect foundation grant-making strategy and shape the opportunities for philanthropic influence within individual districts.

"The Cocoon of Localism"

In their book *Ten Thousand Democracies: Politics and Public Opinion in America's School Districts*, Berkman and Plutzer begin by stating that education is "equated with the American ideals of localism."[12] Locally elected boards govern the vast majority of school districts, and federal funding is a small portion of school district revenues. In other major urban policy areas, such as housing, transportation, and downtown redevelopment, the federal government played a key role at the local level, beginning in the mid-20th century.[13] Yet studies of urban education politics from the past 50 years consistently emphasize the dominance of local actors, including school boards, unions, administrators, the local business community, and mayors.

Dahl's classic *Who Governs?* showed the pluralistic politics of public education in New Haven, involving the mayor, the board of education, the teachers' union, administrators, and parent-teacher associations.[14] In a study of Gary, Detroit, and Newark school politics, Rich describes the public school cartel, which includes "a coalition of professional school administrators, school activists, and union leaders."[15] Reviewing more than 100 years of Chicago Public Schools history, Shipps demonstrates the remarkably consistent and influential education reform agenda of Chicago's corporate elite, who mobilized through business networks to support replication of the corporate structure in school administration and to establish performance targets for finances and educational outcomes.[16] Orr describes the role of the mayor, civic organizations, and the local business community in Baltimore education politics.[17] Additionally, the Civic Capacity and Urban Education Project was designed to assess mobilization around a shared education reform agenda in 11 major cities. The authors consistently emphasize the role of local actors, including elected officials, school district leaders, business, and community organizations.[18] According to Henig and Stone, "For most of American history the cocoon of localism shielded education decision making."[19]

This cocoon for local education had some positive consequences. It sheltered most school districts from paralyzing ideological battles at the national level and promoted close identification between local communities and public schools.[20] Yet localism has also become associated with dysfunction and low standards in public education. As Americans have grown increasingly concerned about international competition in education, nations with highly centralized and standardized education systems, such as Finland, Singapore, and South Korea, are seen as models to emulate.[21] Another perceived failure of localism in public education is the local district as a monopoly provider of education for a given geographic area. As Hess argues:

> Today, every school district is asked to devise ways to meet every need of every single child in a given area. Since they can't tailor their service to focus on certain student needs, districts are forced to try to build expertise in a vast number of specialties and services. Districts then must also become the employers of nearly all educators in a given community.[22]

Thus, criticism of localism in public education has been mounted from multiple directions, highlighting the lack of standardization across local districts and the lack of district capacity to meet the needs of diverse students.

Have urban school districts changed at all since Dahl's 1961 description of education politics in New Haven? Current scholarly opinion appears to differ considerably on this matter. In recently published books, two widely recognized scholars in education policy imagine a Rip Van Winkle scenario involving a superintendent who fell asleep several decades ago and awoke to observe school districts in 2010.[23] According to Hess, "a superintendent who nodded off in 1950 would feel almost uncannily at home in most of today's school districts."[24] Advancing the scenario by one decade, Cuban imagines:

> Were a Rip Van Winkle superintendent of a large urban district to have gone to sleep in 1960 and awakened in 2010, he would have been astounded by the degree of federal and state authority over his district's curriculum, instruction, and testing....Equally stunning to our Rip

Van Winkle superintendent...was learning that private-sector companies, even for-profit ones, now operated some public schools in U.S. major cities.[25]

How do these two scholars come to such divergent conclusions despite their shared affinity for the Rip Van Winkle legend? They are, of course, both correct. As Hess argues, there is remarkable continuity in the basic infrastructure of schooling in the United States—geographically defined school districts, the 180-day school year with summer vacation, the comprehensive high school, and the training and pay scales of teachers. In these respects, public schooling has changed little since it was reformed and expanded by Progressive era educators at the beginning of the 20th century.[26] Acknowledging this continuity, urban districts have never been more open to outside influence. The federal government and market-based reforms have pried open the cocoon around school districts, enabling new outside actors to become highly involved in urban school districts, particularly in some of the largest and most troubled school systems.

No Child Left Behind

For most of U.S. history, the federal government left public education entirely to states and localities. Prior to the Great Society legislation of the 1960s, "no long-term, general federal aid program for elementary and secondary education" had been approved.[27] Three key issues produced extensive debate and little action at the federal level: (1) the likelihood that federal aid would lead to federal control, (2) the potential impact on the parochial school system, and (3) the system of racial segregation in the South.[28] With President Lyndon Johnson's Great Society programs and the rights-based education legislation that followed, targeted funding began to flow from the federal government to the states and to local districts. Yet programs such as Title I, the Bilingual Education Act, and the Education for All Handicapped Children Act focused on serving specific populations: the poor, English language learners, and the disabled.[29] Republicans supported some of these programs, but they remained opposed to expanding the federal role in broader or more intrusive ways. The federal Department of Education was not established until 1979, by President Jimmy Carter. The formation of a cabinet-level department was seen largely as payback to the National Education Association for working on Carter's election.[30]

The position of the Secretary of Education was primarily a bully pulpit under Republican presidents in the 1980s. As Ronald Reagan's newly appointed secretary of education, Terrel Bell did not expect to be on the job for long, due to Reagan's campaign promise to abolish the Department of Education. Soon after taking office, Bell recalled seeing a political cartoon depicting the chairs in the cabinet room, but "the one for the secretary of education down at the end of the room was an electric chair."[31] Despite this unpromising beginning, Bell made use of his bully pulpit by appointing "a first-rate panel to study the problems of American education."[32] In April 1983, the National Commission on Excellence in Education released *A Nation at Risk: The Imperative for Educational Reform*, addressed as "An Open Letter to the American People." The authors of the report did not mince words in calling attention to a "crisis" in education, characterizing the issue of educational quality as a national security threat: "If an unfriendly foreign power had attempted to impose on America the mediocre educational performance that exists today, we might well have viewed it as an act of war."[33] The impact of this language and the report's striking conclusions about the decline of American education reverberated widely in the press. As Bell recalls, "The commission's report was on the front page of all the major newspapers in every city—small, medium, and large—across the nation."[34]

A Nation at Risk is commonly cited as the rallying cry that initiated a new sense of urgency and wave of education reform in the United States. During the 1980s and 1990s, most of this reform activity proceeded at the state and local level.[35] In particular, Southern states began adopting policies that foreshadowed the policy design of No Child Left Behind. For example, Kentucky enacted an "educational bankruptcy" law, which permitted "the state to take control of school districts that do not meet certain standards, including a high school drop-out rate of no more than 30 percent, maximum absentee rates of 6 percent and a maximum failure rate on basic skills tests of 15 percent."[36] Districts in Kentucky were required to submit improvement plans indicating their deficiencies, along with timetables and measures for correcting them. By 1987, Alabama, Arkansas, Florida, Kentucky, Mississippi, South Carolina, Tennessee, Texas, and Virginia had adopted state-mandated curriculum standards.[37] Meanwhile, during the 1988 election, George H. W. Bush proclaimed his intention to become the "Education President." Once elected, his efforts were largely symbolic, including the Charlottesville Education Summit involving governors who had led education reform in their states. President Bill Clinton, known as an "education governor" in Arkansas, promoted voluntary national education goals through the Goals 2000 legislation, passed in March 1994.

Until 2000, the federal role in local education was still primarily limited to categorical grant programs and voluntary action. States had become more active by establishing their own accountability and testing regimes, but state-level action varied considerably depending on political conditions, and policies were often developed incrementally.[38] The NCLB bill was the first legislation introduced to Congress by the newly elected President George W. Bush. It was promoted as Bush's plan to bring the education policy reforms he led in Texas to the national level. The bill had bipartisan backing; Democratic Senator Edward Kennedy coauthored the bill and was highly involved in ensuring its passage through Congress. Yet Congressional Republicans had to reverse their long-standing opposition to federal involvement in education. The electoral benefits of supporting Bush's plans for education were not lost on the Republicans. Republican Senator Mitch McConnell noted that Bush "has taken us [from] a 20-point deficit on education to a point in which we lead on education."[39] The bill passed in the House by a vote of 384–35 and in the Senate by a vote of 91–8.

No Child Left Behind included several provisions that considerably strengthened the federal role in public education. First, the law required annual testing in reading and math in grades three through eight. Second, the law identified several subgroups of students and required that progress toward meeting standards be measured for each, including Whites, African Americans, Latinos, Asian and Pacific Islanders, American Indians, students receiving free/reduced lunch, English language learners, and special education students. Third, the law required each subgroup to meet or exceed standards set by the states by 2014. States were required to define measures of adequate yearly progress (AYP) toward the achievement of full proficiency in 2014.

Title I schools—meaning schools where 40 percent or more of the students come from households defined as low-income—that fail to achieve AYP for all subgroups can face a range of corrective measures under NCLB. After two consecutive years of failing to meet AYP, the school is designated as "needing improvement." After four consecutive years of failing to achieve AYP, the district is required to take "corrective action" in the school, such as replacing staff or implementing a new curriculum. When a school has not achieved AYP for five consecutive years, the district is required to initiate plans for "restructuring" the school. Options for school restructuring include conversion to a charter school, replacing relevant school staff, turning over control of the school to the state, contracting with a private management company to operate the school, and any other major restructuring of the school's governance.[40] In practice, the vast majority of districts have chosen the less intrusive options, such as replacing key staff, rather than state takeover or conversion to charter status.[41] Due to these provisions, NCLB has turned the federal government into the new sheriff in local education, with states acting as deputies charged with monitoring districts and schools and identifying those that fall short on requirements. According to Henig and Stone, "With NCLB, national politics has truly changed the nature of the game. For local school leaders as well as states, the results can be bewildering. Superintendents and school boards can no longer concentrate on local problems, resources, and constituencies."[42]

Although the passage of NCLB did include an initial increase in funding for Title I, funding increases have not been sustained.[43] Instead, the enforcement mechanisms of NCLB have consumed the attention of urban district leaders. Following the 2005–2006 school year, almost two-thirds of the 2,700 schools nationwide that were facing corrective action or restructuring were in urban districts.[44] Furthermore, these schools are highly concentrated in the nation's largest urban districts; Chicago, Detroit, Los Angeles, Philadelphia, and New York City contained more than 25 percent of all schools facing corrective action or restructuring following the 2005–2006 school year—10 percent of the schools were located in Chicago alone.[45] By 2009, Detroit had more than 40 schools that had not made AYP for five or more years. Once these schools are identified, as required by federal law, the task of improving the schools is largely in the hands of the local district. According to the Government Accountability Office report on NCLB, school districts bear the "primary responsibility" for assisting schools that require corrective action or restructuring, and districts "must ensure that each school identified for improvement receives technical assistance based on scientifically based research in three areas: analysis of student assessment data, identifying and implementing instructional strategies, and analysis of the school budget."[46] Yet NCLB has provided few additional resources to districts to support significant improvements in these schools.

By focusing on testing and accountability as policy mechanisms but providing little support for school improvement, NCLB has created an enormous gap between the goals of the policy and the capacity of practitioners to achieve these goals. According to Cohen and Moffitt, "The collision among NCLB's rigid regulatory regime, weak technical capability in measurement, and weak school systems created a policy context marked by high risk and low capability."[47] Furthermore, this collision has significant consequences for large urban school districts with high concentrations of schools facing NCLB sanctions. In particular, NCLB has "eroded the schools' legitimacy" by shining a spotlight on the weak capacity of schools and districts to improve failing schools.[48] The issue of legitimacy extends the impact of NCLB sanctions beyond education practitioners and raises the question: where do public schools stand in the eyes of the public?

Although NCLB was intended to increase standards in the public schools, public opinion about the quality of public schools nationally has actually declined since its implementation.[49] The annual Phi Delta Kappa/Gallup poll asks respondents to grade the public schools nationally on a scale from A to F. Figure 1.1 displays the proportion of respondents awarding high grades (A or B) or low grades (D or F) to public schools nationally. After the passage of NCLB, grades for the public schools briefly climbed, suggesting that the public initially expected positive results from the new law. This sentiment is reflected in responses to the 2002 PDK/Gallup survey regarding the anticipated consequences of NCLB. In 2002, 80 percent of respondents said that it is "very likely"

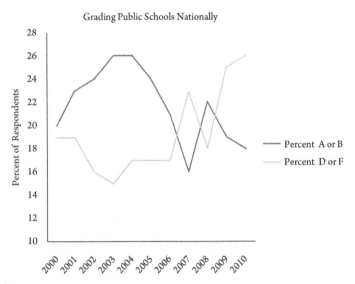

Figure 1.1
Source: PDK/Gallup Poll.

or "somewhat likely" that every student in their community will pass state proficiency tests by 2013–2014.[50] Fifty-seven percent responded that the federal
government's involvement in local public education was "a good thing." Yet by
2005, the proportion of respondents grading public schools nationally at an A
or B level began to decline sharply, and the proportion giving grades of D or F
began to steadily increase. This trend was briefly interrupted in 2008—a presidential election year when the economy was the top issue—but continued in
2009 and 2010. In fact, the proportion of respondents giving a D or F to public
schools nationally in the PDK/Gallup poll is currently at its highest levels in two
decades. Attitudes toward NCLB have also grown more negative. In the 2010
poll, 28 percent of respondents viewed NCLB as "hurting" the performance of
local public schools, and only 22 percent regarded NCLB as "helping" local public schools; the remainder responded that the law was "making no difference."[51]

No Child Left Behind may not be solely responsible for the public's increasingly negative views of public schools nationally, but it would be hard to argue
that the legislation has enhanced the public's confidence in the nation's public schools. The phrase "failing schools" has become increasingly prevalent in
the age of NCLB, despite federal efforts to apply different terminology to the
schools that do not make AYP. In an assessment of the costs and benefits of
NCLB, Mathis explains, "While the federal government has recently announced
that the 'failing' label for schools should be replaced with the more politically
acceptable term 'in need of improvement,' the negative moniker sticks in the
minds of the people and the media."[52] The stickiness of the failing school label

is borne out by an analysis of coverage in the *New York Times* during the past two decades: use of the phrase "failing schools" has grown considerably since 1990.[53] The words *failing schools* appeared in the paper just 11 times in 1990, but the phrase was repeated 80 times in articles published in 2010. A *New York Times* article from June 2, 2009—about Education Secretary Arne Duncan's school turnaround plans—demonstrates the use of this phrase in the context of NCLB:

> Duncan's initiative would seek to correct a troubling legacy of the No Child Left Behind law. The law has identified 6,000 failing schools, yet state and local authorities have left most of them to languish, neither holding their educators accountable nor helping to improve instruction.[54]

On average, the phrase "failing schools" was used 30 times annually in the *New York Times* in the 1990s. In the 2000s, use of the phrase "failing schools" more than doubled to an average of 66 times annually. There is little evidence that U.S. public schools performed worse in the 2000s than in the 1990s, but NCLB has drawn increasing attention to low student achievement in public schools. Thus, both media coverage and public opinion data since the implementation of NCLB reflect similar trends—a rising perception that public schools are failing.

Other aspects of NCLB have advanced the notion that school districts are not equipped to improve student achievement on their own. As Burch explains, "NCLB greatly increased the role of market-based reforms in ways that are not easily visible to the public."[55] For example, students attending schools in need of improvement or corrective action can receive free private tutoring at the district's expense. This provision, not surprisingly, is unpopular with school districts, but it is supported by school choice activists and civil rights organizations, which have lobbied for expansion of access to tutoring services.[56] The requirements for school restructuring under NCLB also introduce new opportunities for private contractors. By 2005, Michigan had contracted with outside organizations to restructure 14 schools; by 2006, California had made similar arrangements for 20 schools that required restructuring.[57] According to Sunderman and Kim:

> NCLB introduces the market principle that competition will create incentives for under-performing schools to improve. Within this framework of competition, [NCLB] also shifts the focus of Title I programs designed to improve schools to programs aimed at individual students by requiring under-performing schools to offer transfers and supplemental education services to eligible students.[58]

Combined with the consequences of NCLB's annual accountability testing, these provisions for private-sector involvement in education highlight the lack of capacity of public school systems and suggest that the capacity for improvement resides in the private sector. Meanwhile, a new set of alternatives to traditional public education has emerged as market-based reforms have gained momentum.

Markets, Charters, and Contracting

Market-based ideas have a long history in education, but they have only recently gained traction through the expansion of charter schools and private contracting by school districts. In the 1950s, Milton Friedman proposed the idea of vouchers for education. In subsequent essays and interviews, he argued that his proposal would promote parental choice, introduce competition into the education sector, and increase innovation and diversity among schools. Yet there was little political momentum for the voucher idea. The first major school voucher program was implemented in Milwaukee, Wisconsin, in 1990, but few districts have followed suit. The most significant political roadblocks for voucher programs at the state level are the lawsuits concerning the legality of vouchers under state constitutions; voucher programs in several states, including Florida, Indiana, and Louisiana have been challenged in the courts.

School choice proponents gained additional support from academia with the publication of Chubb and Moe's *Politics, Markets, and America's Schools*. The book argues that pluralistic politics strangle public school districts with layers of bureaucracy, making reform nearly impossible, and school choice is the only way to improve the system.[59] According to Chubb and Moe, "Without being too literal about it, we think reformers would do well to entertain the notion that choice *is* a panacea.... It has the capacity *all by itself* to bring about the kind of transformation that, for years, reformers have been seeking to engineer in myriad other ways."[60] The Bradley Foundation, an early philanthropic supporter of school choice research and advocacy organizations, helped fund Chubb and Moe's work.[61] Yet school vouchers have never gained broad public support. Meanwhile, school choice proponents found a new policy approach with the potential for much broader appeal: charter schools.

Adoption of charter school policies has spread rapidly among the states. Since Minnesota passed the first charter school law in 1991, 41 states and the District of Columbia have passed charter school legislation. According to Henig, charter schools were easier to sell than voucher programs because they were "still public schools" in three respects: (1) their funding is primarily public, (2) access is public, and (3) there is public oversight.[62] Nonetheless, charter schools are private in a couple of important ways: they are operated by private entities, and they are exempt from many government regulations. Republicans, who were the strongest supporters of vouchers, have also promoted charter schools, but the Democratic Party is divided on the issue. Old-line Democrats, those most associated with union interests, have been wary of charter schools as "a precursor to vouchers, or an element in a strategy to weaken teachers' unions generally by creating a mirror system in which contracts and collective bargaining did not apply."[63] Meanwhile, New Democrats have viewed charter schools as consistent with their agenda to shake up the public sector.

President Obama is a vocal supporter of charter schools, and he has visited several charter schools since his election to the presidency. Political pundits have viewed Obama's support for charter schools as a signal that he is willing to break from traditional Democratic Party interests, particularly teachers' unions. Public opinion polling suggests that Obama is in good company in his stance on charters. According to the 2010 Phi Delta Kappa/Gallup poll, 68 percent of respondents favor the idea of charter schools and only 28 percent oppose them.[64] This is a substantial change from 2000, when the same poll reported 42 percent in favor of charter schools and 47 percent opposed.[65] Additionally, in the 2010 poll, 60 percent of respondents said they would support a large increase in the number of public charter schools in the United States, and 65 percent would support new public charter schools in their community.

Thus, charter schools have become the primary mechanism for introducing school choice into public education. The growth of the charter school sector has been particularly rapid in several large urban districts. In New Orleans, more than half of students are enrolled in charter schools. More than 30 percent of students in Detroit and Washington, D.C., attend charter schools. Los Angeles has the largest number of students attending charter schools—more than 82,000 during the 2011–2012 school year, approximately 12.5 percent of students in the district. Additionally, some mayors have adopted charter schools as part of their political agenda.[66] For example, Newark, New Jersey, Mayor Cory Booker promoted the creation of the Newark Charter School Fund, which raised money from the Gates Foundation and the Walton Family Foundation for charter school expansion.

Another key development in the charter school sector is the formation of charter management organizations (CMOs). The earliest charter schools were typically mom-and-pop ventures—independently operated schools started by individuals or teams of teachers. The CMOs are nonprofit or for-profit entities that operate networks of charter schools and attempt to replicate new schools based on a common model, similar to franchising. KIPP is among the most widely recognized of CMOs, but there are dozens of others. A recent report estimated that 82 CMOs were operating 496 schools at the end of the 2007–2008 school year.[67] The CMO model is intended to "meld the benefits of school districts—including economies of scale, collaboration among similar schools, and support structures—with the autonomies and entrepreneurial drive of the charter sector."[68] The CMOs have the potential to rapidly expand the charter school sector, although some reports have questioned the capacity of CMOs to rapidly scale up without compromising quality.[69] As I show in subsequent chapters, philanthropy has been an essential partner for CMOs.

School vouchers and charter schools are reforms aimed at expanding choice for parents and students as consumers of education. Another aspect of the rise of market-based reforms in education focuses on developing the market for the school district as a consumer. School districts have contracted with private entities for services such as food, maintenance, and transportation for many years. Private contracting for the provision of services directly related to education—such as tutoring, professional development, and full school operations—is a newer development. No Child Left Behind included some mechanisms for private contracting in school districts.[70] An additional push has come from proponents of the portfolio management model (PMM) for urban school reform. The idea of PMM was articulated by Paul Hill and several colleagues in the 1990s. As Hill explained:

> [Schools would] be operated by a variety of public and private organizations, based on school-specific contracts that would define each school's mission, guarantee public funding, and establish standards and procedures for accountability....A school board would not directly run schools, but would contract with independent organizations to run them. A local public school system would manage many different contracts....Every school's contract would specify the amount of public funds it would receive, the type of instructional program it would provide, and the student outcomes it expects to produce.[71]

As Henig has argued, PMM is a "contracting regime," placing "government into the role of consumer supreme."[72] Unlike charter schools, PMM has not spread rapidly through the passage of new state laws. Instead, it has emerged more gradually, as the ideas promoted by PMM have been incorporated to varying degrees by urban districts, including New York City, Oakland, Philadelphia, Los Angeles, Chicago, and New Orleans.[73] In these districts, nonprofit and for-profit organizations are highly involved in supporting and operating public schools.

The combined effects of NCLB and the rise of market-based reforms have created a window of opportunity for philanthropists in two key ways. First, these trends have diminished the authority of urban school district leaders and increased negative perceptions about their capacity to improve schools. Second, these trends have created new levers for influence in urban education—particularly, charter school operators and district contractors—that allow philanthropists to bypass traditional actors in urban school districts. Thus, the first decade of the 2000s offered philanthropists new and expanding opportunities for access and influence in urban education politics.

Bigger, Bolder Philanthropy

Philanthropic foundations are not obvious contenders for influence in a democracy; they lack two vital resources: a constituency to represent and formal political power. Foundations do, of course, have vast financial resources, but these dollars are relatively insubstantial compared with public-sector budgets. Yet according to Marris and Rein, foundations have another key resource:

> [A] national philanthropy [is] a prestigeful and uniquely well-placed broker of new ideas.... Less spontaneous and accessible than the salons or coffee houses of other civilizations, the discreetly luxurious offices [of a national philanthropy]...are still a market place of intellectual exchange.[74]

To act as brokers of policy ideas in the public sphere, or policy entrepreneurs, foundations must develop relationships with political actors and engage in the political process. Yet the relationship between philanthropy and politics has been contested since the origins of large private foundations in the United States.[75] Judges, legislators, and bureaucrats have repeatedly attempted to define the distinction between tax-exempt charitable work and political advocacy. Often, these regulatory efforts occurred in response to philanthropic activity that appeared too political or concerned controversial issues of the time, such as civil rights.

Meanwhile, the relationship between philanthropy and the public sector has evolved as government has grown. A century ago, government was much smaller and less active in social policy, including health, welfare, and education policy. In this context, philanthropists could play a significant role in creating and supporting new educational institutions. Today, local, state, and federal levels of governments are each involved in financing, operating, or regulating public schools. Education politics is a crowded and contested field, with interest groups vying for influence at all levels of government. Philanthropists today have considerably less elbow room, and they face substantially more complexity in the political system.

Early-20th-century education philanthropists were often bold—building new universities, libraries, and schools—but they accomplished much by working cooperatively through elite networks, rather than courting political controversy. Zunz refers to the "pact between the rich and reformers," which supported the formation of secular educational institutions and a new university-based research infrastructure.[76] Even in areas where philanthropists worked most directly against the prevailing political establishment—as in the Jim Crow South—accommodation often trumped confrontation. The Rosenwald Fund was a major supporter of school construction for African Americans in the rural South; by 1932, as many as "40 percent of all black children enrolled in school that year attended Rosenwald schools."[77] Rosenwald required local contributions from African American communities to share the costs of school construction, even though they already paid taxes that largely funded White schools.[78] The schools were "organized around specific notions of what African Americans' social status should be," emphasizing industrial education and training for manual labor.[79] Thus, rather than directly challenging state and local officials, Rosenwald opted to work within a system of segregated and limited education for African Americans.

By the 1960s, the federal government had grown substantially, and philanthropy's era of major institution building was over. In the context of increasing policy activism at the federal level, the Ford Foundation made a notable shift to more political grant-making activities—supporting voter registration, community action programs, and civil rights groups. Within education policy, Ford led an initiative to reform New York City's schools, focused on decentralization and community control. In 1967, the foundation provided planning grants to community organizations to develop three community-based demonstration school districts in Harlem, Brooklyn, and Manhattan's Lower East Side. In the Ocean Hill–Brownsville district in Brooklyn, the meaning of community control was hotly contested between community leaders and the United Federation of Teachers (UFT). This conflict was laden with instances of racial and religious resentment, with a predominantly Jewish teacher population working in predominantly African American and Puerto Rican neighborhoods.[80] During the summer of 1968, the governing board in Ocean Hill–Brownsville hired 350 new teachers to replace UFT teachers, and a series of lengthy districtwide strikes ensued.[81] The long strikes and open racial conflict sparked by the situation in Ocean Hill–Brownsville influenced future grant-making decisions at Ford and probably caused ripples at other foundations as well. The Ford Foundation was chastened by the events of 1968. In a recent Ford Foundation report, Petrovich states: "In the wake of the failure of school decentralization in New York, the Ford Foundation withdrew support for these efforts and largely stopped funding major initiatives in big cities."[82]

Ford's experiment with school decentralization also became part of a Congressional investigation of philanthropy. School decentralization, funding for voter registration, and grants to Senator Robert Kennedy's staff were regarded as "having explicit political intentions and consequences."[83] In the eyes of members of Congress, Ford had crossed the invisible boundary separating tax-exempt charitable work from political advocacy. The Congressional investigation led to the passage of the Tax Reform Act in 1969, which "prohibited foundations from supporting any efforts that might 'influence the outcome' of legislation or political campaigns."[84] This prohibition excludes foundations from direct lobbying and involvement in electoral politics. Still, a wide range of political activity remains available to foundations, allowing them to play a role in "framing issues, developing public will, supporting advocacy organizations, and funding policy implementation and evaluation."[85]

Despite the relatively low barriers to involvement in several political activities, foundations have remained extremely cautious about giving grants to organizations that actively engage in politics and public policy.[86] Jenkins finds that social movement organizations receive less than 1 percent of total foundation giving.[87] In a study of peace grant making by U.S. foundations, Aksartova shows that the largest foundations overwhelmingly supported elite institutions, such as universities and research institutes, as opposed to grassroots and advocacy organizations.[88] Similarly, Lagemann's history of the Carnegie Corporation describes how Carnegie's grant making supported several research institutions and commissions of academic researchers on key topics of public interest.[89] Assessing the consequences of this grant-making strategy, Lagemann explains that "important and controversial public questions were debated within Carnegie commissions or the Carnegie Corporation itself," rather than among a broader community of interests or in the public sphere.[90] In his book on the conservative legal movement, Teles outlines the "elite-focused strategy" of the Olin Foundation, which supported the expansion of law and economics programs in top law schools.[91] Distributing grants to research institutions and academia has allowed major foundations to fund influential research, promote new areas of study, and in some cases—such as the conservative legal movement—achieve significant policy influence in the long run. Yet this grant-making strategy generally does not lead to direct philanthropic engagement in politics and the policy process.

The role of major foundations in education policy has evolved dramatically in the past decade. Three key changes in the nature of philanthropy have allowed major education grant makers to play a more public role and have greater policy influence: (1) major foundations are giving away more money, (2) individual philanthropists and education philanthropies have become more openly involved in policy advocacy, and (3) major foundations have tried to emulate business practices and develop more selective and targeted grant-making strategies. In combination, these changes mean that major foundations have more resources to promote their policy ideas, they are more openly political about supporting their ideas, and they are learning to be more effective in the ways they distribute funds to advance their ideas.

Despite the faltering recovery of the national economy since the 2008 recession, major philanthropy appears to be thriving. In 2006, Warren Buffett, an investor worth $40 billion, pledged to give more than $30 billion over a period of several years to the world's largest foundation—the Bill and Melinda Gates Foundation. The pledge was attached to a condition: that the Gates Foundation must spend the total value of the previous year's gift each year. With Buffett's gift, the projected assets of the Gates Foundation doubled, and the foundation's responsibility to give away large sums in grants each year grew enormously. According to the Gates Foundation's financial statements, the amount of grants paid out by the foundation more than doubled in five years, from $1.4 billion in 2005 to $3 billion in 2009. This massive growth is not fully reflected in the foundation's giving for K-12 education; global health is the fastest growing area of giving by the Gates Foundation. Yet grant making in education grew as well, from $280 million in 2005 to $370 million in 2009. The Gates Foundation is undoubtedly a philanthropic giant, both among U.S. foundations and within K-12 grant making. The next largest U.S. foundation based on assets—the Ford Foundation—has about a third of the resources of Gates.

Many other top education grant makers have also increased their giving during the past decade. In 1998, the 50 largest K-12 education grant makers distributed $383 million in grants for education; by 2005, grant making by the 50 largest K-12 funders had more than doubled to $817 million.[92] Based on the most recent data available from the Foundation Center, in 2010, the total funds distributed by the 50 largest K-12 grant makers was nearly $1 billion.[93] This trend is not just the result of increased grant making by the Gates Foundation. According to the Foundation Center, the Eli and Edythe Broad Foundation gave $26.9 million for K-12 education in 2005 and $44.3 million in 2008.[94] Carnegie Corporation of New York nearly tripled its K-12 grant making from 2005 to 2008—from $10.3 million to $30.8 million.[95] Buffett's gift has certainly increased the dominance of the Gates Foundation among philanthropies, but other education grant makers are also raising their levels of giving.

In the summer of 2010, Buffett and Gates teamed up again as a billionaire fund-raising duo, with the announcement of the Giving Pledge. Starting with the Forbes 400 list of wealthiest Americans, Buffett and Gates asked billionaires to pledge to give at least 50 percent of their net worth to charity during their lifetimes or at death. Based on the net worth of the Forbes 400 in 2009, the potential total charitable giving from these individuals would be $600 billion. Just over a month after the announcement of the Giving Pledge, 40 people had signed on, including Eli and Edythe Broad, Michael Bloomberg, Paul Allen, T. Boone Pickens, and David Rockefeller.[96] The pledge has received some criticism—as a PR stunt at a time when the superwealthy are held in low public esteem and as an undemocratic gesture to avoid taxes on large fortunes.[97] Yet most of the response to the Giving Pledge has been celebratory, noting the amount of money it could generate for charity and that public pledges could produce social pressure for more giving.

The effects of the Giving Pledge on K-12 education grant making are difficult to estimate at this stage, although some of the early pledges are from individuals with a track record of K-12 education giving, including Eli and Edythe Broad, John Doerr (cofounder of New Schools Venture Fund), and Julian Robertson (founder of the Robertson Foundation, which funds dozens of charter schools and other education organizations in New York City). Overall, the massive growth of the Gates Foundation and the newly announced Giving Pledge suggest that philanthropic funding for K-12 education should remain at high levels and possibly grow larger in the coming decade.

Alongside the growth in philanthropy since the 1990s, there has been a shift in the role of the philanthropist. Newly wealthy individuals have taken charge of giving away their own money, and they are actively seeking to change public policy. A living philanthropist can take public positions on policy in ways that extend the work of the foundation as an institution. Bill Gates exemplifies this trend. In 2010, Gates delivered keynote speeches at the National Charter Schools Conference, the American Federation of Teachers Convention, and the Council of Chief State School Officers Annual Policy Forum. These speeches were not announcements of grants from the Bill and Melinda Gates Foundation; Bill Gates was speaking about his personal views on education policy issues, such as merit pay for teachers and replicating charter schools through charter management organizations. Other than Gates, the most publicly vocal education philanthropist is Eli Broad, a strong supporter of mayoral control of schools, who speaks freely about the role of unions in education politics, Obama's education agenda, and his support for particular urban school district leaders.

Nonetheless, the public role of the philanthropist does not directly translate to a more public or transparent approach to grant making in the foundation that bears the philanthropist's name. Neither the Bill and Melinda Gates Foundation nor the Eli and Edythe Broad Foundation accepts unsolicited grant proposals for education grants; their program officers remain reserved and circumspect in their public comments. These philanthropists are taking a very selective approach to adopting more visible political role—separating the individual philanthropist as a spokesperson and position taker from the foundation as an institution.

Looking beyond recognizable public figures like Bill Gates, involvement in policy advocacy is increasing within education philanthropy more generally. Grantmakers for Education is a membership organization of 260 education philanthropies, including large private foundations, family foundations, community foundations, and corporate funds. According to a 2010 report by Grantmakers for Education, a "high percentage of funders—72 percent—[are] supporting [policy] advocacy, which has traditionally been considered a higher risk area for grantmakers."[98] This level of involvement in policy advocacy represents a considerable change in perspective among education philanthropies. Christine Tebben, executive director of Grantmakers for Education, recalled a 2002 Grantmakers for Education conference where foundation officials were reluctant to discuss policy; according to Tebben, "People would say, 'We don't like to use the word *policy*.' People were very, very anxious about it."[99] Tebben went on to explain that "the discussion has shifted from whether philanthropies should engage in the policy realm to how to do so effectively, what roles to serve, and how to evaluate their impact."[100] Thus, policy advocacy has recently become an integral and accepted component of education philanthropy.

Additionally, many major philanthropists are focusing more on evaluating the effectiveness of their grants and seeing themselves as investors in social ventures. Among education grant makers, this shift can be traced to a couple of developments: disappointment with the results of the Annenberg Challenge grants in the 1990s and the adoption of businesslike practices by major education philanthropies. The $500 million Annenberg Challenge, announced in 1993, involved grants to 18 project sites to support locally developed education reforms. Several reports evaluating the impact of the Annenberg Challenge have questioned whether large philanthropic initiatives could significantly change the education system.[101] According to Fleishman, "Virtually all of the foundation professionals with whom I spoke cited the Annenberg Education Challenge as one of the major failures in foundation history."[102] Millot provides an incisive reflection on education philanthropy that echoes the perspective of many observers of the Annenberg Challenge:

> At best, [foundation] investment has yielded the rare and too often temporary "islands of excellence"—schools with a brief, shining moment of exemplary practice and performance that usually revert to the norm. Little in the way of improvement seems to stick. Today, there is little dispute among leaders in the field of school reform that the social return on philanthropic investment has been grossly inadequate.[103]

Since the Annenberg Challenge, the landscape of major education philanthropies has shifted, and the Gates Foundation is currently the dominant grant maker in the field; other new foundations, such as Broad and Walton, became top 10 grant makers after 1998. These foundations observed the outcomes of the Annenberg Challenge and responded with a different approach. According to Eli Broad, "[The Annenberg Challenge] was a non-confrontational approach to reform. [It] was not set up to challenge the status quo."[104]

Broad, Gates, and Walton are each associated with the move toward "venture philanthropy" or "results-oriented" giving.[105] This approach to philanthropy draws on a business model, particularly strategies for investment in successful start-up ventures in the technology sector. As Broad Foundation managing director Dan Katzir stated at a Democrats for Education Reform event in March 2009, "[Eli Broad was] interested in venture philanthropy: funding or creating out-of-the-box solutions to chronic problems, and then measuring the student 'return on investment.'"[106] Of course, using the language of "investments" and "returns" does not directly translate to full-fledged business practices. None of the major practitioners of venture philanthropy actually report a return on investment in their annual reports.[107] Yet this does not mean that the rise of venture philanthropy as a common framework among foundations is inconsequential. Rather, it demonstrates that foundation leaders have new and heightened expectations for the output of their charitable endeavors—significant policy change and measurable results. Undoubtedly, tracking significant results in a field as complex as education is extremely challenging, and these foundations may never report a return on investment figure. Despite the difficulties involved in achieving and documenting measurable results, venture philanthropy has had measurable effects on foundation grant-making strategies.

Another area where major foundations and their grantees have applied practices more common in the business world is the use of management consultants. With the launch of Bridgespan Group in 2000, a nonprofit consulting firm spun off from Bain & Company, the market for applying business strategies to the philanthropic and nonprofit sectors has been on the rise. Major foundations have sought advice from management consultants early and often as they develop grant-making and evaluation strategies. A Harvard Business School case study from 2000 on Bridgespan's first year describes its work in the philanthropic sector:

> Bridgespan's largest client was a major foundation. Bridgespan had completed a strategy project to assist the foundation in adopting a "venture philanthropy"-type approach to its grant-making—fewer grantees, bigger investments, and higher engagement with its grantees. As Bridgespan became involved in the implementation of this new strategy, the foundation had also agreed to a seven-figure engagement with Bridgespan to assist its high-potential grantees in developing their growth strategies.[108]

This statement may refer to the Gates Foundation, which has been a regular client of Bridgespan, spending several million dollars for foundation strategy documents and on behalf of grantees. In 2001, the Broad Foundation commissioned

RAND to develop an evaluation strategy for the foundation. The report includes four logic models for assessing various types of programs designed to measure the Broad Foundation's impact.[109] Several management consulting firms have recently developed specialized education consulting "shops," including McKinsey & Company, the Parthenon Group, Boston Consulting Group (BCG), and Booz Allen Hamilton, as well as Bridgespan.[110] The use of management consultants further demonstrates the growing preoccupation with applying business strategies and demonstrating effectiveness among major foundations.

Still, talk of investments and hiring consultants could be symbolic gestures—making philanthropy appear more businesslike without producing observable changes in practice. In chapter 2, I show that significant changes have occurred in education grant making in the past decade. Education grant making has converged in three ways as top foundations have claimed to adopt the practices of venture philanthropy: foundations are giving less money to the public sector and more money to private-sector education organizations, they are targeting their resources at fewer school districts, and they are favoring districts with particular political characteristics and nonprofit capacities.

With more money, a bolder approach to involvement in policy, and a new focus on applying business practices and evaluating effectiveness, major foundations have positioned themselves to be more influential in education policy. Yet these changes do not erase old challenges to philanthropic involvement in policy. Foundations and individual philanthropists do not represent a broader political constituency. Thus, they are highly vulnerable to charges of elitism or accusations that they are outsiders bringing unwanted changes to a local community. In many respects, a greater role in policy advocacy only increases the vulnerability of foundations to these charges. The more philanthropists show support for particular policy approaches, the more they raise public attention to their role and draw questions about why wealthy private foundations should have significant influence on public education policy. Philanthropic efforts to influence education policy involve the lives of millions of students, parents, and teachers, who often believe that they are closest to the problems and best equipped to determine the course for the future.

Conclusion

The opportunity for greater foundation influence in education policy—especially in urban school districts—is a story of converging circumstances, akin to a perfect storm. No Child Left Behind changed the politics of urban districts, market-based reforms changed the stream of ideas for reforming education, and changes in philanthropy made foundations more capable of engaging directly in education policy. The events that led to these changes mostly emerged independently, but these changes are complementary in many respects and increasingly intertwined. As I have argued, NCLB and market-based reforms changed school district politics in significant ways, making districts more open to outside influence and making traditional district leaders appear unequipped and ill prepared to deal with failing schools. Meanwhile, the changes in philanthropy made education foundations more engaged in public policy and more strategic in leveraging their wealth.

In the remainder of this book, I trace how foundations intervene in urban school districts. I begin with a national perspective—"following the money" to see which school districts attract the most foundation grants and which types of organizations receive the most funds. Then, I look more closely at the intersection of foundation grant making and urban education politics in case studies of New York City and Los Angeles. I show the grant-making strategies that foundations have adopted in each place, track their interaction with local political actors, and assess the political and policy consequences of foundation involvement. This approach draws on previous work that emphasizes how local conditions can shape the consequences of federal policies in different urban areas.[111] Rather than focusing on federal policies, I regard foundation grant making as a broad multicity intervention that works through local political actors to produce policy change.

Although NCLB and market-based reforms have opened the door for outside involvement in urban districts, they have not fully homogenized urban education politics. Negotiating the politics of urban school districts with a cookie cutter is not a recipe for success. Philanthropists have accounted for some political variation across districts in their grant-making strategies. The most obvious political differences involve the governing systems of urban school districts: the majority of districts are governed by elected school boards, but a growing number are governed by boards appointed by the mayor or are under state control. As I show in chapter 2, major foundations have used this difference in governing systems to help guide grant-making strategies. But districts also differ in much more complex ways that can be difficult to observe without extended involvement in local politics. For example, there are considerable differences across urban school districts in the perspectives of the teachers' union leadership, the quality and diversity of the charter school sector, and the history of engagement and collaboration with community organizations in education. Race and ethnicity also play a significant role in the politics of urban school districts, given the long and contentious history of unequal education and segregation in schools.[112] Furthermore, foundation intervention in urban education can affect the existing politics of urban districts and even change the balance of power among different groups. Major foundations have adopted a steadfast focus on achieving significant policy outcomes and other measurable goals from their investments. Yet foundation involvement in urban education policy also produces political consequences; these consequences can feed back into the political system in ways that may either bolster or undermine foundation-supported policies in the long term.

CHAPTER 2

Following the Money from Foundations to Urban School Districts

In 2005, Boston received more than $11 million in major foundation grants supporting K-12 education, but Detroit—a district more than twice as large and in much worse condition—received just 1 percent of Boston's total. Why do some large urban districts receive scarcely any major foundation grants, while others collect more than $10 million in grants in a single year? Major foundations choose certain districts as targets for investment, and there is systematic variation in the types of districts that do get substantial grant dollars and the types that do not. The source of this variation is not entirely evident based on the public pronouncements of foundation directors and program officers, although two foundation heads—Bill Gates and Eli Broad—have recently offered personal support for mayoral control of school districts.[1] Foundation program officers' specific grant-making preferences are often not widely known, and the process of selecting grantees at many major foundations is typically hidden from public view. Hoffman and Schwartz provide a particularly vivid account of foundation decision making:

> Grantees are rarely privileged to know how decisions are made and by whom, starting with decisions to fund their own projects, although they usually know with clock-like precision the day and hour of the board meeting in which the decision will be made. Because foundations take action in sealed rooms, their decisions have an air of authority....And to seal the curtain around foundations, good program officers are schooled in decorum. They are socialized to be pleasant, to listen well and respectfully, and not to disclose doubt, confusion, or dissatisfaction. And the elegantly argued white papers on strategy that appear on foundation Web sites simply underscore the reserved, consistent message of those with power, money, and choices.[2]

This account largely mirrors my own experience as a researcher who interviewed several foundation program officers; they were agreeable and interested in being helpful, but most program officers did not stray far from the material already available on the foundation's Web site.

Although transparency is not a hallmark of philanthropic giving, it would be inaccurate to imply that foundations have strict formulas for identifying grantees or school districts for investment that they simply refuse to disclose. Constancia Warren, the former senior program officer and director of urban high school initiatives at Carnegie Corporation of New York, explained that "there are a range of factors that influence the choice of where to invest."[3] Warren described five factors that could shape major foundations' decisions. First, foundations may focus on sites that offer "good laboratories" to test their preferred solution. Warren attributes this emphasis to a shift from "more traditional charitable giving (based primarily on need) to strategic giving (based more on demonstrating approaches and solutions that will have wider applicability)."[4] A second consideration, Warren explained, is selecting a range of places with "an appropriate distribution of geographic and demographic characteristics" to exhibit national impact. The third factor Warren mentioned involves capacity: "Do the sites have the underlying professional and political capacity to implement the change the foundation is supporting—or any kind of meaningful reform?" In particular, Warren added, foundations may avoid sites that are "fragmented and disorganized." Fourth, Warren explained that national foundations may seek sites with local foundations that are potential collaborators. Fifth, according to Warren, foundations may ask: "What is the track record of past education reform in this site?"[5] She noted that some districts gain reputations for misusing grant dollars, and a good reputation could override other considerations.

Many of these characteristics are difficult to measure and offer broad discretion for program officers. Yet these guidelines boil down to a simple premise: foundations, not surprisingly, prefer to invest funds in cities where they believe that their policy agenda has some hope of success. Although they may not have a checklist or scorecard for identifying the right cities, I argue that foundations do operate with a set of underlying expectations about the political and organizational characteristics that make some places ripe for reform and others a dead end; these expectations are particularly linked to the "professional and political capacity" of school districts that Warren highlighted. The first expectation is that centralized authority is preferable to fragmentation. Districts with mayoral or state control, as opposed to an elected school board, have a clear advantage in this regard. Mayoral or state-controlled districts rely on more centralized decision-making processes and avoid the political uncertainties of bargaining and public scrutiny that are more typical with elected school boards. An added bonus for foundations seeking greater national prominence for their agenda is the opportunity to partner with a well-known big-city mayor who is seeking to build a reputation by promoting extensive education reforms. The second expectation is that a high level of professional capacity and expertise outside the school district is more essential than capacity within the district; in other words, a place should have a strong local nonprofit advocacy sector and a sizable local pool of highly educated individuals.[6] These local resource endowments provide assurance to foundations that the right kinds of organizations and the right kinds of people will be available to work on foundation-supported initiatives. Major foundations do not fully specify who or what the right kinds of people and organizations might be, but the frequent mention of "entrepreneurs," "change agents," and "innovators" in foundation annual reports sends a strong message: experience working inside a school district bureaucracy may not be necessary or even preferred.

Using an original data set of foundation grants from the top 15 donors to K-12 education for 2000 and 2005, I show where foundations invest the most grant dollars and why. I highlight evidence that foundations have grown increasingly selective in allocating grants to districts since 2000. Focusing on the 2005 grant data, I assess the relationship between school district characteristics and grant dollars per student for each of the 100 largest school districts. I show that district need has only a small effect on the distribution of foundation grants; instead, foundations give more funding to districts with political and organizational features that appear to increase the likelihood of foundation influence.

Data

"How much philanthropic funding goes to each of the 100 largest school districts?" seems like a simple question. Yet neither districts, state departments of education, nor the U.S. Department of Education compiles these data. In contrast, district revenue from all public sources (federal, state, and local) is compiled annually by the National Center for Education Statistics. Other researchers have found that district-level data on education grant making is difficult to gather. In a study of philanthropic involvement in district reform in Charlotte, Houston, and San Diego, Jenkins and McAdams explain:

> When we began, we expected the task of collecting information about philanthropic giving in these districts to be straightforward. These expectations were quickly dashed. In each district, different people (and in some cases, different organizations) were responsible for different grant projects, and no one seemed to have a grasp of the whole.[7]

A study that puts forward a systematic method to collect these data also begins by stating some hurdles. According to Greene, "It is impossible to know precisely how much philanthropic giving to K-12 education there is. Nonprofit organizations face only limited disclosure requirements when it comes to the purposes of their expenditures."[8] Greene notes that the data gathered by the Foundation Center, an organization supported by foundations to collect and track information on grant making, is incomplete and potentially biased. The Foundation Center allows its member organizations to categorize their own grants, meaning that grant categorization can be inconsistent from one foundation to the next. Greene's solution to this problem was to collect data from the tax returns (the 990-PF form) of the largest donors to K-12 education for 2002.[9]

Drawing on Greene's method, I collected data from the 2000 and 2005 990-PF forms filed by the 15 foundations that gave the most money for K-12 education.[10] I used lists compiled by the Foundation Center to identify the 15 largest donors in both years; the lists of the 15 largest donors for each year are in Appendix A.[11] On the 990-PF, foundations report every grant they disbursed during the fiscal year. In some cases, they also report the location of the recipient and the purpose of the grant. For each grant that directly funded K-12 education, training and support for K-12 personnel, K-12 policy advocacy or research, or supplementary education services for K-12 students, I recorded the amount of each grant, the recipient, the recipient's location (when available), and the purpose of the grant (when available). When the recipient's location and/or the grant purpose were not included in the tax form, I conducted a Google search to identify the grantee and obtain the information about the grantee's location and purpose.[12] For 2005, the data set includes nearly 1,600 grants totaling more than $660 million. The Foundation Center reports that about $1.18 billion in grants was distributed for K-12 education in 2005, so the data set accounts for more than half of this estimate of total grant dollars. For 2000, the data set includes more than 1,200 grants totaling more than $380 million. According to the Foundation Center, about $1.2 billion in grants was distributed that year, so the 2000 data account for nearly a third of the total grants estimate. These totals suggest that a considerably greater share of grant dollars for education was distributed by the largest foundations in 2005 than in 2000.

I coded each grant recipient into one of 46 categories; the full list of categories is available in Appendix B. The categories are based on the grantee's function or role, such as school districts or after-school programs. To determine the total grant dollars devoted to grantees in a given school district, I isolated all the grants in categories that were geographically constrained at the school district level, including grants to public schools, charter schools, nonprofits, advocacy organizations, and any other local group. I also searched in all of the other grant categories for grants that mentioned a specific school district in the description of their purpose. I grouped all of these grants based on the locations of the grantees and then totaled the grants for each school district. Using these data, I worked to

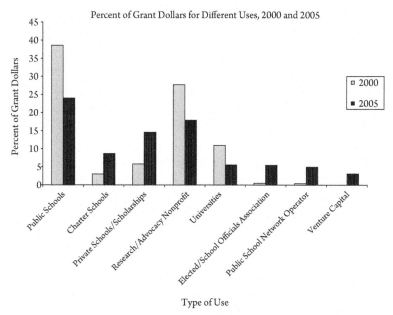

Figure 2.1
Source: Author's data gathered from foundation tax returns.

determine which school districts receive the most foundation grants and assess the relationship between school district characteristics and grant dollars.

Funding the Competition

Since 2000, major foundation grant making has shifted away from supporting public school districts directly and increasingly toward sectors that may compete with traditional public schools, such as charter schools. To assess trends in funding priorities among the major K-12 grant makers, I aggregated the funding totals for 2000 and 2005 to several types of grantees.[13] Then I calculated the percent of funding to each grantee type out of the total funds distributed that year. The results are displayed in figure 2.1. Several contrasts between grant making in 2000 and grant making in 2005 are evident in the graph. First, the amount of funding directed to public schools (via individual public schools, school districts, state education departments, and their respective foundations) was nearly 40 percent of grant dollars in 2000 but less than a quarter of grant dollars in 2005. In other words, foundations that are giving millions of dollars for K-12 education are increasingly unwilling to give those dollars directly to public schools and school districts.

The share of grants supporting nonprofit organizations focused on research or advocacy, as well as grants for universities, fell from 2000 to 2005.[14] Yet the proportion of grant dollars for charter schools and private schools rose considerably from 2000 to 2005. In 2000, grants to private schools, private school scholarships, charter schools, charter management organizations, and charter school associations accounted for less than 10 percent of all grants; in 2005, the share of grants in these categories grew to nearly a quarter of all grants. By 2005, the largest foundations invested nearly equal shares of their grant dollars in organizations that create alternatives to school districts and in the public institutions that run the schools.

Other categories received scarcely any funds in 2000, including Elected/School Officials Associations, Public School Network Operators, and Venture Capital. Each of these categories received more than $20 million in grants by 2005. The rise in grants to Public School Network Operators is almost entirely a function of the Gates Foundation's emphasis on creating small public high schools. Gates executed this strategy by funding nonprofit organizations, such as Big Picture Company, Envision Schools, and High Tech High, which replicate specific small school models across different districts. Venture Capital is a new category for 2005; none of the grants in 2000 fits that description. Most of the grants in this category went to a single organization, the New Schools Venture Fund, based in San Francisco. Founded in 1998, its purpose is to apply the principles of venture capital investing in technological innovation to education reform by funding new education organizations and tracking returns on their investments. New Schools Venture Fund has provided funding for charter management organizations, Teach for America, and organizations focused on principal training, such as New Leaders for New Schools.

The increased funding for Elected/School Officials Associations, such as the National School Boards Association and the National Conference of State Legislatures, suggests increasing foundation involvement with policy makers and political leaders. For example, a 2005 grant of nearly half a million dollars from the Gates Foundation to the National League of Cities was intended to "stimulate municipal leadership for the development of alternative secondary schools in diverse communities across the nation." The Gates Foundation also gave $108,376 to the National Conference on State Legislatures for "a conference on high school redesign and reform."[15] In both cases, the foundation provided funding to promote high school reform among elected officials. Thus, in addition to funding organizations to start new small high schools, the Gates Foundation attempted to influence political leaders at the state and local levels to support high school reform.

Although it does not stand out among the categories reported here, the idea of accountability played a much larger role in 2005 grant making than it did in 2000. In 2000, only five grants mention data or accountability in the description of their

K-12 Grants from Old and New Foundations in 2000 and 2005

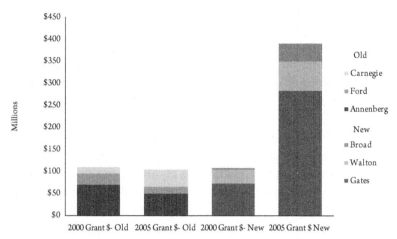

Figure 2.2
Source: Author's data gathered from foundation tax returns.

purpose. In 2005, more than 30 grants mention data or accountability. For example, an $8.3 million grant from the Gates Foundation to the Council of Chief State School Officers was designated "to provide states with sophisticated, web-based tools that will strengthen accountability and improve results through data-driven decision making." Taken together, the shift in targets for education grant making from 2000 to 2005 demonstrates the rise of the Boardroom Progressive agenda. Foundations are increasingly funding alternatives to public schools and accountability systems and avoiding grants directly to public school bureaucracies.

The Boardroom Progressive agenda is most ardently promoted by a new group of philanthropists tied to new wealth—Bill Gates with Microsoft, Eli Broad with KB Homes, and the Walton family with Wal-Mart. East Coast foundations once dominated philanthropy. Currently, some of the largest donors border the Pacific, such as Gates in Seattle and Broad in Los Angeles. These West Coast foundations just began to enter the ranks of the top 20 education grant makers starting in 2000.[16] In 2000, the $500 million Annenberg Challenge was still underway, and older foundations—Annenberg, Carnegie, and Ford—gave more than $110 million in grants combined (figure 2.2).[17] In the 1990s, the Annenberg Challenge grants supported public-private partnerships between school districts and collaborating nonprofit intermediaries. Since the Annenberg Challenge, there has been "a changing of the guard" in K-12 philanthropy.[18]

According to figure 2.2, the total amount of grants given by older foundations remained stable from 2000 to 2005, but the grant dollars given by the newer foundations, Gates, Broad, and Walton, nearly quadrupled. The massive increase in funding is not the only thing that sets these foundations apart;

these foundations have also adopted a more forceful approach to grant making. According to Ravitch:

> [The new foundations] wanted nothing less than to transform American education. They would not leave local communities to design their own reforms and would not risk having their money wasted. Their boldness was unprecedented.[19]

The large infusion of grant dollars from new foundations and the focus on new types of grantees both represent an important shift in education philanthropy and the rise of a new agenda, and my data clearly support this conclusion. Yet I do not want to overstate the difference between old and new philanthropy. Although the Gates, Broad, and Walton Foundations are more frequently identified with the venture philanthropy approach, many of the largest foundations are adopting similar grant-making strategies. For example, the grant-making preferences of old philanthropy sometimes resemble new philanthropy. According to Janice Petrovich, who served as Ford's director of education, sexuality, and religion until April 2008, "Most foundations are not providing direct support to the school system. They are supporting organizations outside the school system that have an impact inside the school system."[20] Petrovich explained that large urban districts, such as New York City, have very large budgets, "so giving money to a school system is a drop in the bucket." She also commented that the strength of outside organizations is their innovative capacity.

In 2000, major foundations provided a large share of grant dollars directly to public schools. By 2005, a new group of education philanthropists had substantially increased their grant making and focused their grant dollars in a new direction—supporting organizations that compete with school districts and supporting engagement with elected officials. At the national level, these changes have helped to build the charter school movement and fund the nationwide growth of new organizations such as Teach for America and KIPP. Yet the impact of this new direction can be even more potent at the local level when foundations selectively target certain districts with substantial funds.

More Dollars, Fewer Districts

The distribution of major foundation grants among large urban school districts favors a small number of districts. In 2005, grantees in fewer districts received funding from the top 15 foundations than in 2000, despite the increase in the total grant dollars allocated. In 2000, grantees in 47 of the 100 largest districts received some philanthropic support. By 2005, grantees in only 34 of the 100

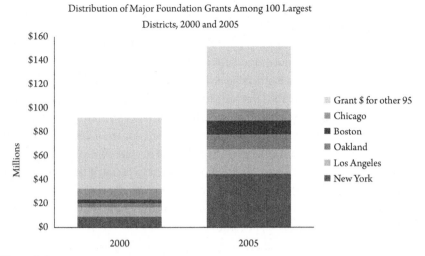

Figure 2.3
Source: Author's data gathered from foundation tax returns.

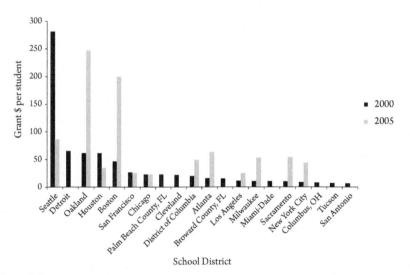

Figure 2.4
Source: Author's data gathered from foundation tax returns.

largest districts received funding. Although the total grants allocated by the 15 largest donors grew by more than $300 million from 2000 to 2005, these grants were less widely distributed among the 100 largest districts in 2005.

Therefore, it is not surprising that the level of support for grantees in certain districts increased substantially from 2000 to 2005. Figures 2.3 and 2.4 compare funding to grantees in specific districts in 2000 and 2005: figure 2.3 provides total grants in dollars, and figure 2.4 displays grant dollars per student. The top five recipient districts for 2005 are distinguished from the other 95 largest districts in figure 2.3. In 2005, these five districts—New York City, Los Angeles, Oakland, Boston, and Chicago—received more foundation grants than all of the 100 largest districts in 2000. Also, the top five districts received 65 percent of major foundation grant dollars distributed to the 100 largest districts in 2005. The total grants to districts in 2005 offer preliminary confirmation of the importance of mayoral or state control. Four of the five districts receiving the most grant dollars in 2005—New York City, Oakland, Boston, and Chicago—had mayoral or state control.

Given the vast differences in student enrollment in many of these districts, it is useful to compare the total dollars to grantees in each district on a per student basis. Figure 2.4 presents the top 20 districts based on grant dollars per student in 2000, along with the grants per student that grantees in each district received in 2005. Although grantees in New York City and Los Angeles received the largest total amounts of grant dollars in 2005, these districts are also very large: New York City has more than 1 million students, and Los Angeles has nearly 700,000 students. On a per student basis, Oakland and Boston stand out in 2005 because both have grants per student totaling more than $200. This graph also emphasizes the spike in additional grant dollars from 2000 to 2005 in certain districts; in addition to Oakland and Boston, grants per student to grantees in Washington, D.C., Sacramento, and Atlanta increased substantially. Meanwhile, other districts, such as Seattle and Detroit, lost foundation funding from 2000 to 2005. The Seattle case demonstrates the willingness of the Gates Foundation to cut funding to a district that no longer appears to be a good investment, even when it is the foundation's home turf. According to Clemens and Lee, "Repeatedly, [the Gates Foundation] has declined to extend—and has even cut—grants to districts where the leadership appears either in disarray (as in nearby Seattle) or less than committed to the small high school initiative."[21]

The decrease in the total number of districts receiving philanthropic dollars, combined with an increase in funding to grantees in certain districts, demonstrates that many foundations are increasingly selective about their investment in districts. Simultaneously, these foundations are interested in fueling ambitious reforms, and they are willing to invest large sums to do so. The clustering of investments in a shrinking set of large districts suggests that many foundations make their investment choices based on specific district characteristics.

Why Boston but Not Detroit?

The total foundation funds for grantees in specific school districts clearly show that certain school districts take in the bulk of grant dollars. Yet it is possible that the difference between these districts and the districts that get few grants is arbitrary or that districts serving large numbers of low-income students get most of the grants. A multivariate model offers an initial assessment of the relationship between school district characteristics and major foundation grants. I argue that two key factors guide foundation grant making—mayoral or state control and nonprofit capacity/expertise—and I test these expectations with two models. To evaluate whether mayoral or state control of districts and nonprofit capacity/expertise are significantly related to foundation grants, we need to first account for some alternative explanations.

I explore a few other explanations for variations in foundation grant making to school districts. The most salient is that foundations fund districts that have the greatest needs—districts with the poorest students and lowest graduation rates. This is the most intuitive explanation for why some districts would get major foundation investments while others would not. After all, foundations are philanthropic institutions, and philanthropy is often motivated by helping those in the greatest need. Yet I expect that many of the neediest districts also lack the characteristics that foundations regard as promising for promoting reform—centralized governing and nonprofit/expert capacity. Thus, some struggling districts will be left behind, receiving few or no grant dollars from foundations.

Another alternative is that restrictive teacher union contracts bar the type of reforms the donors would like to advance, such as merit pay. Thus, foundations would be less likely to invest in districts with highly restrictive teacher contracts. Yet given the powerful position of unions in most large urban districts, I do not expect union contracts to be an important factor. According to Hess and Loup, only 5 of the 50 largest school districts have flexible labor agreements, including three districts in Texas.[22] To avoid powerful unions, foundations would be restricted to making grants in Texas and a few other Southern states that prevent collective bargaining for teachers. Furthermore, some major foundations are providing grants directly to unions to encourage their leaders to adopt new merit pay systems or collaborate on charter schools. In these cases, foundations seem interested in seeking out powerful unions to promote policy change through these organizations.

A third alternative is that foundations prefer to fund reforms in districts governed by nontraditional superintendents—individuals with backgrounds in business or law, for example, rather than education. Perhaps these individuals are more likely to be viewed as reformers because of their unconventional backgrounds. Fourth, I assess whether major foundations give more grant dollars to school districts that are close to the foundation's headquarters. Foundations may show a preference for their home city or neighboring cities, due to relationships with local leaders or an interest in maintaining good relations with the surrounding community. Appendix C includes a detailed description of the sources and data collection processes for each independent variable.

Table 2.1 presents two Tobit regression models predicting 2005 grant dollars per student to the 100 largest districts.[23] Model 1 incorporates most of the alternative explanations; model 2 is more limited and offers support for both mayoral or state control and nonprofit capacity/expertise as explanations of foundation grant-making patterns.[24] Model 1 includes the number of top 15 education grant makers in the metropolitan area of each school district. This variable is not statistically significant, showing that major foundations do not give more grants in their immediate vicinity, controlling for other factors. A dichotomous variable indicating whether a district has a nontraditional superintendent is also included in model 1, and it is not statistically significant. On average, districts with nontraditional superintendents received about $23 in grants per student, and districts with traditional superintendents received about $9.50; the difference in means is not statistically significant. In contrast, districts with mayoral or state control received an average of $67 in grants per student, compared with only $6.50 per student in districts governed by an elected school board; this difference in means is statistically significant ($p < 0.01$). I chose not to include the teacher labor agreement flexibility variable in this model because it is available for only 50 cases. The bivariate correlation between this variable and grants per student is insignificant, and the variable is also insignificant when included in the multivariate model.

The models include three independent variables to test my two initial expectations: mayoral or state control, nonprofit advocacy density, and the percent of individuals with postgraduate degrees (on a scale from 0 to 100). I expected that each of these variables would increase grant dollars per student. Each of these variables is positive and statistically significant in both models, and the predicted effect of mayoral or state control on grants per student is particularly large.

Nonprofit advocacy density and the percent of individuals with postgraduate degrees are intended to capture a community's capacity to develop and support organizations that foundations prefer to fund. We can assess the combined impact of these variables by comparing two very different school districts in Texas: Austin and San Antonio. These districts are similar in one key respect—both have elected school boards. Yet the poverty rate of 5- to 17-year-olds in San Antonio is 37 percent; in Austin, it is much lower, 21 percent. These districts also vary considerably in the percent of individuals with postgraduate degrees—only 8 percent in San Antonio, compared with 15 percent in Austin. There is similar variation in the nonprofit advocacy organization density in each area: 2.6 per 100,000 in San Antonio and 7.4 per 100,000 in Austin. In 2005, grantees in San Antonio received only 35 cents in foundation grants per student, but grantees in Austin received nearly $25 per student. Although San Antonio has a much larger share of low-income youth than Austin, San Antonio is well below Austin on indicators of nonprofit capacity and expertise. Based on this comparison, the

Table 2.1 Tobit Regression on Grants per Student to 100 Largest Districts, 2005

	Model 1	Model 2
Mayoral/state control	55.87*	61.12**
	(24.51)	(21.83)
Nonprofit advocacy density	5.62*	6.04*
	(2.87)	(2.80)
Percent postgraduate degrees	8.54**	8.87**
	(2.43)	(2.32)
Percent poverty, 5- to 17-year-olds	2.02*	2.14*
	(1.08)	(1.07)
4-Year high school graduation rate	−1.29	−1.28*
	(.80)	(.76)
Top 15 foundations in region	7.21	——
	(11.41)	
Nontraditional superintendent	1.32	——
	(18.68)	
Constant	−99.84	−106.63*
	(63.56)	(61.24)
Likelihood-ratio X^2	51.30**	50.83**
N	94	94

Note: Table entries are unstandardized regression coefficients. For a one-tailed test of significance, $*p < 0.05$; $**p < 0.01$.

stronger capacity for a highly professionalized nonprofit sector in Austin appears to have attracted more foundation grants than San Antonio's high rate of youth poverty.

The largest predicted coefficient in both models is for mayoral or state control. Why do major foundations show such a strong preference for districts with mayoral or state control? Although most foundations do not publicly endorse a particular mode of governing school districts, the Broad Foundation's first publicly released annual report—in 2008—is quite explicit on this matter:

> Our work in this handful of cities—including Chicago, New York City and Oakland, Calif.—has deepened over time as we watched their progress. These cities have a common distinction: the school systems in New York City and Chicago are under the control of the mayor, and the school system in Oakland was placed under state control after facing

bankruptcy. We have found that the conditions to dramatically improve K-12 education are often ripe under mayoral or state control.[25]

The Broad Foundation 2009–2010 Annual Report reiterated and elaborated on the foundation's preference for mayoral or state control:

> But observing the frequent political turnover on school boards (and often the resulting shakeup in a school district's leadership or reform agenda) and the lack of focus on student achievement led us to conclude that a more successful governance structure than the country's 14,000 school boards was mayoral, gubernatorial or state control. So our work evolved into supporting mayors and governors in cities and states like New York, Boston, Washington, D.C., Chicago and New Orleans, where their education reform efforts are supported politically in a more sustainable way.[26]

These comments from the Broad Foundation reports and my interviews with program officers point to two seemingly contradictory factors that make districts with mayoral or state control attractive to grant makers—continuity and change.[27]

First, foundations prefer mayoral or state control because they assume that stable and centralized leadership offers greater security for their investment and the opportunity to develop relationships with district leaders over time. Foundation program officers speak of district leaders in some mayoral-led districts with great familiarity and confidence, for example, frequently referring to former New York City Chancellor Joel Klein as "Joel" and explaining that his leadership was "critical to making the district a good place to invest." Nonetheless, mayoral or state control does not always go hand in hand with leadership continuity. During five years of state control in Oakland, the district had three different state administrators. A few prominent examples of mayoral control in cities with well-known multiterm mayors (Daley in Chicago, Menino in Boston, and Bloomberg in New York City) may have advanced the notion that school governance change can foster leadership continuity. Yet even a "mayor for life" eventually moves on; Daley did not run for reelection in 2011, and Bloomberg completes his final term as mayor in 2013—after persuading the city council to pass a term limit extension that allowed him to run for a third term.

Second, in districts where foundations hope to catalyze dramatic reform, the disruption provided by a change in governance offers a window of opportunity to shape new policies. Some program officers described how a change in governance could enable significant policy change. According to Michele Cahill, vice president for national programs and program director of urban education at Carnegie Corporation, the reorganization of New York City's school district governance in 2002 enabled "a major mayoral-led reform that was a break with the status quo."[28] Following the state takeover of Oakland's public schools, philanthropists decided that conditions were "ripe to try something big."[29]

Although mayoral or state control has the largest effect on foundation grants per student, one alternative explanation is supported by the models in table 2.1. District need does matter, but its effect on grant dollars per student is much smaller than the effect of mayoral or state control, other things being equal. I used two indicators of district need in both models: one is a measure of youth poverty, and the other is a measure of academic performance. Youth poverty is statistically significant in both models, and graduation rate is statistically significant in model 2, the limited model. Both are significant in the expected direction: youth poverty has a positive relationship with grant dollars per student, and graduation rate has a negative relationship. Yet the estimated effects of each variable are quite small. Table 2.2 displays the predicted grant dollars per student based on district poverty and governing structure. High poverty was calculated at one standard deviation above the mean, or average, for district poverty. All other variables were held constant at their means. Based on the results for estimated grants per student, mayoral or state control has a much larger effect than poverty in a district. A high-poverty district with an elected board is predicted to receive about $20 less in grants per student than an average poverty district with mayoral or state control. This predicted difference is exemplified by comparing Detroit and Boston. Detroit is a high-poverty district, with a poverty rate of 31 percent for 5- to 17-year-olds, and Detroit had an elected school board in 2005. Boston's poverty rate for 5- to 17-year-olds is 22.5 percent, closer to the average for the 100 largest districts, and Boston has mayoral control. In 2005, grantees in Boston received $200 in grants per student, but grantees in Detroit received only $1.27 per student.

Evidence drawn from examples of governance changes also supports the importance of mayoral or state control. Consider the trajectories of two districts where political control changed between 2000 and 2005. In 2000, the majority of the members of Oakland's board of education were elected (although the mayor did appoint three members). Grantees in Oakland received about $2.4 million from the 15 largest grant makers that year. By 2005, Oakland's schools were fully taken over by the state, and grantees in Oakland received $11.4 million. In contrast, the Detroit public schools were controlled by the mayor in 2000, and grantees in Detroit received about $10.5 million. Yet in 2005, a voter referendum reinstated an elected school board in Detroit, and there was a single major foundation grant of $179,814 to a charter school that year. Of course, mayoral or state control is not always a direct route to philanthropic support. Two districts under mayoral or state control in 2005—Cleveland and Prince George's County—received no direct support from major philanthropies that

Table 2.2 Estimated Grant Dollars per Student by District Poverty and Governing Structure

	Elected Board	Mayoral/State Control
Average poverty	$5.31	$31.29
High poverty	$10.35	$45.48

Note: Estimates calculated using model 2 in table 2.1

year. Yet the dollars devoted to districts with mayoral or state control are substantial. Of the six other districts controlled by the mayor or the state, grantees in five of the districts received a total of more than $9 million in 2005.

By concentrating grants in districts with mayoral or state control, foundations have focused their efforts for reform where opportunities for democratic deliberation over policy change are least available. Districts with mayoral control primarily enroll African American and Latino students, yet a study of mayoral control in Cleveland and Chicago finds that centralization of district governance reduces minority political participation.[30] Certainly, if foundations seek to catalyze dramatic reforms, these changes can often be implemented more quickly in a district where fewer people must agree to the change. Yet there are consequences to enacting change when few of the critical stakeholders have a role in the process. This approach can turn potential allies into enemies and create pushback against reforms that might otherwise be effective. Foundations have largely overlooked these consequences, preferring the anticipated rewards of swift policy change.

Conclusion

The pattern of giving among the largest K-12 grant makers changed substantially from 2000 to 2005. First, grant dollars were distributed more heavily to public-sector education grantees in 2000; in 2005, charter and private school grantees received nearly the same share of funding as the public schools. This shift in priorities matches the rising Boardroom Progressive agenda, with its emphasis on competition for public schools and lack of faith in public bureaucracies. Second, among the 100 largest school districts, the number of districts with grantees receiving foundation funds dropped 28 percent from 2000 to 2005. Foundations became more selective by 2005, giving more grants to fewer districts. Third, the 15 largest grant makers distributed $300 million more in 2005 than in 2000, and certain districts received a much larger share in 2005, including New York City, Los Angeles, Oakland, and Boston.

Districts that predominantly enroll students from poor households were not necessarily the largest recipients of major foundation grants in 2005. Many of the 100 largest school districts enroll high numbers of poor students; the average percentage of students receiving free and reduced-price lunches in these districts is 47.6. Thus, foundations can choose among many districts with large numbers of students in poverty. The findings here show that foundations choose the districts that have a greater capacity to support nonprofits to provide education services and expertise. As a result, cities that have high educational inequality—struggling public school systems and large numbers of individuals with postgraduate education—typically receive more grant dollars. Districts like Austin, Oakland, Atlanta, and Washington, D.C., fit these criteria. In contrast, places like Detroit, Cleveland, San Antonio, and Santa Ana, California, with high rates of poverty and fewer highly educated individuals, are less likely to get many grants from major foundations.

The other key factor shaping major foundation grant making in 2005 is mayoral or state control. Given this funding pattern, we can expect greater pressure for mayoral or state control of struggling districts. Education Secretary Arne Duncan recently urged Michigan leaders to return the Detroit public schools to mayoral control.[31] Furthermore, in a district like New York City, where mayoral control was revisited by the state legislature in the summer of 2009, there is a strong incentive for the foundations invested in the district to find ways to lobby for maintaining mayoral control. By giving heavily to districts with mayoral or state control, foundations and their leaders become invested in supporting a particular arrangement of governance, as well as particular individuals who hold the office of mayor. Otherwise, they risk seeing their investments lost in the turbulence of electoral politics and a likely shift in priorities by the new district leadership. Yet this political risk can be avoided if foundations are willing to look beyond city hall for allies by working through a more transparent democratic process, persuading local constituents to support policy reforms, and garnering significant investments in reforms from local groups.

In chapters 3, 4, and 5, I examine philanthropic involvement in New York City and Los Angeles education reform. A close analysis of these school districts provides an opportunity to compare foundation strategies and their political consequences in a district with mayoral control to a district with an elected school board. Although both districts have a long history of foundation involvement in education policy reform, there are sharp differences in the funding relationships and political relationships between foundations, district leadership, and education organizational leaders in each district.

CHAPTER 3

From Annenberg to Gates

EDUCATION REFORM IN NEW YORK CITY AND LOS
ANGELES, 1990–2005

Foundations have provided substantial funding for education reform initiatives in both New York City and Los Angeles during the past decade. Yet underlying the fairly continuous stream of private funds to organizations in both districts are important changes in the strategy behind the grant making and the grantees targeted for funding. These changes include an increase in the total amount of grant dollars distributed within each district, increasing convergence in grant-making strategies across different foundations, and greater emphasis on organizations that focus on school replication, as well as human capital development and recruitment of noneducators into the education field.

Much like the changes in grant making shown in the previous chapter, these changes are driven by the rise of new foundations and their adherence to Boardroom Progressive education reform strategies. Nonetheless, there are also important differences in the strategies that major foundations have adopted in each city. Nearly the same group of major funders has been involved in both New York City and Los Angeles, but these foundations largely fund nonprofits that operate public schools in New York City while funding charter school organizations in Los Angeles.

Beginning with the reforms of the early 1990s and the Annenberg Challenge grants, I trace the direction of education reform in both districts and highlight the growing importance of major national foundations. Using social network analysis, I present funding networks for each district in 2000 and 2005 that illustrate the expansion of foundation funding in New York City and Los Angeles and the converging grant-making strategies of major foundations. I also highlight specific grants in 2005 tied to Boardroom Progressive priorities, such as developing charter schools and nonprofit education service providers. Last, I discuss how the reform of governing institutions in each district—the successful change to mayoral control in New York City and the failed attempt in Los Angeles—have shaped each district's political context.

Roots of Reform

Nearly one of every 30 public school children in the United States attends school in either New York City or Los Angeles public schools. Almost one in 10 Latino public school children are enrolled in these two districts. The size of both districts is daunting, whether one focuses on their budgets, staff, bus routes, food service systems, or, perhaps most often, their challenges. Based on data from 2004, both districts had four-year high school graduation rates below 50 percent.[1] In both districts, the share of students enrolled in the free or reduced-price lunch program during the 2004–2005 school year exceeded 70 percent.[2] The student body in both districts is exceptionally diverse, with large numbers of students who are first- or second-generation immigrants. In Los Angeles, the majority of students—more than 70 percent—are Latino. In New York City, no single racial or ethnic group composes a majority of the student enrollment, though Latinos are the largest group at nearly 40 percent.

Both districts are also caught in perpetual cycles of reform. Since the 1990s, reformers in New York City and Los Angeles have proposed both decentralization and centralization of administrative functions, mayoral control, increasing the involvement of nonprofit intermediaries, and expansion of charter schools. The role of major national foundations in education reform in both New York City and Los Angeles has grown substantially. Local actors generally promoted the ideas that drove education reform in both districts in the early 1990s.[3] These ideas have formed the roots of present-day reforms. New York City was the base of a movement to create small, personalized schools.[4] In Los Angeles, a community coalition—the Los Angeles Educational Alliance for Restructuring Now (LEARN)—developed a plan for district restructuring and decentralization adopted by the school board in 1993.[5] Key aspects of these reform efforts in both cities—small schools in New York City and decentralization in Los Angeles—have been broadened and deepened by new sets of actors in each district, including major foundations.

SMALL SCHOOLS IN NEW YORK CITY

New York City's public schools had a highly decentralized system of governing and elected representation from 1969 until the beginning of mayoral control under Mayor Bloomberg in 2002. The district was divided into 32 local districts, each governed by an elected board with broad discretion over hiring

and budgets.[6] Within the decentralized system, reform efforts were fairly disconnected and varied. The school district had many serious problems; most noto-
rious was the rampant corruption within some of the local school districts. In
some districts, local board members demanded kickbacks in exchange for jobs
in the district, and teachers were drafted to work for board members' political
campaigns.[7] Meanwhile, some districts became known for fostering new and
innovative schools. District 4 in East Harlem gained widespread recognition for
the development of small, personalized schools and public school choice.

The innovations in District 4 began in the 1970s, when East Harlem's schools
were among the worst in the city. A few small alternative schools were opened
there, including the famous Central Park East School founded by Deborah Meier,
and District 4 superintendent Anthony Alvarado encouraged the formation of
more alternative schools.[8] Although small schools may be the most enduring
aspect of the reforms in District 4, school size was only one dimension of a broader
school reform approach. Schools had autonomy to develop distinctive missions
and programs; families could choose among junior high schools in the district;
parent orientation and visiting opportunities were designed to inform choices.[9]
Additionally, schools such as Central Park East drew on the progressive education ideals of John Dewey, applying a model of democratic schooling with interac-
tive learning, portfolio assessment systems rather than standardized testing, and
extensive teacher involvement in school-level decisions.[10] Test scores improved
substantially in District 4 from 1974 to the late 1980s, and the share of students
from District 4 admitted to selective New York City high schools also increased.[11]

By the late 1980s, the success story of the District 4 schools was gaining wider recognition. In 1987, Deborah Meier was selected for a MacArthur
Foundation "genius" grant, and a flurry of media coverage followed. New York
City's new chancellor, Joseph Fernandez, looked to District 4 as a model for a
broader reform effort focused on small schools.[12] In the early 1990s, Fernandez
enlisted the Fund for New York City Public Education to support the creation
of additional new small schools. These schools were known as New Visions
schools, and the Fund for New York City Public Education changed its name
to New Visions for Public Schools.[13] Meanwhile, following the announcement
of the massive Annenberg Challenge in 1993, representatives from Annenberg
approached Deborah Meier to solicit a grant proposal for New York City.[14] Meier
brought together four organizations that collaborated on the proposal: New
Visions for Public Schools, the Center for Collaborative Education, the Center
for Educational Innovation, and Association of Community Organizations for
Reform Now (ACORN).[15] These four groups joined to form the New York City
Networks for School Renewal (NYNSR) and received a five-year $25 million
grant from the Annenberg Challenge, along with 2–1 matching grants from the
New York City Department of Education and private donors.[16]

The primary reform strategy of the NYNSR was the creation of networks of small schools. For Meier, who founded her first small school nearly two decades before the Annenberg Challenge grant, the infusion of funding and support from powerful organizations was a thrilling prospect. In a 2008 *Education Week* blog post, "The Collapse of the Annenberg Challenge," she states:

> I was just recently going through the documents from [the Annenberg Challenge] and recalling my disbelief and joy—could it possibly be (I kept pinching myself) that all the powers-that-be have signed on to such a serious and visionary effort to innovate on a sufficient scale to really influence future policy?[17]

In the proposal, the four sponsoring organizations promised to open more than 100 new small schools. The project ultimately involved 5 percent of the district's students and 10 percent of the schools. The final evaluation largely judged the effort to be a success:

> Through the Annenberg Challenge grant, NYNSR created, restructured, or reorganized almost 140 schools serving almost 50,000 students, a sector of the New York City school system larger than most districts across the nation. Those 50,000 students, as an aggregate, were well-served by the NYNSR schools.[18]

This rosy picture is not fully supported by other accounts of the Annenberg Challenge in New York City. The strategy to work through intermediary organizations, rather than directly through the district, presented political challenges in New York City, as well as other Annenberg Challenge sites. In New York City, the Annenberg reforms initially had the support of Chancellor Cortines, but they stumbled after the appointment of a new chancellor, Rudolph Crew, and "the dream died."[19] According to Meier, the officially sanctioned autonomy that the network schools had enjoyed ended under the new chancellor. She also states that the change in leadership fractured the collaboration between the four supporting organizations.[20] Meier elaborates on the demise of the Annenberg Challenge in New York City in her *Education Week* blog post, explaining that "the Annenberg Foundation and the sponsors saw no other solution but to take the money and salvage what they could."[21] According to Raymond Domanico, senior education policy advisor for the New York City Industrial Areas Foundation affiliate, Metro IAF, another weakness in the staying power of the Annenberg Challenge was the lack of investment in constituency building. In an interview, Domanico explained that his organization tried for almost a year "to get the Annenberg people to put some money into constituency building—it never got anywhere."[22] He cited the "lack of constituency building and road-blocks thrown up by Board of Education" as the main reasons the Annenberg Challenge reforms were not sustained.

Nonetheless, a core idea of the NYNSR and the District 4 reforms—small schools—has been a key component of the recent education reform efforts in New York City. Yet the new strategy for opening small schools in New York City—enlisting nonprofits to replicate particular school models and restructuring existing large high schools—is several steps removed from the original small school reforms of the 1970s. A new governing system and a new set of funders, particularly the Gates Foundation, have reshaped the way small school reforms are developed and implemented in New York City.

DECENTRALIZATION IN LOS ANGELES

For decades, the Los Angeles Unified School District (LAUSD) was governed by a system developed during the Progressive Era: board of education members were elected at-large with a superintendent managing the district.[23] Yet the district's highly centralized authority began to erode slightly in the 1960s. Desegregation lawsuits, teacher strikes, and public data showing the district's failure to educate many of its students "brought the District under increasingly hostile scrutiny" during the 1960s and 1970s.[24] Starting in 1978, the state mandated district elections for the seven members of the board of education, though this was a far cry from the more radical decentralization of elected representation that occurred in New York City.[25] Despite this electoral reform, the governing structure and bureaucratic organization of the district changed relatively little. According to Menefee-Libey, Diehl, Lipsitz, and Rahimtoola:

> The central elements visible in the Los Angeles school district by the end of the Progressive period remain today. Although restructured somewhat, the school board remains essentially divorced from the city's government.... The central office remains large, professionalized, and hierarchical, working to keep schools in compliance with the mandates of their various missions.[26]

During the 1980s, LAUSD developed two reform plans, Priorities for Education and The Children Can No Longer Wait, following release of the famous national report, *A Nation at Risk*. Two different superintendents requested each of the two reports, and both reports recommended decentralization by increasing the authority of principals and teachers at school sites. The second report, *The Children Can No Longer Wait*, also included a number of recommendations for spending priorities, such as reducing class size and increased funding for specialty staff such as librarians, nurses, and art teachers; this plan was adopted by the school board in 1989.[27] This plan guided district spending once the state-wide economy recovered in the late 1990s, but "hardly any of the ideas behind the reforms took root in immediate practice."[28]

Although the reform plans of the 1980s demonstrated recognition of the need for change, LAUSD seemed unable to effectively implement reform internally. By the 1990s, the momentum for school reform in Los Angeles was generated by three main sources outside the school district—charter schools, a community reform coalition, and the Annenberg Challenge. Unlike the reform proposals of the 1980s, the district leadership played little role in these reform efforts and remained resistant to change. As a result, these reforms served to further erode the capacity of the district and hastened new forms of decentralization by giving new actors control over schools within the district's boundaries.

In 1992, California was the second state to enact charter school legislation, following Minnesota.[29] Although the expansion of charter schools in Los Angeles began slowly, the district now has more charter schools than any other district nationally. Most of the early charter schools in the district were "conversion" charter schools: traditional public schools where teachers petitioned to convert the school to a charter school. Many of the conversion charters maintained affiliated status with LAUSD and retained "a fiscal and a service relationship with the District, purchasing services, utilizing district teachers, and participating in collaborative programs and professional development."[30] The expansion of charter management organizations (CMOs), which was well under way by the mid-2000s, led to the rapid growth of independent charter schools that have greater autonomy from LAUSD.

Although charter schools remained a relatively small development in the early 1990s, the Los Angeles Educational Alliance for Restructuring Now (LEARN) was a large, well-organized community coalition that demanded immediate reform of LAUSD. LEARN began with an unlikely alliance between business-man and future mayor Richard Riordan and United Teachers of Los Angeles (UTLA) president Helen Bernstein.[31] These two were drawn together by a common interest in reform; Riordan had been frustrated by previous attempts to help the district, and Bernstein had engaged in contract negotiations that led to implementation of site-based management in schools, an effort to decentralize some authority to school sites.[32] Early on, LEARN developed into an explicitly political organization, designed to build a broad coalition and put pressure on the school district. California Assembly Speaker Pro Tem Mike Roos was hired to lead the organization, and he operated it in ways that resembled both a political campaign and a social movement.[33] The heart of the organization was the Working Group, which included Riordan, Bernstein, several business leaders, a few community organization leaders, the superintendent of LAUSD, and the board of education president. To build a broader consensus for a reform plan, LEARN recruited more than 600 Angelenos to participate in seven task forces. Once a plan was developed, 90,000 signatures were collected to demonstrate community support.[34] The final LEARN plan drew on the previous reform plans developed by the school district; decentralization remained the core reform strategy. The school board adopted the plan in 1993 and "pledged to create a decentralized network as a form of organization in place of its well-established command and control hierarchy."[35] Of course, achieving adoption was not even half the battle—there was still the far more difficult process of implementation.

LEARN remained an outside organization charged with implementing reform within the district, although LEARN leaders had close ties with the district leadership. The implementation strategy for LEARN involved three components: "offering schools a choice to participate in the reform; decentralizing decision-making; and providing financial and professional development resources to schools."[36] The first LEARN cohort had 34 schools, although these schools were not fully representative of LAUSD as a district. In particular, predominantly Latino schools in East Los Angeles were not involved, an outgrowth of LEARN's failure to reach out to Latino groups during the political mobilization process.[37] Meanwhile, LEARN also faced the unwillingness of the central bureaucracy to relinquish authority; for example, based on the LEARN plan, the district had promised to grant schools control over 85 percent of their budgets, but this did not happen.[38]

The Annenberg Challenge claimed the spotlight for education reform at the point when LEARN was barely getting off the ground. Although initial discussions about developing an Annenberg Challenge grant proposal for Los Angeles involved some LEARN Working Group members, the final decision was to form an independent reform organization—the Los Angeles Annenberg Metropolitan Project (LAAMP).[39] The scope of LAAMP's work extended beyond the boundaries of LAUSD to include other districts in Los Angeles County; the teachers' union and school district leaders were not included in the LAAMP leadership. Also, rather than involving leaders in the business community, LAAMP's leadership drew more heavily from major universities—the University of California, Los Angeles and the University of Southern California.[40] In spite of the explicit organizational separation from LEARN, the reform agenda proposed by LAAMP was quite similar to LEARN. Specifically, LAAMP aimed to create decentralized networks of schools. According to the LAAMP final evaluation:

> The LAAMP proposal centered on the creation of the School Family, a new, intermediary organization that would bring sets of schools together in stable, intimate, learning communities to provide all children a quality, integrated K-12 experience and assure their continuous progress

toward high standards. Rooted in a commitment to decentralization, LAAMP asked School Families to combine professional development, parent and community involvement, rigorous standards-based curriculum, and assessment and accountability mechanisms in a coordinated effort to improve teaching and student learning.[41]

Thus, Los Angeles had two nonprofit organizations pushing similar agendas to support school-level decision making and liberate schools from bureaucratic rigidity. Due to the substantial size of the Annenberg Challenge grant—$53 million, matched 1–1—LAAMP was able to hire a staff of about 40, and LEARN remained a tiny organization.[42] LAAMP recruited LEARN schools to form school families within LAAMP, such that all of the LAUSD schools participating in LAAMP were also LEARN schools.

The schools affiliated with these reform efforts remained in the district but not entirely of the district. LEARN's training pushed schools "further away from historic behaviors and beliefs. District procedures, rules, and, in the end, the incentive system pulled them back."[43] Similarly, LAAMP helped develop new collaborative practices among schools within the School Families, but these changes did not affect ordinary district operations.[44] Although LAAMP reformers set out to catalyze systemic reform, those aspirations faded by the end of the initiative.[45] Neither reform effort fundamentally changed district practice. The LAAMP Board Chair Virgil Roberts did not mince words when asked what he learned from his experience: "That Los Angeles Unified as a school district is totally dysfunctional, and you probably can't fix it."[46] LEARN was declared "dead" by 1999, and LAAMP funding ended in 2000. One remaining vestige of LAAMP is a nonprofit organization, Families in Schools, which was created in 2000 and carries forward aspects of LAAMP's parent involvement agenda.[47]

Perhaps the most far-reaching legacy of these reform attempts is their reinvention as a blueprint for charter school management. Now, rather than working within the district for reform, the inheritors of LEARN's and LAAMP's legacies are more likely to be working on developing networks of charter schools. William Ouchi, a management professor at UCLA who served as LEARN chair in the late 1990s, attended a meeting of the New Schools Venture Fund where he learned about charter management organizations (CMOs): "I heard that and this light bulb went off in my head, ding! And I said, branded charter schools, federations of autonomous schools under a loosely knit central umbrella.... That's the LAUSD [as] we would like it to be. That's the LEARN plan."[48] During the past decade, a burgeoning group of CMOs has further advanced the decentralization of control of Los Angeles schools by developing networks of independent charter schools within district boundaries. Meanwhile, Roy Romer, the former governor of Colorado who served as LAUSD superintendent from 2001 to 2006, attempted to recentralize control of LAUSD. Yet major foundations have not focused grant dollars directly on reforming LAUSD since the conclusion of the Annenberg Challenge. Instead, the CMOs have attracted the bulk of major grants, promoting further growth of charter schools in the district.

Following the Money

In both New York City and Los Angeles, the influx of Annenberg Challenge grants helped to support and broaden existing streams of reform—small schools in New York City and decentralization in Los Angeles—but neither district was fundamentally changed by the Annenberg Challenge. Since the Annenberg Challenge, new major foundations have overtaken Annenberg as top grant makers in K-12 education, including the Gates Foundation, Broad Foundation, and Walton Foundation. With the additional funding from these new foundations, grant making for education has increased in both districts. Since 2003, a single organization focused on New York City education reform, New Visions for Public Schools, has received more foundation funding than the total amount of the five-year Annenberg Challenge in New York City—$75 million.[49] In 2005 alone, just three major education grant makers (Gates, Broad, and Annenberg) gave more than $18 million to support charter schools and education nonprofits in Los Angeles. By comparison, the total funding for the Los Angeles Annenberg Metropolitan Project, including the 1–1 matching grants, averaged about $17 million a year. Thus, current levels of foundation investment in these districts top the private funding generated by the Annenberg Challenge.

Yet the dollars alone do not account for the increasing foundation influence on education policy in each district. As grant making has increased, funders have also converged on a shared set of grant recipients and shared funding strategies. Thus, funding originating from multiple foundations tends to support a common policy direction, rather than promoting various pet projects. With these shared grant-making approaches, foundations have greater potential to influence policy.

A close examination of grants for K-12 education in New York City and Los Angeles offers a window to observe this shift in philanthropic strategy. Using the data gathered from the 2000 and 2005 tax returns of the 15 largest K-12 grant makers, I identified each grant focused on education in New York City or Los Angeles, including grants to charter schools, nonprofits, advocacy organizations, and universities, as well as the New York City Department of Education and Los Angeles Unified School District. I present the grants from major foundations to grantees in each city using social network analysis. The network data was analyzed using UCINET Version 6.216.[50] I used the NetDraw program available in

UCINET to create visual representations of each social network.[51] These social network diagrams highlight instances of convergence in grant making—when more than one foundation supports the same grantee. There are four networks— one network for each city displaying grants from 2000 and a separate network for each city with 2005 grants (figures 3.1, 3.2, 3.3, and 3.4). In each network, the foundations and their grantees are represented with circles, or nodes— foundations are white nodes and grantees are black nodes. Grantees that receive grants from more than one major foundation are distinguished with gray nodes. The thickness of the lines linking the foundations to their grantees indicates the relative size of the grant—thicker lines represent larger grants.[52]

In 2000, the Annenberg Foundation was the main grant-maker in both cities (figures 3.1 and 3.3). The Annenberg Challenge was winding down in New York City by 2000. A key organization in the Annenberg Challenge—New Visions for Public Schools—received support from both the Ford Foundation and the Annenberg Foundation related to the Annenberg Challenge (figure 3.1). The Ford grant was designated for evaluation of the New York City Networks for School Renewal. The other major Annenberg grant, to the Center for Arts Education, was part of a separate Annenberg Challenge initiative in New York City focused on arts education. The Gates Foundation had just launched its education programs in March 2000.[53] The creation of "smaller, more personalized learning environments" was part of the Gates Foundation's mission at the outset.[54] In 2000, Gates funded a nonprofit organization in New York City called Community Studies "to support 39 New York City high schools in educational reform for small schools and performance assessment."[55] Thus, as early as 2000, the funding for small schools reform

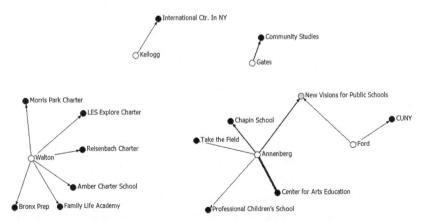

Figure 3.1 New York City Grant Network, 2000, Total Grants: $9 million. The figure depicts a two-mode network of foundations and grantees. Links indicate grants given; white nodes are foundations; black nodes are grantees; gray nodes are grantees receiving funding from more than one foundation.

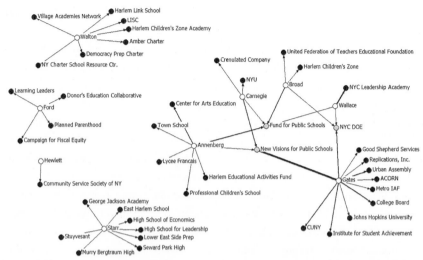

Figure 3.2 New York City Grant Network, 2005, Total Grants: $44.5 million. The figure depicts a two-mode network of foundations and grantees. Links indicate grants given; white nodes are foundations; black nodes are grantees; gray nodes are grantees receiving funding from more than one foundation.

in New York City was already shifting from Annenberg to Gates, although the role of the Gates Foundation remained limited. The Walton Family Foundation, a major supporter of school choice, supported several charter schools in New York City. One grant, from the Kellogg Foundation to the International Center in New York City, focused on community and parent organizing; according to Kellogg's tax return, the grant's purpose was to "expand and enhance programs to develop the capacity of immigrant youth and parents to become engaged in public education in New York City."[56] Overall, with the exception of Ford and Annenberg, the major foundations involved in New York City in 2000 pursued independent reform strategies through grants to different organizations.

By 2005, the grant-making picture in New York City became considerably more crowded (figure 3.2), and the grant-funding total from major foundations was five times the total in 2000. The Annenberg Challenge grants were no longer driving grant making, and the role of the Gates Foundation had expanded considerably. Three grantees received funding from more than one foundation in 2005 (indicated by gray nodes): New Visions for Public Schools, the New York City Department of Education (NYC DOE), and the Fund for Public Schools—the school district's education fund. Five foundations gave grants to at least two of these three entities: Gates, Broad, Wallace, Annenberg, and Carnegie. New Visions for Public Schools was a key organization in the Annenberg Challenge; this organization's involvement in New York City education reform has changed and grown substantially with increased philanthropic support.

Compared with 2000, there was considerable convergence of foundation grant-making agendas in 2005. The descriptions of specific grants from foundation tax returns explicitly demonstrate this convergence. For example, both the Gates Foundation and Carnegie Corporation gave grants to New Visions for Public Schools supporting the New Century High Schools initiative. This initiative involved the conversion of large New York City public high schools into campuses supporting several small high schools. Similarly, both the Gates Foundation and Broad Foundation gave grants to reform the Department of Human Resources within NYCDOE in 2005. According to each foundation's tax return, the Broad grant's purpose was "to analyze and redesign the New York City Department of Education Department of Human Resources,"[57] and the Gates grant's purpose was "to transform New York City Department of Education Human Resources from a personnel unit to a highly strategic, efficient, and effective organization."[58] Thus, foundations were not only committing grants to the same institutions but also, in this case, targeting the same division within the very large NYCDOE. These examples suggest that foundations intentionally coordinated their grant making to target more resources at specific reform initiatives.

Most of the grants from the Gates Foundation to grantees in New York City— around $20 million in 2005—were devoted to nonprofits to support the creation of small schools. In addition to more than $10 million for New Visions for Public Schools, several other organizations received grants of more than $1 million from the Gates Foundation for small schools, including the College Board, Urban Assembly, the Institute for Student Achievement, and Replications Inc. It is the last organization—Replications Inc.—that most explicitly distinguishes the Gates Foundation's strategy from the earlier approach to small school formation in New York City. The small schools formed in District 4 in the 1970s relied on the emergence of local leaders with a vision for a new school; the result was a diverse set of alternative schools. Yet the venture philanthropy model calls for rapidly scaling up reforms.

Replication was a strategy that allowed the Gates Foundation to reconcile the distinct visions of school founders with the goal of achieving broader impact. The result bears only slight resemblance to the small school reforms of the 1970s, and the Gates Foundation has received sharp criticism for its approach from some earlier adherents to the small schools movement.[59] The Gates Foundation selected nonprofit intermediaries, such as the Institute for Student Achievement and Replications Inc., which supported the formation of dozens of similar small schools based on a shared model or vision. The idea of replication was mentioned in annual reports of the Gates Foundation. In 2003, the annual report states: "Throughout the year, the foundation worked to replicate proven school models to expand access to great schools, especially in urban areas."[60] The 2004

Annual Report explains: "We also pursued ongoing work with intermediaries to help them replicate proven new school models and strategies for improving schools."[61] The strategy appears again in a 2004 newspaper article about former Gates Executive Director of Education Tom Vander Ark and the small school reforms: "These days, in fact, a lot of Vander Ark's time is spent on replication. 'One of the most important things we're trying to understand in our work is how to scale up success,' [Vander Ark] says."[62]

A few other foundations pursued relatively independent grant-making strategies in New York City. Walton continued its focus on supporting charter schools in New York City. Also, the Broad Foundation provided a small grant to the United Federation of Teachers to support two union-led charter schools—through a partnership with Green Dot Public Schools—in New York City. The Starr Foundation, based in New York City, primarily supported existing public schools in the city. Among major grant makers, only the Ford Foundation's grants focused heavily on advocacy organizations. In 2005, the bulk of the funding for grantees in New York City came from the new leader in education philanthropy, the Gates Foundation.

Turning to Los Angeles, the grant network for 2000 was dominated by the Annenberg Foundation (figure 3.3), much like New York City's grant network in 2000 (figure 3.1). The largest grant in the network, from the Annenberg Foundation to the California Community Foundation, was for the Annenberg Challenge in Los Angeles. Annenberg also directly funded both the Los Angeles Annenberg Metropolitan Project (LAAMP) and LEARN in 2000. LAUSD was

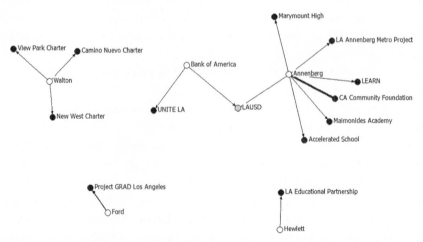

Figure 3.3 Los Angeles Grant Network, 2000, Total Grants: $8.1 million. The figure depicts a two-mode network of foundations and grantees. Links indicate grants given; white nodes are foundations; black nodes are grantees; gray nodes are grantees receiving funding from more than one foundation.

the only recipient of grants from more than one foundation—Annenberg and Bank of America Foundation—but both grants were relatively small and unrelated to one another. The Walton Family Foundation provided grants to charter schools in Los Angeles. The Gates Foundation did not give any K-12 education grants in Los Angeles in 2000. The Los Angeles–based Broad Foundation was founded in 1999 and had not yet begun large-scale grant making in 2000.

Both the Gates Foundation and the Broad Foundation were significant grant makers in Los Angeles by 2005 (figure 3.4). Annenberg also remained a large grant maker in 2005, providing ongoing support to Families in Schools, the organizational descendent of LAAMP. The grant to LEARN appears to be in name only—the purpose of the grant was for school playground construction. Rx for Reading, the common grantee for Annenberg and Broad, is a literacy program supported by the Riordan Foundation, started by former Los Angeles mayor Richard Riordan.

The strongest evidence of converging grant making in Los Angeles is in the charter school sector. Large grants from the Gates Foundation and Broad Foundation supported the growth of CMOs in Los Angeles, including KIPP, Green Dot Public Schools, and Aspire Public Schools, while Walton funded individual charter schools. Yet the largest grant from each foundation was for Pacific Charter School Development Inc. (PCSD). These three grants from Broad, Gates, and Walton were intended to support the primary mission of PCSD— the construction of facilities for charter schools. The buildings constructed by PCSD typically house schools operated by CMOs in Los Angeles; the PCSD Web site lists partner organizations, which are also "tenants," including Aspire Public Schools, Green Dot Public Schools, Inner City Education Foundation, KIPP, the Alliance for College Ready Public Schools, and Partnerships to Uplift Communities.[63] PCSD has already built or is planning to build facilities in and around Los Angeles for each of these CMOs. Of the $20.7 million in major foundation funding for grantees in Los Angeles, $16.2 million went to organizations supporting charter schools.

Another common thread linking PCSD, CMOs in Los Angeles, and major foundations such as Broad and Gates is the New Schools Venture Fund. Founded in San Francisco in 1998, the New Schools Venture Fund has provided funding to more than 30 nonprofit and for-profit education organizations. Gates and Broad are both investors in the New Schools Venture Fund, and starting in 2002, the New Schools Venture Fund raised about $50 million to support CMOs.[64] The New Schools Venture Fund was also a cofounder of PCSD in 2003. Thus, it is likely that the network of grants (figure 3.4) understates the web of relationships linking the actors involved in charter school expansion in Los Angeles, including major foundations, CMOs operating in Los Angeles, PCSD, and New Schools Venture Fund. For example, some of these organizations have overlapping

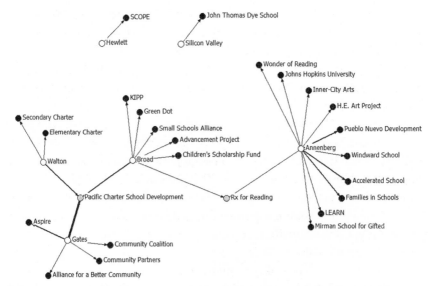

Figure 3.4 Los Angeles Grant Network, 2005, Total Grants: $20.7 million. The figure depicts a two-mode network of foundations and grantees. Links indicate grants given; white nodes are foundations; black nodes are grantees; gray nodes are grantees receiving funding from more than one foundation.

boards of directors. Representatives of the Broad Foundation, New Schools Venture Fund, and Green Dot Public Schools sit on the board of PCSD.[65]

From a national perspective, the geographic concentration of foundation funding for charter schools in Los Angeles is striking. The grants to organizations supporting charter schools in Los Angeles compose 28 percent of the total grant dollars for charter schools and charter-related organizations from major foundations in 2005.[66] Los Angeles is a hub for charter school expansion, particularly for charter schools operated by CMOs. The idea of replication is also evident in the funding for CMOs. Much like the nonprofits forming small schools in New York City, the CMOs operating in Los Angeles support the formation of charter schools based on a specific model. Some CMOs, such as the Alliance for College Ready Public Schools and Aspire Public Schools, operate schools with extended instructional time and develop their own assessments of student learning. The Inner City Education Foundation is known for an analytical writing program used in all of its schools. In some respects, CMOs are analogous to franchisers, a comparison that occasionally is made explicit. According to Kerchner, Menefee-Libey, Mulfinger, and Clayton, "Aspire's business model combines principles of entrepreneurship and standardization. [Aspire's cofounder] Shalvey likens it to the notion of the Starbucks model, where a cup of coffee at 6:00 AM tastes the same as one at 10:00 PM."[67] Thus, the strategy to scale-up reforms by funding nonprofits engaged in replication is used by the Gates Foundation in

New York City and by the Gates and Broad Foundations in Los Angeles. In New York City, these schools are typically small public schools, and in Los Angeles, they are charter schools.

In addition to replication, major foundations have also placed increasing emphasis on funding organizations that deal with human capital—teacher, principal, and district leader recruitment and training—in both New York City and Los Angeles. Of course, districts have had traditional routes for recruiting and training their staff for decades, typically involving local universities that provide teacher training and coursework for graduate degrees, as well as internal training and promotion. The foundation-funded organizations depart from traditional practices by recruiting individuals with experience outside education and by providing their own training and mentoring experiences. These organizations have played a significant role in recruiting and training staff that go on to work for education organizations tied to Boardroom Progressive priorities, including CMOs.[68]

Most of the human capital grants went to national organizations, so they do not show up in the networks, but these organizations have significant roles in each district. For example, Teach for America consistently raises millions of dollars from major foundations, including Broad, Walton, Gates, and Carnegie. Both New York City and Los Angeles have hundreds of Teach for America corps members and alumni serving as teachers. New Leaders for New Schools is a national organization that recruits and trains school principals. New Leaders does not work in Los Angeles, but in New York City, the organization has been involved with training principals for new small schools since 2001.[69] Last, the Broad Foundation created the Broad Residency Program, which recruits individuals with business experience to work in high-level management positions within school districts and charter school organizations. The first Broad Residency cohort was recruited in 2003. Eight current or former Broad residents are working in the NYCDOE, and four are working in LAUSD. Six current or former Broad residents are working in Los Angeles–based CMOs.[70]

Despite the convergence of foundation grant making to similar grantees and the increasing focus on school replication and human capital, there is an important difference in the targets of major foundation funding in New York City and Los Angeles. None of the major foundation grants in 2005 directly supported the school district in Los Angeles. The bulk of grants in Los Angeles in 2005 supported nonprofits involved in charter school expansion; thus, most of the major foundation resources for school reform were targeted at organizations that compete with LAUSD. Meanwhile, the New York City Department of Education received some direct support from major foundations for reform, and nonprofits received grants to create new small public schools within the district. This difference in funding strategies is likely a consequence of the different governing systems in each district

Mayoral Control

In 2005, districts with mayoral or state control received more major foundation grants, on average, than districts with elected school boards. The mayors of both New York City and Los Angeles have tried to gain control of the schools, but only New York City's mayor successfully gained full control of the school system. Complications due to overlapping jurisdictions and a lawsuit prevented mayoral control in Los Angeles.

New York City, which had a decentralized system of 32 local districts, was placed under mayoral control by state legislation passed in 2002. Mayor Bloomberg, who was elected in 2001, sought control of the schools soon after he took office.[71] New York City has a particularly centralized form of mayoral control. The mayor has the power to appoint the chancellor and to appoint the majority of an advisory board, known as the Panel for Educational Policy; there is no elected school board in New York City. Under this system, the mayor and his appointed chancellor have extensive authority to shape education policy in New York City.

In Los Angeles, Mayor Villaraigosa proposed a plan for mayoral control in 2005. In 2006, the California State Legislature passed a bill giving the mayor partial control over Los Angeles schools. Jurisdictional complications made full mayoral control unlikely: LAUSD encompasses cities other than Los Angeles, such as Huntington Park, Inglewood, and West Hollywood. Thus, the state legislation included provisions for a "council of mayors" representing the cities within LAUSD; additionally, the board of education would remain in place and retain limited powers. Villaraigosa was given direct control over three low-performing high schools and their feeder schools.[72] This law was challenged by a lawsuit filed by LAUSD, the California School Boards Association, and others, including parent organizations.[73] Ultimately, the law was ruled in violation of the state constitution. In 2007, Mayor Villaraigosa and LAUSD announced a new plan: the mayor would create a nonprofit organization, the Partnership for Los Angeles Schools (PLAS), and he struck a deal with LAUSD for PLAS to control a set of failing schools in the district. Sixteen schools, mostly in East Los Angeles and South Los Angeles, are under the direct control of the new mayoral-affiliated nonprofit.[74] The partnership also started to raise outside funds to support these schools, including a $50 million, 10-year grant from the Lundquist Foundation.[75]

The contrasting outcomes of these attempts at mayoral control in New York City and Los Angeles have shaped the way certain major foundations support education reform in each district. Some major foundations, such as Annenberg and Walton, pursue relatively similar grant-making strategies in each district. Walton generally supports charter schools, and Annenberg has continued some funding for the descendants of the Annenberg Challenge, along with grants for arts education and nonprofits working with each school district. Yet the Broad Foundation and Gates Foundation have pursued sharply contrasting strategies in New York City and Los Angeles. These strategies mirror the statements of the heads of each foundation regarding their preferences for mayoral control. Both Bill Gates and Eli Broad have publicly expressed support for mayoral control of schools in New York City and suggested that their grant making in New York City is linked to mayoral control. In a December 2008 interview on CNN with Wolf Blitzer, Bill Gates stated, "The cities where our foundation has put the most money in is where there is a single person responsible. In New York City, Chicago, and Washington, D.C., the mayor is responsible for the school system."[76] At a March 2009 event in New York City, Eli Broad spoke about his foundation's investments in New York City, adding, "I'm a big believer in mayoral control."[77] Both foundations have directly supported district-level reform in New York City.

In Los Angeles, the Broad Foundation and Gates Foundation have concentrated their investments in charter schools. Broad was a strong proponent of mayoral control in Los Angeles, though he and Mayor Villaraigosa had somewhat different ideas about how to pursue it through the state legislature.[78] Since the failure to institute mayoral control in Los Angeles, the Broad Foundation has channeled more grants to charter schools. According to an article in the *Los Angeles Times* about a recent announcement of a new charter school grant:

> Broad's gift to [the] Alliance [for College Ready Public Schools] is the latest indication that he views the work of charters, and not the efforts of Mayor Antonio Villaraigosa or the district's Board of Education, as the best chance to reform the nation's second-largest school system. "Certainly the brightest hope for students in Los Angeles are high-performing charter school organizations," Broad said in prepared remarks.[79]

Neither Bill Gates nor the Gates Foundation has indicated a preference for mayoral control in Los Angeles publicly, but the foundation's grant-making strategy in Los Angeles mirrors that of the Broad Foundation.

Thus, mayoral control in New York City and the absence of mayoral control in Los Angeles appear to shape foundation grant-making strategies. Some foundations, such as Annenberg and Walton, have fairly consistent grant-making strategies in both places. Meanwhile, the Broad Foundation and Gates Foundation have clearly adopted different funding approaches in each district—funding the district and partner organizations in New York City while funding charter schools in Los Angeles.

Conclusion

Current education reform agendas in New York City and Los Angeles have roots in reform initiatives that began more than a decade ago. By the early 1990s, local education reformers in New York City were developing small schools, and reformers in Los Angeles proposed plans for district decentralization. Each of these reform trajectories was picked up by the Annenberg Challenge. Despite its size, the Annenberg Challenge did not produce deep, lasting changes in either of these very large school districts. The Annenberg Challenge produced some changes at the school level but had little impact on the district bureaucracies. Since the Annenberg Challenge, foundation grant-making strategies have changed, giving foundations the potential to influence education policy in more significant ways. Foundations have converged on similar grantees and shared grant-making strategies. By supporting school replication, foundations are able to promote more rapid scaling-up of particular reform approaches. Through human capital organizations, foundations are supporting the pipeline for recruitment of staff with experience outside education; many of these individuals go on to work for new education organizations, including CMOs.

Although major foundation grant-making strategies have converged within New York City and Los Angeles, there is some divergence in funding approaches between the two districts. The layering of different governing systems and different major foundation grant-making strategies is likely to produce different policy-making processes in each district. In New York City, public-sector authority over the school district is highly concentrated in the hands of the mayor and the school district chancellor. Major foundation grant making, which largely supports reform within the district, has also converged on a core set of actors. When foundations and district leaders in New York City develop common priorities, the alliance of private resources and public authority can guide rapid policy change in the district. In Los Angeles, the layers of public authority and private investment are mismatched. The school district, which has faced erosion of its authority for decades, must oversee a diverse set of organizations running schools, including the mayor's nonprofit and CMOs. Private funding has largely focused on CMO expansion.

Within these very different political environments, advocacy groups, neighborhood associations, parents, business leaders, unions, and students are also developing proposals and responding to changes in school district policy. Unlike the major foundations, which can choose their preferred venues for involvement, locally based interests are bound to the political landscape of their home city. The complementary layering of mayoral control and foundation funding in New York City produces a very different set of political opportunities for local actors than the disjointed layering of public authority and foundation funding in Los Angeles. Furthermore, these different political contexts create very different dynamics for policy feedback in each district. In the next two chapters, I look beyond the major foundations and their grantees to understand how education politics is shaped by foundation involvement in each city.

CHAPTER 4

A Shadow Bureaucracy

FOUNDATION DOLLARS AND NEW YORK CITY
SCHOOL REFORM

The New York City public school system has long been synonymous with bureaucratic complexity and cumbersome size. More than 1 million students are enrolled in the district, and they are taught by more than 70,000 teachers.[1] In the 2005–2006 school year, the district spent more than $16 billion; this is more than the total expenditures of 12 state governments.[2] Yet since 2000, the governance of the district has been transformed from a decentralized system of community districts to centralized mayoral control, and the investment of philanthropic foundations in the district has increased substantially. New York City has become a testing ground for a host of new ideas in education reform supported by philanthropic dollars, such as rapidly increasing the numbers of small public schools and charter schools, developing a new principal training program, performance bonuses for teachers based on gains in student test scores, and experiments in rewarding students with cash for academic performance.[3]

The Bill and Melinda Gates Foundation invested more than $150 million in high school reform in New York City. The plans for the investment were far-reaching, according to the foundation's 2003 annual report:

> The citywide program will double the number of high schools with fewer than 600 students and create 80,000 new seats in small schools. Ultimately, this investment will affect 25 to 30 percent of all high school students in New York City, and almost 90 percent of schools in central Brooklyn, the Bronx, and Harlem.[4]

The Broad Foundation Web site described how reforms in New York City aimed "to transform a top down decision-making system into one that empowers the department's 1,450 principals and holds them accountable for ensuring that all students make academic progress."[5] These foundations intended to support ambitious ideas. Yet they lacked political or bureaucratic authority in the district, and their grants composed a small share of district expenditures. How have these grant dollars supported policy change in the school district? What are the political consequences of foundation involvement in New York City education policy?

In New York City, major foundations have primarily funded nonprofit organizations that work in close partnership with the school district; they have also given a few large grants to the school district itself. This funding strategy has helped to elevate the role of certain nonprofits in the district, involving them in policy development and implementation. Similar to Honig's account of nonprofit involvement in school reform in Oakland, foundation-funded nonprofits in New York City have had "formal and informal roles and responsibilities in implementation that in many ways positioned them as school system insiders."[6] Honig finds that the insider role of a major nonprofit organization in Oakland helped considerably in advancing reforms such as developing small autonomous schools and reorganizing the school district's central office. Similarly, insider nonprofits in New York City have enabled rapid implementation of the district's Children First reform agenda, including opening hundreds of new small schools and creating an organization to train hundreds of new principals.[7]

Thus, the New York City education policy community is composed of an essential cadre of insider nonprofit groups, and major foundations are highly involved with this group. Meanwhile, key stakeholders, including parent leaders and local advocacy organizations, have often found themselves relegated to outsider status. This tension between insiders and outsiders continues to underlie education politics in New York City, and it flared into an open conflict during the 2009 debate over the reauthorization of mayoral control, as well as subsequent debates over school closures and restructuring. These conflicts underscore the policy feedback dynamic in New York City. Rather than fostering positive policy feedback by gaining investments from diverse constituencies, the sustainability of New York City's reforms depends on a strategy of entrenchment by the top district leadership.

In this chapter, I show how foundation influence has affected education policy and politics in New York City in three ways. First, I trace foundation grant dollars to specific organizations, and I explain the role of foundations and their grantees in the development and implementation of major policy reforms in New York City. Second, using the results of my survey and social network analysis, I show how insider nonprofits and the district administration are divided from parents and advocacy organizations in their networks of policy information exchange, as well as their attitudes toward education politics. Third, I examine how major education policy reforms in New York City have been entrenched, despite political challenges and ongoing conflict over the consequences of these reforms.

Following the New York City Grants

In 2005, New York City education nonprofits received $29 million in major foundation funding (see table 4.1). Other categories of grantees, including the NYC Department of Education, charter schools, and advocacy organizations received far fewer grants dollars.[8] Education nonprofits are organizations that offer services or provide supplemental capacity and expertise to the school district. Charter schools and charter management organizations are organizations that operate a single charter school or networks of charter schools in New York City. Advocacy organizations claim to represent a broader group in the community, such as a neighborhood or a racial or ethnic group, or a particular issue position, such as reducing class size.

The foundation funding for nonprofits included organizations with close ties to the school district; these nonprofits played central roles in implementing district reforms. For example, in 2005, the Wallace Foundation gave a $5 million grant to the nonprofit New York City Leadership Academy, which was designated as the primary provider of principal training for the district in June 2008. The largest grantee in 2005 was New Visions for Public Schools (New Visions), a nonprofit that received more than $13.5 million from three major foundations—the Gates Foundation, Annenberg Foundation, and Carnegie Corporation. The grants to New Visions funded the organization's work in developing new small high schools in New York City. The school district itself received more than $10 million in grants in 2005: $4.6 million went to the NYC Department of Education and $5.8 million went to the district's education fund, the Fund for Public Schools. Charter

Table 4.1 Funding for NYC Grantees from Top Fifteen K-12 Grant Makers, 2005

Organization/Institution	Total Funding
NYC Department of Education and Fund for Public Schools	$10.4 million
Education nonprofits	$29.0 million
Charter schools and charter management organizations	$1.1 million
Advocacy organizations	$1.1 million

Source: Author's data gathered from foundation tax returns. Grants to private schools have been excluded from the table.

schools and charter management organizations were a relatively small share of major foundation grantees in 2005, but foundation support for charter schools in New York City has grown in recent years. In 2005, the Walton Family Foundation was the main funder of charter schools. Walton has maintained its support for charter schools in New York City, particularly in Harlem; in 2011, the foundation gave nearly $2.5 million in grants for expanding Harlem-based charter schools.[9] Other major foundations have recently increased their funding for New York City charter schools. For example, in 2009, the Broad Foundation announced $2.5 million in grants for two New York City–based CMOs: Uncommon Schools and the Success Charter Network.[10]

Only a small share of funds in 2005 supported advocacy organizations— less than 3 percent of all funds from the major K-12 grant makers to New York City education. The funding for advocacy organizations included a grant of $50,000 to ACORN and a grant of $56,000 to Metro IAF, both from the Gates Foundation. According to the Gates Foundation 2005 tax return, the purpose of these grants was to conduct outreach and increase applications for "new and existing small high schools" and "Gates-sponsored new small high schools."[11] Metro IAF Senior Education Policy Advisor Raymond Domanico explained the grant in an interview.[12] Domanico said that Metro IAF was approached by the Gates Foundation to "raise awareness [of small schools] in the Bronx and drum up applications." Domanico indicated that community organizing was not part of a broader strategy for the Gates Foundation; rather, it was used to fill a last-minute need in relation to the foundation's small schools reform. Metro IAF received the grant after the "application process for high schools was already underway," Domanico said. He characterized this as a "common [experience] with foundations and school systems—they get in crisis mode and think community organizing is the answer." According to Domanico, this is the only education organizing grant that Metro IAF has received from the Gates Foundation. Other grantees involved with community organizing have encountered pressure from foundations to link their work to specific measures of student achievement. Norm Fruchter, former director of the Community Involvement Program at the Annenberg Institute for School Reform, explained that the Gates Foundation wants to see "how our organizing will lead to increases in student graduation rates and college attendance."[13] He added, "Foundations are increasingly outcome oriented, but it's very hard to tie the work that we do to specific increases in outcomes, because it's mediated through the school system."

Although grants to advocacy organizations composed a very small share of overall grant making from major foundations, the relationship between grant makers and advocacy groups in New York City has been strengthened by the presence of the Donor's Education Collaborative (DEC), a joint grant-making effort involving several foundations that provides funding to advocacy organizations in New York City. In 2005, the Ford Foundation gave $250,000 to DEC. Janice Petrovich, director of education, sexuality, and religion at the Ford Foundation until April 2008, spoke about DEC in an interview.[14] She explained that DEC chose not to support "different models of reform that tended to come and go; [instead] they would support groups that tried to build public understanding and public will to improve schools." In a report for the Ford Foundation, Petrovich stated that "more than $11 million has been invested in New York City groups" through DEC since 1995, which amounts to just under $1 million per year.[15] Why would foundations support advocacy organizations through DEC rather than funding them directly? According to Norma Rollins, coordinator for DEC, funding constituency building through DEC allows some foundations, whose guidelines might steer clear of grassroots work that does not readily translate into concrete outcomes, to support community activism and organizing. She added that DEC "gives them opportunities to interact and learn from a new and different set of grantees, without establishing a direct relationship with them."[16]

Although the Ford Foundation has made constituency building a key part of the foundation's strategy for involvement in education, their level of funding in 2005 was quite small compared with Gates, Annenberg, Wallace, and Broad. Working through parent groups and advocacy organizations has not been the main channel for foundation involvement in education policy. Instead, major foundations supported nonprofit organizations with close ties to the district leadership. These nonprofit organizations have been highly involved in school district policy development and implementation.

Children First

The set of reforms implemented in New York City since the start of mayoral control in 2002 are known as Children First. This agenda has evolved continuously since 2002, and there have been three reorganizations of the district administration in the past eight years.[17] Despite the numerous reorganizations, the general trajectory to the Children First reforms involves two components: (1) increasing school-level autonomy and accountability while removing middle layers of bureaucracy and (2) use of market-oriented strategies such as school choice, contracting for services, and charter schools. Aspects of both reform trajectories have been supported with foundation grant dollars and guided by foundation-funded nonprofits, though foundation funding for the market-oriented strategies has been greater. The Children First reforms were developed under the leadership of Chancellor Joel Klein, Mayor Michael Bloomberg's first appointee to lead the district. Klein's background is not in education—he previously worked as assistant attorney general for antitrust in the U.S. Justice Department. In this capacity, he served as lead prosecutor in the antitrust case against Microsoft, although this clearly did not dissuade Bill Gates from giving millions to New York City schools. After leading the development and implementation of Children First, Klein resigned from his post in November 2010.

After Klein's appointment as chancellor, he quickly sought outside expertise for reforming the district; he asked Michele Cahill of Carnegie Corporation to join the senior leadership team in 2002. Previously, Cahill had developed Carnegie Corporation's Schools for a New Society initiative, a seven-city urban school reform project. In 2007, Cahill left the NYC Department of Education and returned to Carnegie. Cahill was not the only individual from a major foundation speaking with Klein as he developed reform strategies in the fall of 2002. At an event in New York City on March 9, 2009, Eli Broad of the Broad Foundation stated, "From the first day Joel [Klein] took office, literally, we met with him."[18] Also, Eli Broad paid half of the $3.75 million price tag for the study that led to the Children First reform agenda.[19]

Publicly available documentation of the Children First planning process is very limited; the reports that do exist, as well as the recollections of one participant, suggest strong links between lead actors in the planning process, major foundations, and foundation-funded nonprofits. Initial reports mentioned a few members of the "working groups" who would develop Children First, including Norm Fruchter and Beth Lief, former president of New Visions.[20] Yet later news coverage from the fall of 2002 suggests that the planning for Children First was cloaked in secrecy: "Aside from five open parent meetings, the plan has come together in long, private meetings at Tweed Courthouse, the school system's new downtown headquarters."[21] The full membership of the Children First working groups was not reported in the local press. An advocacy organization focused on improving the district's mathematics curriculum, New York City HOLD, submitted a freedom of information act (FOIA) request to find out the composition of the Children First working groups and posted the information retrieved from the NYC Department of Education on their Web site.[22] Most of the members of the 10 Children First working groups were affiliated with the NYC Department of Education.

Yet the affiliations of the other working group members suggest that foundations and certain nonprofits, particularly New Visions, played an important role in developing Children First. Chancellor Klein chaired only one working group, "Leadership and Organization." Fifteen of the 21 members of this working group were affiliated with the NYC Department of Education; those with outside affiliations included Kathryn Downing (affiliation, Broad Foundation), Shivam Shah (affiliation, New Schools Venture Fund; Shah became a senior program officer at the Gates Foundation in 2003), Bob Hughes (affiliation, New Visions), Warren Simmons (affiliation, Annenberg Institute for School Reform), and Norm Fruchter.[23] Fruchter recalled that the working group was a "very scripted, very managed process."[24] According to Fruchter, Jim Shelton was one of the "chief planner/managers of the process," although he was not listed in the Department of Education's response to NYC HOLD's FOIA request. Shelton had worked for McKinsey & Company and New Schools Venture Fund; he became education program director at the Gates Foundation in 2003, and in 2009, he was appointed assistant deputy secretary for innovation and improvement in the federal Department of Education. In response to the tightly managed working group arrangement, Fruchter, Hughes, and Simmons wrote a document to "protest about the nature of the planning process," Fruchter recalled.[25] Fruchter eventually chose to stop attending the working group meetings, out of frustration with the process. Cahill cochaired three working groups, including "Choice Models," "Secondary School Restructuring," and "Community and Parent Partnerships." Representatives from New Visions participated in five of the ten working groups.

Mayor Bloomberg announced the Children First agenda in January 2003, although implementation was largely delayed until the following school year.[26] In an interview, Cahill described the Children First reforms as an effort "to create a system of good schools, rather than a good school system."[27] Toward this end, many of the Children First reforms have devolved both authority and responsibility to the individual school level—particularly to the principals. The Children First reforms aim to create a bottom-up system that grants greater authority to individual schools. Yet much like the planning process, the implementation of Children First has largely occurred from the top down. According to Fruchter's written account:

> Teachers, students, and parents had little input into the processes through which Children First was implemented. Cabinet members, often aided by cadres of consultants, designed most new initiatives. The school system's practitioners and its parent, student, and community constituencies usually learned about these new initiatives through media coverage, press conferences, and web-site releases.[28]

Major foundations have played a key role in facilitating Children First implementation. As the district's senior leadership team developed the reform strategies for Children First—including bureaucratic reorganization, a leadership academy for principals, and high school reform—they sought extensive funding support from private foundations.

Economics Meets Education

Three distinct areas of policy reform in New York City have been supported with foundation dollars to education nonprofits or directly to the school district. To varying degrees, these reform efforts draw on ideas from economics and business to reform schools. The first involves creating schools of choice within the district. There are two components to this reform: the formation of hundreds of new small high schools linked to nonprofit partners, as well as opening dozens of new charter schools. Second is the increased outsourcing of school support functions paired with increasing school-level autonomy. The administrative reorganization in 2007 allowed schools to choose among a set of nonprofits to contract for professional development and other academic services.[29] Also, a foundation-funded nonprofit, the New York City Leadership Academy, operates the district's principal training program, which applies ideas from business leadership training. Third, there have been two pilot projects involving pay for performance programs: one for teachers and one for students, both based on standardized test scores. The school choice and contracting policies are largely based on market-oriented ideas; pay for performance draws on the accountability portion of the Boardroom Progressive agenda. An additional accountability policy, implemented without extensive foundation involvement, was a new school grading system based predominantly on state test scores.

SCHOOLS OF CHOICE

The largest recent investment of foundation dollars in New York City education was the high school reform supported primarily by the Gates Foundation. The Gates Foundation's U.S. high school reform initiative was massive—it dwarfs the 1993 Annenberg Challenge of $500 million. In the first decade of the 2000s, the Gates Foundation committed more than $1 billion to high school reform throughout the United States.[30] In New York City alone, the foundation spent $150 million to support the creation of small high schools.[31] More than 200 new small high schools have been opened in New York City since 2002. Typically, the new small high schools are formed in partnership with a nonprofit organization, which replicates a particular school model. In 2005, several nonprofits, including New Visions, Urban Assembly, Replications Inc., Institute for Student Achievement, and Outward Bound, received grants of more than $1 million to support new small schools. With support from the Gates Foundation, Carnegie Corporation, and the Open Society Institute, New Visions opened 86 New Century High Schools.[32] These schools were created by phasing out large comprehensive high schools and opening new small high schools on the same campus—one campus often houses three to five small schools. The Urban Assembly manages 20 small high schools and junior high schools, five of which are also New Century High Schools.[33] Replications Inc. and the Institute for Student Achievement each support more than 20 small high schools and junior high schools in New York City, and Outward Bound operates 11 schools.[34]

These high schools have added substantially to the citywide high school choices available to New York City eighth graders. The high school admissions process in New York City is quite complex: the district provides an 18-page guidebook to assist parents and students; for those seeking more information, there is a 242-page guide to New York City high schools.[35] Students can list up to 12 high schools on their application, and different schools have varying eligibility requirements and selection mechanisms. Within this market, many schools and their nonprofit founders promote themselves with brands and themes. Small high school themes include the environment, humanities, law, and sports careers. These schools are now a substantial portion of the district's high schools—about 25 percent of the city's high school pupils in 2009 were enrolled in small schools.[36] Although the Gates Foundation is no longer funding the development of new small high schools in New York City, the district administration continues to close large high schools and convert them into small schools.

Recent evaluations of New York City's small schools reform suggest some positive results, as well as some drawbacks. The largest study of New York City's small schools, funded by the Gates Foundation, was conducted by MDRC and released in June 2010.[37] The study uses lotteries of oversubscribed small schools to compare the outcomes of students who "win" the lottery and those who do not. The vast majority of the students who enrolled in small schools are black or Latino and eligible for free or reduced-price lunch. The results show improved progress toward graduation for the students who enrolled in small schools, as well as a 6.8 percent increase in the four-year graduation rate. Results on test scores were more mixed. In math, significantly more small school students—5.3 percent—achieved the necessary scores on the New York State Regents exam to be exempt from remedial classes at City University of New York (CUNY). On the English exam, there was no significant difference between small school enrollees and other students.

Meanwhile, other studies have demonstrated that although the small schools may be helpful to students who enroll in them, they can be harmful to others. A study released by the Center for New York City Affairs at the New School found higher attendance and graduation rates in small schools, but "the gains for students at the small schools came at the expense of other students, some of whom were even needier than those who attended the new small schools."[38] In particular, English language learners (ELL) and special education students have faced difficulties during the implementation of small school reform. From 2002 to 2007, new small schools were not required to serve ELL and special education students during their first two years of operation.[39] Schools that opened after 2008 were required to serve these students. A 2009 report issued by Advocates for Children of New York and the Asian American Legal Defense and Education

Fund focused on the experience of ELL students in two restructured high schools in Brooklyn—Tilden and Lafayette.[40] Both schools were well known for their English as a second language (ESL) programs and large numbers of recent immigrant students. The report shows that the small schools that replaced Tilden and Lafeyette enrolled few, if any, ELL students, and these schools failed to provide adequate ESL instruction. As Tilden and Lafayette were phased out, the proportion of ELL students remaining in each large school increased, but these schools began to phase out ESL programs and encourage ELL students to transfer elsewhere.[41] The report suggests that the small schools reform has had a negative effect on ELL students citywide: "While the City's overall graduation rate climbed to 52.2% in 2007 from 46.5% in 2005, the rate for ELLs dropped from 28.5% to 23.5% over the same period."[42] Although the MDRC study provides strong evidence that small schools do help their students, it is not clear how these schools will fare when they are required to serve ELL and special education students at the outset.

In addition to the hundreds of new small schools in New York, by the 2010–2011 school year, New York City had 125 charter schools enrolling students. This is the result of a concerted effort by Mayor Bloomberg and former Chancellor Klein to increase the number of charter schools operating in New York City. Charters were not a key element of the original Children First reform strategy in 2003, "but they have emerged as one of the administration's signature initiatives."[43] The district leadership's focus on charter schools has coincided with several major foundations'—including the Gates Foundation, Broad Foundation, and Walton Family Foundation—increased funding for charter schools. The first New York City charter school opened in 1999, and the city had 58 charter schools by 2006.[44] The growth of charter schools in the city has been limited by statewide charter school caps set by the state legislature, but in May 2010, New York state legislators agreed to raise the cap to 460 schools, allowing continued expansion of charter schools in New York City. Several of New York City's charter schools are operated by charter management organizations, including Achievement First, Uncommon Schools, and KIPP NYC.

Some charter school organizations based in New York City, such as KIPP NYC, had well-established reputations and ready access to philanthropic dollars. Newer organizations often struggle to gain the attention of funders. Yet one charter school leader, former New York City Councilwoman Eva Moskowitz, found that her close connection to Chancellor Klein could also facilitate her efforts to raise philanthropic grant dollars.[45] Moskowitz founded Harlem Success Academy in 2006, and she has since expanded the Success Charter Network to 12 charter schools in Harlem, Brooklyn, and the Bronx. According to e-mails between Moskowitz, Klein, and officials at the Broad Foundation, which the *New York Daily News* obtained through a FOIA request, Klein assisted Moskowitz in obtaining a large grant from the Broad Foundation. Moskowitz e-mailed Klein on October 8, 2008, about her recent contact with Broad Foundation officials and asked for Klein's assistance:

[I] have had a very good response from Broad. As mentioned [I met with Eli Broad in L.A.] last week and he was interested but concerned that our work was aligned with yours. Broad holds you in very high regard and doesn't in any way want to disrupt your efforts. This week [Broad Foundation managing director] Dan Katzir reached out and asked me for more materials and to visit our schools next week when [he is] in town. [I] am arranging. Again he seems enthusiastic but has concerns about our alignment. [I] think your input would be very significant. [I] am hoping you can put in a strong good word. [I] think it will really help and I need the money to get my replication efforts off the ground. [I] will be very aggressive growth and advocacy wise if can get over the financial hump in this bad financial climate. While your weigh in [is] always valuable, [I] think in this case particularly so [because] Broad [likes] district change. To me what has the potential for power is 1) willingness to change within and good climate for [charter school] suppliers 2) creating demand from parents. This one-two punch is much more powerful than either alone. On this one [I] would REALLY, REALLY appreciate your help.[46]

Klein appeared to respond to the request from Moskowitz with an e-mail on October 8, 2008, to Broad Foundation Managing Director Dan Katzir:

I'm a big supporter of what [Moskowitz is] doing, not just in terms of her charters (which appear to be very strong) but also in terms of the political sophistication she brings to the overall effort. She's done more to organize parents and get them aligned with overall reforms than anyone else on the outside. [I'm] happy to discuss if you'd like. See you next week. Regards, jk[47]

The e-mails illuminate two key aspects of the Broad Foundation's involvement in New York City school reform and the development of charter schools there. First, given the foundation's substantial investments in district-led reforms in New York City, Broad Foundation officials wanted reassurance that the charter schools would be complementary to the district-level reforms. In this case, it appears that Klein provided the assurance that Broad Foundation officials were seeking. Second, part of Moskowitz's pitch for funding—and part of Klein's expression of support—is a political argument. Moskowitz discusses her plans to be aggressive "advocacy wise" and the importance of "creating demand from parents"; Klein compliments Moskowitz for her "political sophistication" and applauds her efforts to "organize parents and get them aligned with overall reforms." These arguments from Moskowitz and Klein suggest that Broad Foundation officials were also interested in hearing about efforts to build political support for the reforms they have funded.

Moskowitz did succeed in getting funding from the Broad Foundation—the Success Charter Network received a $1 million grant in 2009. Overall, philanthropic support for charter schools in New York City has grown substantially in recent years. Most of this growth has occurred since 2005, the latest year of data available from my foundation grant data set. An independent analysis by Kim Gittleson and Ken Hirsh (on gothamschools.org) shows a 23 percent growth in philanthropic funding for charter schools from 2008 to 2009.[48] Charter schools in New York City received $25 million in philanthropic funds in 2008 and $31 million in 2009. Thus, although foundation funding for the small-schools reforms has fallen off, foundations are continuing to support the formation of new schools in New York City by funding charter schools.

PRINCIPAL AUTONOMY AND NONPROFIT CONTRACTING

In addition to restructuring at the school level through small-schools reform and charter schools, Children First involved restructuring at the district level. According to Hemphill and Nauer, "Schools Chancellor Joel Klein has presided over three major reorganizations of the Department of Education since the state legislature gave Mayor Michael Bloomberg control of the city's schools in 2002."[49] In the first reorganization, Klein consolidated the city's 32 districts into 10 regions, combining stronger local districts with weaker ones. In 2007, Klein removed the regional offices, and devolved additional authority to school principals. Principals could select among several providers for academic services: the Empowerment Support Organization, Learning Support Organizations, and Partnership Support Organizations. Empowerment schools were free to select their own outside affiliations and collaborate with one another. Learning Support schools could choose to affiliate with one of four networks operated by administrators in the Department of Education. Partnership Support Organizations (PSOs) include six outside entities that schools could choose among, including major foundation grantees such as New Visions, CUNY, and Replications Inc.

Foundation grant dollars supported the services that PSOs offer to schools. For example, New Visions has received grants from the Gates Foundation to support the development of an online data management system; as a PSO, New Visions promotes the assistance it offers to schools for using student achievement data.[50] This reform was explicitly designed to mirror a market model for academic services. University of California Los Angeles Management Professor William Ouchi consulted with the Department of Education on the implementation of this model, which draws on Ouchi's research.[51] As Chancellor Joel Klein stated, "We are creating a competitive market for support, in which schools will be able to make the smart decisions that help students make real academic progress."[52]

Once again, in 2010, Klein reorganized the district to create Children First Networks. These networks combine the services of the school support organizations and the district's Integrated Services Center, which offers operations management in areas such as payroll and food services. The new arrangement maintains the network approach of the 2007 reorganization, offering principals extensive flexibility and little oversight. According to an analysis of principal autonomy in the district by Hemphill and Nauer, "The decision to abandon geographically based districts and to free principals from the day-to-day supervision of a superintendent has substantial costs."[53] For example, this policy reform has created difficulties for parent groups and community organizations, which are typically organized at the neighborhood or borough level. The structure of the Children First Networks is not based in geography, and most of the organizations that support schools are scattered throughout the city. According to Fruchter:

> The support organizations are in support roles without any governance or accountability mechanism—their relationships are solely with the individual schools. Our organizers are trying to figure out what [the support organizations are] doing or how effective they are, but there are not any accountability levers directly through the support organizations.[54]

A public school parent and leader of an advocacy organization stated in an interview that the school support organization model "undermines the notion of community involvement in the schools."[55] The 32 community education councils (CECs), which are representative bodies for parents and the community, are geographically defined. This parent leader observed that there was "no point in having a CEC" if support organizations for the schools did not mirror arrangements for parent and community representation. It is too early to tell whether the latest administrative reorganization will create mechanisms to more effectively link schools, parents, and community groups within the same neighborhood, but currently there are no indications that it will.

Principal training in New York City also draws on a business model by preparing aspiring principals to be managers of their schools. The New York City Leadership Academy, a nonprofit organization, has developed a program to provide this training, which includes simulations and a school-based residency. The Leadership Academy was started in 2003 as part of the Children First reforms and largely supported with foundation dollars. Since 2004, the Wallace Foundation has given more than $18 million in grants to the Leadership Academy. The first CEO of the Leadership Academy, Robert Knowling, came from the business world; he was previously CEO of Covad Communications.[56] Some accounts of the Leadership Academy strongly emphasize the business angle. A business magazine article on the Leadership Academy opens with a description of former General Electric CEO Jack Welch exhorting principals that "your job is harder than running a company."[57] The training methods of the leadership academy also draw on expertise from General Electric; Noel Tichy, who helped create the GE Leadership Development Center, also worked with the Leadership Academy.[58]

Yet Knowling's successor as Leadership Academy CEO, Sandra Stein, has a doctorate in education and wrote a well-regarded book about principal training. Her appointment suggested that the Leadership Academy was beginning to emphasize educational expertise along with business. Stein argued that the corporate leadership model must be translated to apply to education. According to Stein:

> Most successful corporations invest in talent development, and the Department of Education wanted an arm that did that. As far as the actual business principles, some strategies need to be translated so that they apply to an education environment. There are a lot of tools that you can take that are more common to corporate America, but you can't just take them as they are—they need to be adapted.[59]

In June 2008, the New York City Leadership Academy was awarded a contract to be the "primary provider" of principal training for the district, according to a Department of Education press release.[60]

PAY FOR PERFORMANCE

Pay-for-performance programs also draw on a business approach—using monetary incentives as motivation for improved outcomes and holding individuals accountable for their performance. New York City has piloted two pay-for-performance programs supported by philanthropic funding—one for teachers and one for students.

The pay-for-performance program for students was called the Spark Program. The Broad Foundation provided funding for this program through the Education Innovation Laboratory at Harvard University, or Ed Labs, headed by Harvard

University Economics Professor Roland Fryer. The total budget for the program was $6.1 million, entirely funded with private donations.[61] According to the Ed Labs Web site, the program awarded fourth-grade students up to $250 per year and seventh-grade students up to $500 per year based on their performance on reading and math assessments.[62] There were 8,583 students enrolled in the program in New York City.[63] The Spark Program, as well as variations piloted in Chicago, Dallas, and Washington, D.C., provoked extensive media coverage and controversy. In a column in *Forbes* magazine, Diane Ravitch commented on the potential high costs of the program and its dampening effects on student motivation, adding, "This is money that might otherwise be spent reducing class size (New York City has the largest classes in the state), improving the quality of tests and technology and refurbishing obsolete facilities."[64] Meanwhile, Fryer argued that it is essential to try radical new approaches in education. "We will have the willingness to try new things and be wrong," he said.[65] Each city's program was designed with different incentives tied to different behaviors and outcomes. The New York City and Chicago programs incentivized "outputs," that is, test scores and grades. The Washington, D.C., and Dallas programs incentivized "inputs," that is, reading books, attendance, and behavior.[66] By 2010, Fryer acknowledged that the Spark Program had failed to raise test scores in New York City, and the program was cut.[67] Yet Fryer's research revealed that the input programs in Washington, D.C., and Dallas did improve student achievement.[68]

The pay-for-performance program for teachers in New York City was a three-year pilot program that began in 2007. After extensive negotiations with the teachers' union (UFT) over the program, the UFT and the district agreed to performance bonuses for teachers based on overall school test scores in schools with a high proportion of low-income students.[69] In the first year of the program, teachers received $19.7 million in bonuses supported by philanthropies, including the Broad Foundation.[70] During the second year, the program shifted to public funding. An initial study of the program by two researchers at Columbia University indicated that the bonuses had little impact on teacher effort or student performance.[71] In January 2011, the program was suspended by the Department of Education due to budget constraints.[72] An evaluation by RAND, released in July, 2011, showed that the teacher incentive program did not improve student achievement.[73] Thus, both the student-focused and the teacher-focused experiments with pay for performance failed to produce significant academic gains for students in New York City.

For each of these three areas of policy reform—increasing the number of schools of choice, outsourcing for school leadership and support services, and experimenting with pay-for-performance initiatives—foundation dollars provided start-up funds for the district to try out new programs led by nonprofits. In some cases, such as the New York City Leadership Academy and the teacher bonus pilot, the program eventually transitioned to public funding. Without foundation support, it is unlikely that many of these policy changes would occur as rapidly or as extensively. As Joel Klein has stated, "Outside money is much more flexible than government money."[74] For Klein, foundation funding for education in New York City is clearly positive—it allows policy change to occur in the district without committing public funds up front. Meanwhile, these policy changes have drastically changed the experiences of New York City public school teachers, students, and parents. Their reaction to these reforms—and the processes that led to the enactment of these policy reforms—has produced a sharply divided political climate surrounding New York City education.

"Where You Stand Depends on Where You Sit"

In the spring and summer of 2008, I conducted a survey of key players in the New York City education policy community to assess how major foundations relate to other actors involved in education policy.[75] I identified five sectors of the local education policy community: the New York City Department of Education, unions, nonprofit service providers, advocacy organizations, and parent leaders. I developed a list of survey contacts covering each of these five sectors by including all of the foundation grant recipients from 2005 and consulting with experts on New York City education politics. My contact list included 44 education nonprofits and advocacy organizations in New York City. The parent leaders who received the survey were the presidents of the 32 CEC districts and the two citywide councils for high schools and special education. Within the NYC Department of Education, I focused on contacting individuals in leadership roles, particularly those in charge of divisions implementing district reforms. I received a total of 40 responses to the survey, representing each of the five sectors of the New York City education policy community (table 4.2); the response rate was approximately 37 percent.[76] I also conducted 19 interviews with education policy leaders and constituents in New York City and attended three public meetings on education. I also conducted a focus group with parent leaders at CUNY in September 2008.

Based on the survey responses, I found that attitudes about education politics in New York City are divided. Groups that receive major foundation grants generally share one set of views about the direction of district reform and the roles of specific actors, and groups that do not receive major foundation grants hold a different set of views. More specifically, groups that receive major foundation grants generally think the district is improving, that philanthropies play an important role, and that the teachers' union is a barrier to reform. Groups that do not receive major foundation grants are less optimistic about the school

Table 4.2 Survey Responses

NYC Education Policy Sector	Survey Responses
NYC Department of Education	7
Unions	5
Nonprofit service providers	7
Advocacy organizations	8
Parent leaders	13

district's trajectory and less likely to regard philanthropies as important, and they generally do not regard the teachers' union as a roadblock to reform. In the presentations of the survey results, I divide the five sectors of the education policy community into two groups: (1) the two segments that receive a large share foundation funds, that is, the district bureaucracy and nonprofits, and (2) the three segments that do not receive much foundation support—advocacy organizations, unions, and parent leaders. Using this division, I can assess how attitudes toward reform and the role of foundations vary between the two groups.

One survey question was designed to gauge respondents' overall attitudes toward school reform in New York City: "In your opinion, is this school district improving, staying about the same, or getting worse?" Among the 14 respondents who were district administrators or nonprofit leaders, only 1 stated that things were getting worse, and 9 responded that the district is improving. Among the 26 respondents who were advocacy organization, union, and parent leaders, opinions were more divided: 8 responded that things were getting worse, and 8 responded that things were getting better. Using a T-test, we can compare the mean attitude of each group and test for statistical significance by coding the responses as improving (1), staying the same (0), and getting worse (−1). The group mean for the administrators and nonprofit leaders is 0.57, and the group mean for the advocacy, union, and parent leaders is 0.0; the difference between the group means is statistically significant ($p < 0.05$ for a two-tailed test). In general, the groups with greater funding ties to foundations have a more positive view of the progress of the school district than groups that receive little foundation funding.

The survey also included a question about the role of foundations in school reform in New York City. Respondents were asked whether foundations (1) had an important role in funding and setting the direction for reform, (2) had a role in funding alone, or (3) not a very important role. Once again, the responses were split (table 4.3). Most district and nonprofit leaders responded that philanthropies have an important role in funding and setting the direction for reform;

Table 4.3 Survey Responses on Role of Foundations

	District and Nonprofit Leaders	Parents, Unions, and Advocacy Organizations
Philanthropies provide important source of funding and help set direction for school reform here.	64%	22.5%
Philanthropies provide important source of funding but do not set direction for school reform here.	36%	22.5%
Philanthropies do not have a very important role in school reform here.	0%	55%

parent, union, and advocacy organization leaders largely regarded their role as unimportant. Thus, the set of individuals who receive a larger share of foundation funding tend to agree that foundations are important for their funding and policy roles.

In interviews, leaders in the district bureaucracy and foundations characterized the policy role of foundations somewhat differently. For example, a senior official in the Department of Education stated that "[The] Gates [Foundation] knew five years ago what the vision for New York today was going to be."[77] By contrast, when discussing the origins of the Children First reforms, Cahill—who left Carnegie Corporation to work with the district—emphasized the leadership of Chancellor Klein, rather than mentioning foundations.[78] Given how much foundation funding the district has secured for its reform objectives and the involvement of foundation officials and grantees in the development of Children First, there undoubtedly was a convergence of ideas among both district and philanthropic leaders. Meanwhile, when I discussed the role of foundations with parent leaders in a focus group, they commented that many parents were "naïve" and "unaware" of the nature and extent of foundation involvement in the district.[79]

If opinion is divided about the role of philanthropies, is it also divided regarding the role of other actors? The survey included a series of questions about the role of the teachers' union—the United Federation of Teachers (UFT)—as well as advocacy organizations and parents. The respondents were presented with a statement about each type of actor and asked to respond on a five-point scale: strongly disagree (–2), somewhat disagree (–1), neutral (0), somewhat agree (1), or strongly agree (2). The responses to each statement are summarized in

Table 4.4 Attitudes toward Role of Actors Involved in Schools

	District and Nonprofit Leaders	Parents, Unions, and Advocacy Organizations	T-Test Results, Difference of Means
In this district, the teachers' union obstructs efforts to reform the schools.	0.89	−0.61 (−.40)* *excluding union respondents	$p < 0.01$
Community/advocacy organizations and parent groups are shut out of education politics here.	−0.50	1.0	$p < 0.01$

table 4.4. There is significant disagreement between the two groups regarding the role of unions and the involvement of parents and advocacy organizations. Generally, the district and nonprofit leaders agreed that "the teachers' union obstructs efforts to reform the schools," but parents, unions, and advocacy organization leaders largely disagreed. This disagreement remains statistically significant even when union respondents are excluded from the analysis. Also, most district and nonprofit leaders did not agree that "community/advocacy organizations and parent groups are shut of education politics here," but the representatives of those groups saw things differently. Parent, union, and advocacy organization leaders largely agreed that they are shut out of education politics in New York City. These responses provide further support for an attitudinal divide between the groups that receive a large share of philanthropic support and those that do not.

Responses to the open-ended survey question "What specific roadblocks make it difficult to carry out your objectives for this school district?" indicate that many parent and advocacy organization leaders attribute their limited voice in school affairs to the district's centralization and the actions of the Department of Education. Roadblocks mentioned by parent and community leaders included "Lack of interest by the DOE in the input of parents and other 'lay people'"; "The Administration does not encourage any efforts for parents to be a part of the decision-making process and creates actual policy roadblocks"; "No respect and process to respect input from stakeholders"; and "The Chancellor. He does what he wants, when he wants." Despite these frustrations, it is important to note that some parents, particularly those from neighborhoods with a track record of very low-performing schools, were pleased about academic gains that have occurred since mayoral control in their schools. During the parent leader focus group, one parent praised improvements in graduation rates for high schools in his neighborhood, adding, "Something happened that is good."[80] Nonetheless, the same parent also expressed frustration that there is "nobody at the top representing parents."[81]

Nevertheless, some district leaders viewed the demands of multiple stakeholders as a roadblock to their objectives. Some roadblocks mentioned by district leaders included "population size and variety of local agendas" and "so many stakeholders need to be considered before moving forward." An issue related to the difficult relationship between stakeholder groups and the district administration is the demise of two citywide education advocacy organizations: United Parents Associations of NYC and Educational Priorities Panel (EPP).[82] The EPP served as a coalition of organizations interested in education, and United Parents Associations was a federation of school parent associations and PTAs in the district. Unfortunately, with fewer citywide organizations involved in education in New York City, the voice of stakeholders appears to be weakened even more.

The views of parents and advocacy organization leaders suggest that the district leadership has tried to avoid barriers to implementing the Children First agenda simply by not involving the public. The truncated role of the public in decision making about public education in New York City is particularly evident in the district leadership's handling of the Panel for Education Policy, or PEP. The PEP is a 13-member board that was created when the mayor gained control of the schools. Unlike the CECs, which operate within 32 districts throughout the city, the PEP is a citywide body. There are eight members appointed by the mayor and five others, who must be parents of public school children in New York City, appointed by each of the borough presidents.[83] The PEP is charged with reviewing and approving district policies and regulations related to educational achievement and student performance.

One policy brought before the PEP was a 2004 proposal to use standardized test results as the basis for promotion from the third grade.[84] Joan McKeever-Thomas was a member of the PEP appointed by the Staten Island borough president. In an interview, she described how she initially had a high opinion of Chancellor Joel Klein: "I was the first member appointed to the PEP," she said, "and Klein called me the next day. He said to call him Joel. I believed in him. The system had been very provincial [before mayoral control]."[85] Yet McKeever-Thomas was uncertain about the proposal for new third-grade promotion requirements. "I was asking questions. I did my homework.... [I was concerned] that kids were going to be left back based on one high stakes test," she explained. McKeever-Thomas decided that she "wanted more time" for the PEP to consider the proposal, but the chancellor would not delay the vote. On the day of the meeting to vote on the third-grade promotion policy, McKeever-Thomas received a cell phone message from the Staten Island borough president instructing her not to attend that evening's PEP meeting. McKeever-Thomas attended anyway and was ushered out, along with two other former PEP members. All three were replaced by newly appointed members who were willing to support the new promotion policy. The new policy passed by a vote of 8–5.[86] McKeever-Thomas explained that the district is "rich with parent resources on paper, but none of it works." She added that the district leadership assumes that "stakeholders will just slow you down."

Advocacy organization and parent leaders clearly disagree with district leaders on the need for stakeholder input in district decision making. The district leadership views public involvement as a stumbling block that could prevent urgent policy reforms. Parents and advocacy organizations leaders view the district as unresponsive and undemocratic. Although parent leaders on the CECs and members of the PEP argue that they are not consulted on matters of education policy, the Department of Education is not implementing district policy on its own. The Department of Education relies on several partners for funding and services in the development and implementation of reforms. District leaders work with a network of nonprofit and philanthropic allies, and these organizations share policy information with one another.

A Divided Network

Social network analysis offers a tool to visualize the relationships between actors sharing policy information about New York City education. Using data from the survey responses, I created two networks of policy information exchange for the New York City education policy community. I asked each respondent to identify organizations and institutions that provided them with "useful data or research" and to identify organizations and institutions that provided them with information about "local community needs or preferences." These questions were designed to identify the sources of two different types of policy information. The data and research question was designed to highlight expert-oriented or research-based sources of policy knowledge. The local needs or preferences question was designed to highlight sources of grassroots or community-based policy knowledge. All of the referents named by my survey respondents are included in the networks. I created visual representations of the networks using the Netdraw program available in UCINET Version 6.166.[87]

Figure 4.1 presents a network of information exchange of policy expertise ("useful data and research") between education policy actors in New York City. I have aggregated the survey responses from individuals into their main organizational or institutional affiliation;[88] for example, all respondents who work for the New York City Department of Education are grouped together as "NYC DOE," and all of the parent representatives on the community education councils are grouped together as "CEC." The arrows indicate the direction of information flow from source to recipient. The thickness of the lines indicates the number of survey respondents who mentioned a particular information source; a thicker line means that more respondents from the same organization mentioned the same source of information. The size of the nodes is based on the outdegree centrality of each organization; larger nodes have higher outdegree centrality. *Outdegree centrality* is a measure of the number of paths from one node to other nodes in the network. Organizations with high outdegree centrality were designated sources of policy expertise for many respondents in the network; organizations with low outdegree centrality were regarded as sources of information by only a few. Last, the shading of the nodes indicates whether the organizations received major foundation funding. Black nodes represent organizations and institutions that did not receive a grant from one of the 15 largest K-12 grant makers in 2005; gray nodes represent major foundations, as well as organizations and institutions that received at least one grant in 2005 from a major foundation.

In figure 4.1, the grant recipient organizations and the organizations that did not receive grants appear in somewhat distinct clusters. The organizations that did not get grants predominate around the CEC node in the bottom right portion of the network, and the grant recipients predominate in the top right, around the NYC DOE node. There is also a small cluster of grant recipients around the UFT, which received a grant of $250,000 from the Broad Foundation to start a unionized charter school.[89] Throughout the network, foundation grantees seem to share more information with other foundation grantees; similarly, the organizations that did not receive major foundation grants share information with one another. For example, there are several foundation grant recipients with policy expertise ties to the NYC DOE, including nonprofits like Outward Bound, Replications Inc., and New Visions, as well as foundations such as Gates and Broad. These organizations were highly involved in the development and implementation of Children First reforms. Meanwhile, advocacy organizations such as Class Size Matters, Future of Tomorrow, and Advocates for Children of New York largely share information with other advocacy organizations representing parents, neighborhoods, or issue positions.

How much are these two subgroups—foundation grantees and nongrantees—separated from one another? By calculating the E-I index of the network, we can examine the proportion of internal ties in the network, linking members within each of these subgroups.[90] The *E-I index* is a ratio of the number of external links between subgroups minus internal links within each subgroup over the total links in the network; it ranges from –1 to 1. Thus, a negative E-I index indicates a greater share of links within each subgroup. Theoretically, we can expect that "the higher the density of internal ties, the greater the identification that members will make with the subunit."[91] The E-I index for the network in figure 4.1, with black nodes and gray nodes indicating the two subgroups, is –0.224,

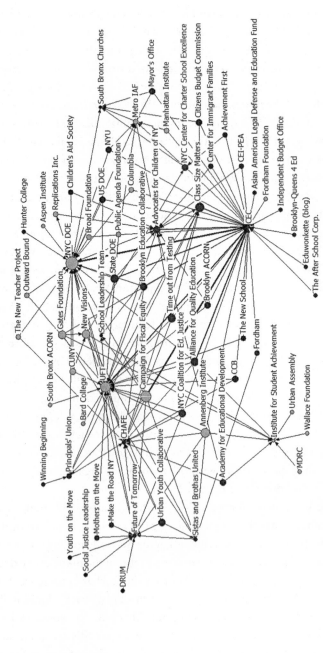

Figure 4.1 New York Education Policy Information Network: Expertise. Node Color Guide, Gray = Major Foundation Grantees; Black = all others. The figure depicts a single-mode network of information exchange. Links indicate the exchange of "data or research"; arrows indicate the direction of information exchange from source to recipient.

meaning there are more internal ties than external ties in the network. The network has a greater prevalence of internal group ties, 61 percent, than external ties linking the two groups, 39 percent. Thus, the network of policy information exchange in New York City education is somewhat divided; groups with funding relationships to major foundations largely exchange policy expertise with one another, and groups that lack this funding primarily exchange expertise among themselves.

Furthermore, there is a significant relationship between sources of policy expertise and attitudes toward education in New York City. Based on outdegree centrality scores, two of the most important sources of policy expertise in the network are the NYC Department of Education (outdegree = 17) and Class Size Matters (outdegree = 12). The Department of Education is the lead actor in the district's policy reforms; Class Size Matters is a citywide advocacy organization focused on reducing class size, which has opposed many of the reforms implemented since mayoral control.

We can test the relationship between these two sources of information and individual attitudes by using the survey question "In your opinion, is this school district improving, staying about the same, or getting worse?" Using an ordered logit model, we can predict the dependent variable, coded as improving (1), staying the same (0), and getting worse (-1). The independent variables in the model are whether the individual respondent mentioned the NYC Department of Education as a source of policy expertise (coded 0,1), whether the individual mentioned Class Size Matters as a source of policy expertise (coded 0,1), and primary affiliation with an organization that received major foundation grants (coded 0,1). My expectation is that individuals who rely on the NYC Department of Education for policy expertise are more likely to view the district as improving, other things being equal. Individuals who rely on Class Size Matters for policy expertise are more likely to view the district as getting worse. Last, I expect that individuals from organizations that received major foundation grants are more likely to view the district as improving. The results are presented in table 4.5.

The results conform to my expectations: relying on the NYC Department of Education for policy information has a significant and positive relationship with attitudes toward district improvement, and relying on Class Size Matters for information has a significant and negative relationship. The grant recipient variable is not statistically significant, but it is positive, which is the expected direction. Of course, the relationship between information sources and attitudes does not show whether the information source causes the attitude, or the reverse. Nonetheless, it provides further evidence of a consistent divide in New York City's education policy community. This divide has many overlapping fault lines: between major foundation grant recipients and organizations that did not

Table 4.5 Ordered Logit Predicting Attitudes with Information Sources

	Is NYCDOE improving (1), staying about the same (0), or getting worse (−1)?
Information source NYC DOE	2.264**
	(.839)
Information source Class Size Matters	−2.221*
	(.876)
Grant recipient	1.580
	(.830)
Pseudo R^2	0.25
N	34

Note: For a one-tailed test of significance, $^*p < 0.05$; $^{**}p < 0.01$.

get grants, between individuals who rely on the NYC Department of Education for policy expertise and individuals who rely on opponents of the district leadership, and between those who view the district as improving and those who view the district as getting worse. In combination, these fault lines suggest that policy reform insiders in New York City have forged relatively little common ground with those on the outside.

Figure 4.2 displays the network of community needs or preferences information exchange. As with figure 4.1, node size is based on outdegree centrality, and the color of the nodes is based on whether the organization is a major foundation grantee. A clear difference between the community network and the expertise network is that the community network has a much greater prevalence of organizations that did not receive major foundation grants (indicated by black nodes). The CEC leaders are the most active seekers of information about community needs or preferences, and many of their sources are advocacy organizations, such as Class Size Matters, Time Out from Testing, and Youth on the Move. Respondents from some of the major nonprofits, such as New Visions and Replications Inc., did not provide any sources of community needs or preferences information on the survey. This lack of response suggests that these organizations are more focused on their policy relationship to the district and less focused on establishing relationships with advocacy organizations and other stakeholders in the district.

Leaders in the Department of Education mentioned several sources of information about local community needs or preferences, including the teachers' and principals' unions (UFT and Council of Supervisors and Administrators), as well as a few advocacy organizations—Mothers on the Move and Brooklyn

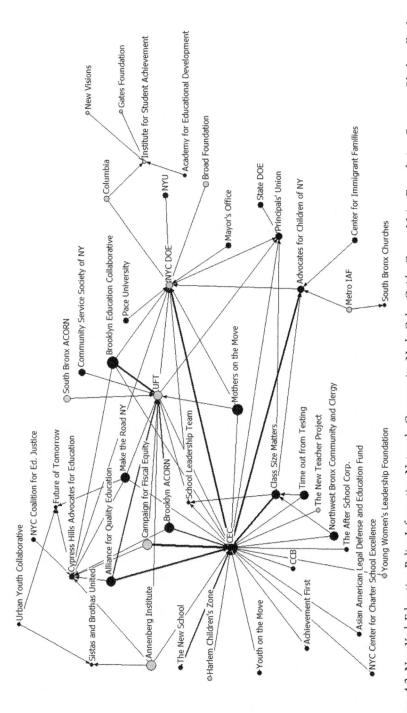

Figure 4.2 New York Education Policy Information Network: Community. Node Color Guide, Gray = Major Foundation Grantees; Black = all others. The figure depicts a single-mode network of information exchange. Links indicate the exchange of "community needs or preferences"; arrows indicate the direction of information exchange from source to recipient.

Education Collaborative. Strikingly absent as a source of information about local needs and preferences for district leaders are the CECs—the official representative bodies for parents in the district. Instead, some of the CEC leaders mentioned the Department of Education as a source of information about community needs or preferences. This provides further evidence that district leaders generally do not see the official mechanism for broad parent and community input—the CECs—as important venues for policy deliberation.

These networks provide some explanation for the differing views on the role of foundations in New York City district reform. Parent leaders are somewhat isolated from the foundations and foundation grantees providing policy information to the Department of Education, whereas Department of Education staff members are embedded in an information network with strong ties to the foundations—including two major foundations and many of their largest grantees, such as New Visions. This network provided New York City administrators with the organizational infrastructure to rapidly implement several reforms—particularly the restructuring of large high schools into small schools. One cost of rapid reform implementation is the lack of involvement and input from parents and advocacy organization leaders.

Entrenchment

Given the divisions in New York City's education policy community, how have many of the Children First policy reforms remained in place? Specifically, the district has continued to close large high schools and restructure them as small schools, even after the Gates Foundation stopped funding this initiative. Charter school expansion in the district has continued, with ongoing support from major foundations. Also, the administrative restructuring, which gives greater autonomy to school principals and offers choices for nonprofit contracting, has been largely maintained. Last, mayoral control of the district has remained in place, with little change to enable greater community oversight of district decision making. The maintenance of these reforms is primarily a product of entrenchment. With the considerable power and autonomy granted to the mayor and the chancellor under mayoral control and alliances with philanthropy and nonprofits, the changes to New York City schools have been protected and maintained in the face of organized opposition.

In June 2009, mayoral control of the New York City public schools was slated to expire unless the state legislature took action to reauthorize it. The debate over reauthorization got under way a full year before the deadline, as advocacy groups began to stake positions and develop coalitions. Two coalitions that opposed mayoral control or supported significant revisions to the mayoral control legislation were the Parent Commission on School Governance and the Campaign for Better Schools.[92] The Parent Commission on School Governance was organized in the spring of 2008 to develop recommendations for the New York State Legislature for revising the school governance law and allowing mayoral control to end.[93] The group involved parents from several CEC boards and other parent organizations. The Campaign for Better Schools was a coalition of parents, youth, and advocacy organizations, such as Advocates for Children of New York, Alliance for Quality Education, Make the Road New York, the NAACP, and Urban Youth Collaborative.[94] This coalition supported significant revisions to the law, including increased checks and balances to give the PEP greater powers and increased transparency.

A new group supporting mayoral control, Learn NY, was founded in 2008. The group brought together local education heavyweights, including Harlem Children's Zone founder Geoffrey Canada, as well as local racial and ethnic advocacy organizations, such as the Hispanic Federation, the Black Equity Alliance, and the Asian American Federation.[95] Other groups that signed onto the Learn NY coalition included major foundation grantees involved in reform implementation in New York City, such as Urban Assembly and Outward Bound. Learn NY also gained support from charter school organizations, including Uncommon Schools and Explore Charter Schools.[96] Many Learn NY supporters were recipients of Department of Education funds or funding from Mayor Bloomberg; with these connections, Learn NY had "limited success in portraying itself as an authentic voice of parents."[97]

In addition to involvement with Learn NY, the charter school community mobilized on its own in support of reauthorizing mayoral control. As Moskowitz had promised in her e-mails with Chancellor Klein, the Success Charter Network helped spawn an affiliated parent organization—Harlem Parents United. A founding member of Harlem Parents United, Natasha Shannon, wrote an op-ed in the *New York Daily News* explaining that she did not want checks on the mayor's power; instead, Shannon argued, "The parent voice I want is parent choice."[98] In March 2009, Mayor Bloomberg, Chancellor Klein, and Geoffrey Canada participated in Harlem Charter Night, which was attended by thousands of students and parents. Bloomberg reminded the crowd of the importance of reauthorizing mayoral control: "We've got to make sure that the reforms that we made don't all get rolled back by the politicians this June."[99]

The enthusiastic support for charters in Harlem shows an emerging divide among parents in New York City—between those who are pleased with the choices offered by new charter schools and those who are frustrated with the top-down governance of the public schools. Although the Learn NY coalition included many advocacy organizations, and charter school parents also mobilized to support mayoral control, the various coalitions taking sides on mayoral control tended to mirror the divisions that emerged from the New York City education policy networks. Public school parent leaders and many of the city's advocacy groups joined coalitions to criticize mayoral control, and foundation-funded nonprofits and charter school supporters joined the coalition favoring mayoral control.

Meanwhile, the role of major foundations was not entirely apparent as the mayoral control debate picked up steam in late 2008 and early 2009. Given the large investments of several major foundations in education reforms that occurred under mayoral control, it is likely that many foundation leaders hoped to maintain the existing system of governance. Interestingly, some of the organizations involved in the Campaign for Better Schools, which criticized aspects of mayoral control, received funding from DEC. Meanwhile, the Broad Foundation funded the "Keep it Going NYC" campaign organized by the Fund for Public Schools.[100] "Keep it Going NYC" was a public relations campaign involving television, radio, and subway advertising. Although the ads did not directly promote mayoral control, they specifically promoted changes that occurred since mayoral control, such as: "Because parents should have more and better options, New York City has opened 354 more public schools since 2002."[101] The ads were prominently displayed on New York City subway trains beginning in the fall of 2008 through the spring of 2009.

Learn NY did not release its list of funders; as a 501(c)(4) organization, it was not required to disclose its donors. Critics of mayoral control, such as Leonie Haimson—founder of the advocacy organization, Class Size Matters—suspected that Bill Gates was a backer of the group.[102] Learn NY seemed to initially face some difficulty raising money, due to expectations that Mayor Bloomberg, "who has lavished handsome sums on many nonprofit groups and spent millions of dollars on his own campaigns, would quietly finance the effort."[103] After mayoral control was restored by the legislature in August 2009, the *New York Post* published an article revealing that Bill Gates and Eli Broad had personally funded Learn NY.[104] According to the article, Gates gave about $4 million to Learn NY, and Broad "also gave millions" that supported "Learn-NY's extensive public-relations, media and lobbying efforts in Albany and the city."[105] Both philanthropists gave to Learn NY personally, rather than through their foundations.

With foundations, nonprofits, and charter school advocates lining up to support mayoral control and groups of public school parents and advocacy organizations criticizing it, the remaining key political force was the UFT. According to Ravitch, the UFT was the "only group" that might have caused the legislature to add significant checks and balances to mayoral control legislation.[106] Yet the UFT leadership owed a great deal to the mayor "because he had awarded the teachers a 43 percent salary increase and a generous boost to their pensions."[107]

Randi Weingarten, president of the UFT, came out in support of continuation of mayoral control, although she was open to reforms regarding the PEP.[108]

The structure of the PEP was a key point of disagreement in the mayoral control reauthorization debate. Critics of mayoral control hoped to decrease the number of mayoral appointees to the PEP or to give PEP members fixed terms, so the board could operate independently and members could not be removed at will. The Campaign for Better Schools organized a protest at a PEP meeting in May 2009 where protestors gave PEP members rubber stamps and one protestor urged board members to "think for yourselves."[109] Meanwhile, Mayor Bloomberg came out strongly against modifications to the PEP and for his power to appoint a majority of its members. In February 2009, during his weekly radio show, Bloomberg explained:

> You can't have it both ways. Either there's going to be somebody in charge, or there's going to be a committee.... Going back [to local district governance] would be a disaster. Not one of the reforms that we did that accounted for all this progress, not one would have ever gotten through.[110]

Bloomberg even warned that if the legislature did not reauthorize mayoral control, there could be "riots in the streets."[111]

The drama surrounding the mayoral control debate heated up considerably in June 2009, as the deadline approached and no bill had passed. On June 17, the State Assembly passed reauthorization of mayoral control until 2015 with minor changes, such as greater PEP oversight of contracts over $1 million. Uncertainty about the future of mayoral control grew as a crisis erupted in the New York State Senate, when two members switched parties and Republicans gained control. The resulting gridlock delayed State Senate consideration of the issue. In early August, the State Senate passed the Assembly's bill reauthorizing mayoral control. The bill included a provision for a parent training center to address concerns about lack of parental involvement in the district, but the bill largely kept the mayor's and chancellor's powers intact.[112]

Since the reauthorization, political conflicts continue to roil the New York City public schools. In January 2010, the chancellor announced plans to close 19 schools due to poor academic performance, including large high schools slated for restructuring. At a marathon PEP meeting on January 26, 2010, lasting until 4 A.M., hundreds of protestors gathered to show support for keeping the schools open, and more than 300 speakers addressed the board.[113] Nonetheless, most of the school closings were approved by a vote of 9–4; the nine yes votes came from the mayor's appointees and the Staten Island borough president appointee.[114] In February 2010, the UFT and NAACP filed a lawsuit against the city, claiming violations of the law governing school closures.[115] A ruling by a State Supreme Court justice in March 2010 sided with the plaintiffs and blocked the school closings. The judge agreed that the Department of Education did not fulfill its requirements under the new mayoral control legislation "to give detailed 'educational-impact statements' describing the effect of each closing on students and surrounding schools."[116]

Despite the outcome of the lawsuit, the district proposed several additional school closures in 2011. Once again, protests were organized, but the closures were approved by the PEP. In March 2011, the UFT and NAACP joined together again to file a lawsuit blocking the closures; additionally, this lawsuit included an argument against proposals for 15 charter school colocations in public school buildings.[117] A ruling by a State Supreme Court judge in July 2011 sided with the district, allowing the closures and colocations to proceed. The school closure debate shows that parent leaders and advocacy organizations still have little power to change the direction of district reforms in New York City without extraordinary measures, such as a lawsuit. Overall, the path that began with the development of Children First in 2003—joining mayoral control with the continuation of foundation-funded policy reforms—remains largely intact.

Interestingly, one of the greatest risks to Mayor Bloomberg's education reform agenda was the product of a decision made by the mayor. When Chancellor Klein resigned in November 2010, Bloomberg selected the chairman of Hearst Magazines, Cathie Black, as Klein's successor. Bloomberg stated that Black was a "world class manager," though Black had no prior experience in education or government. Black's brief tenure as chancellor involved multiple public relations blunders, including a joke about the need for "birth control" to address overcrowded schools and a sarcastic response in a public meeting with parents protesting the closure of neighborhood schools. Furthermore, Black had difficulty to adjusting to the new job, relying heavily on aides in high-level meetings.[118] According to a Marist poll, Black's job approval rating after three months as chancellor was 17 percent.[119] Bloomberg requested her resignation in April 2011, and Black left her post after 95 days on the job. Although Black did little to deviate from Klein's Children First agenda, her time in office was viewed as a period of relative stagnation compared with Klein's frenetic pace. Bloomberg appointed Dennis Walcott—his deputy mayor for education and former president of the New York Urban League—to replace Black.

Despite the recent leadership turnover, the Children First reforms in New York City have remained protected under the existing system of mayoral control. Reform supporters have invested considerable resources and political capital in maintaining policy changes and mayoral control in the face of opposition, leading to entrenchment of Children First. As the restructuring of schools and reorganization of the district administration have progressed, Children First supporters have been unwilling to compromise to build a broader supportive coalition, which could foster civic capacity for reform. The failure to win over key constituencies—including major advocacy organizations and groups representing public school parents—may jeopardize the long-term success of the reforms.[120]

Policy sustainability can occur with entrenchment alone.[121] However, given that Children First reforms continue to rely heavily on top-down leadership and investments, erosion or reversal of the Children First reforms is possible in the future, particularly if the next mayor and chancellor do not maintain investments in public school choice, charter schools, and administrative reforms. According to Patashnik's assessment of policy reforms, sustainable policy change—and avoiding the threat of erosion—is most likely with reconfiguration of interest group alliances and institutions in a policy area.[122] Reconfiguration involves significant investments by various groups in the new system, the rise of new organized groups with a stake in the reformed system, and in some cases, dismantling old institutions and the creation of new institutions. New York City exhibits some steps toward reconfiguration. New interest groups with strong investments in reforms have emerged. In particular, charter school parents are becoming more organized.

Nonetheless, the Children First reforms were layered on top of an older system for parent representation based on the 32 geographically defined CECs. The district leadership has done little to integrate this old geographic representation system with new administrative reforms that are not aligned with geography. The persistence of old institutions like CECs—and the absence of a new venue for parent involvement in district policy making aligned to the new administrative structure—has alienated many parent leaders from the district's reform efforts. As explained by Henig, Gold, Orr, Silander, and Simon, "The demand for a stronger and more clearly defined collective role for parents and community, including the establishment of priorities and the formulation of policies, fueled resentment that was deeper and broader than the administration anticipated."[123] District leaders favored a tightly controlled policy-making process that ensured the adoption and implementation of their most favored reform proposals. Although a select group of nonprofits and philanthropies is substantially invested in the Children First reforms, the district leadership has offered few opportunities for investment or involvement in shaping and implementing reforms to parent leaders and advocacy organizations.

Conclusion

Foundations involved in school reform in New York City have focused their investments on the district bureaucracy and education nonprofit organizations. Several of these nonprofits are involved in implementing key aspects of the district's reform initiatives. Among nonprofit and district leaders, foundations are credited with providing important funding and policy support for school reform. Yet among parents and advocacy organization leaders, there is dissatisfaction with the direction of the district and the lack of opportunities for stakeholder involvement.

Does the strategy to fund nonprofits that become district insiders allow foundations to have policy influence in a large and complex school system? Under the current system of mayoral control, this strategy clearly heightens the influence of major foundations. There is no elected school board in New York City, and the CECs and PEP hold limited powers. Foundation-funded nonprofits—and, more recently, charter school founders—have close relationships with the district bureaucracy. Meanwhile, local stakeholders have been growing more aware of this influence. Patrick Sullivan, PEP member and the appointee of the Manhattan borough president, spoke about philanthropic influence in the district at a New York State Assembly Education Committee public hearing on mayoral control on February 6, 2009:

> In its current form the Panel for Educational Policy does not make policy or even meaningfully advise the chancellor. Those roles are reserved for the chancellor's management consultants and the distant foundations of wealthy men: the Broad Foundation, Gates Foundation and Dell Foundation. But we parents know better. The real insight into the challenges of urban education lies in the communities, school leadership teams, PTAs, community councils.[124]

The alignment of interests involving foundations, the school district bureaucracy, and education nonprofits differs substantially from the pluralist school politics described by Dahl. Regarding public education, Dahl observed:

> [The mayor, the board of education, and the superintendent of schools] consider the reactions of a number of different public school interests who can, if aroused, make themselves felt in various ways—not least through election. The most important of these public school interests are the administrators, the teachers, and the parents of the children in the public schools.[125]

In New York City, the "public school interests" are not only administrators, teachers, and parents but also national foundations and education nonprofit organizations. In Dahl's New Haven, democratic processes involved "ritual and ceremonies" with elected leaders paying heed to spokespersons for local constituent communities.[126] In New York City, foundations mostly support organizations that circumvent these local rituals by working directly as partners with the bureaucracy. For foundations and their partners, the agenda is expert driven, and balancing local competing interests could weaken their ambitious reform agenda.

In the short run, policy sustainability in New York City appears to be assured by successful entrenchment. Longer run sustainability is less certain. Erosion or reversal is a constant threat to significant policy reforms that lack support from heavily invested constituencies. New reform constituencies may continue to emerge and build strength in New York City, particularly in the charter school sector. Yet the district leadership and nonprofit partners have shown little inclination toward public engagement and constituency building. The built-up frustration among many parent leaders and advocacy organizations after years of outsider status means that future efforts could bear little fruit. New York City's school leadership—and the philanthropies that provided support—made a bargain to implement ambitious reforms quickly with a narrow base of engaged stakeholders. The cost of that bargain could be a failure to achieve long-run reform sustainability.

CHAPTER 5

Deliberative Decentralization

FOUNDATION DOLLARS AND LOS ANGELES
SCHOOL REFORM

The Los Angeles Unified School District (LAUSD) is second to New York City in student enrollment, but its geographic size—710 square miles—is more than twice as large. Unlike the New York City Department of Education, which follows the same boundaries as New York City, LAUSD serves the city of Los Angeles as well as 27 other communities, in part or in whole. Thus, the challenges of operating a large district are magnified in LAUSD, given its size, diversity, and jurisdictional complexity.

For decades, the capacity of LAUSD to manage schooling in Los Angeles with top-down bureaucratic authority has been eroding.[1] It has faced multiple secession movements from areas as varied as the suburban San Fernando Valley and urban south-central Los Angeles; advocates for these changes argued that LAUSD was unmanageable and favored creating new districts to serve their local communities.[2] The student population in LAUSD has changed dramatically since the 1970s because of simultaneous Latino immigration and white flight.[3] The district responded to outside pressure for change during the 1990s by partnering with reformers leading the LEARN and LAAMP initiatives. Although these reforms produced some change at the school level, they produced little lasting change in the district administration. Until very recently, much of the funding and momentum for education reform in Los Angeles has been building outside the district bureaucracy.

Major foundations have subsidized the expansion of alternatives to traditional public schools in LAUSD, primarily by giving large grants to charter management organizations (CMOs) and supporting the construction of charter school facilities through Pacific Charter School Development. During the 2011–2012 school year, more than 82,000 students were enrolled in 187 charter schools in LAUSD; more students attend charter schools in Los Angeles than in any other district.[4] By 2010, 42 percent of charter schools in LAUSD were operated by CMOs such as Green Dot Public Schools (Green Dot), the Alliance for College-Ready Public Schools (Alliance), KIPP, and Inner City Education Foundation (ICEF). Only Newark and New Orleans have a larger proportion of charter schools operated by CMOs.[5]

Los Angeles appears to be fertile ground for the divisive politics evident in New York City, as foundation-funded CMOs compete with traditional public schools for students, space, and funds. Debates about charter school expansion in Los Angeles are often heated and frequently involve charges of privatization from charter opponents, while charter supporters argue that the district is beholden to the teachers' union.[6] Nonetheless, the education policy network in Los Angeles is far more inclusive and less divided than the New York City network. Despite the sprawling geography of Los Angeles and the numerous CMOs, there is a well-defined core of actors in Los Angeles education with cross-sector links of information exchange. This core of actors is relatively diverse, including CMOs, major foundations, LAUSD bureaucrats, the board of education, and local advocacy organizations. Compared with New York City, education politics in Los Angeles is considerably more open to involvement from outside groups, and LAUSD operates with greater transparency than the NYC Department of Education. Some CMOs also contribute to the more accessible style of politics in Los Angeles, serving as alternative avenues for advocates to demand change to the system.

Furthermore, there is preliminary evidence of positive policy feedback in Los Angeles in response to the expansion of charter schools. Specifically, district leaders and advocacy groups have sought to extend charterlike autonomy to public schools and further decentralize authority in the district. Policy change in Los Angeles has not proceeded in a logical or linear fashion. Nonetheless, new policies in the district have created paths for public schools to become charter schools or to operate more like charter schools. In 2009, LAUSD adopted the public school choice policy, an unusually bold step allowing outside nonprofit organizations, including CMOs, to submit applications to run newly constructed or low-performing district schools. Public school choice, however, generated political backlash over charter school takeovers of public schools. After two years, charter schools and other outside groups were excluded from the public school choice application process. Meanwhile, in December 2011, LAUSD and the teachers' union adopted a new memorandum of understanding (MOU) that will enable school-level autonomy over decisions like curriculum, the length of the school day, and union contract provisions.[7] Thus, public school autonomy in Los Angeles appears to have shifted onto a new track—from public school choice to the new MOU.

As Patashnik argues, sustainable policy reforms do not endure "because they are 'frozen in place'"; instead, policies endure because they reconfigure interest group alignments and stimulate investment in the new policy.[8] It is too early to tell whether school-level autonomy will produce meaningful benefits for student achievement or generate continued political investments from a diverse set of interests. Furthermore, the policy will continue to evolve as teachers and other groups respond to the new MOU and begin to translate the concept of school-level autonomy into practice. Nonetheless, interest group organizing and advocacy in Los Angeles is increasingly geared toward applying the strategies of charter school reform to public schools in LAUSD. The public school choice policy and the new MOU are products of a political environment that has been reshaped by charter schools, and the charter school sector in Los Angeles is, in turn, a product of extensive foundation investment.

In this chapter, I show how foundation influence has affected education policy and politics in Los Angeles in three ways. First, I trace foundation grant dollars to specific organizations, and I explain the role of foundations and their grantees in the development and implementation of policy reforms in Los Angeles, highlighting the distinct strategies of two major CMOs. Second, using the results of my survey and social network analysis, I show how policy information is exchanged among a relatively diverse core of organizations, while political attitudes do not divide organizations into distinct factions. Third, I examine how recent education policy reforms and the formation of new interest group coalitions suggest the emergence of positive policy feedback.

Following the Los Angeles Grants

Major foundations have adopted a very different strategy for education grant making in Los Angeles than in New York City. The total grant dollars from major foundations to three main categories of grantees in Los Angeles is reported in table 5.1. Charter schools in Los Angeles are clearly the largest grantee category—including charter management organizations as well as nonprofits that support charter schools, such as Pacific Charter School Development. The Broad Foundation and Walton Foundation each gave more than $3 million for charter school expansion in 2005, and the Gates Foundation gave $8.5 million. The main category that is missing is the public sector; in 2005, no major foundation grants for K-12 education in Los Angeles went directly to the school district.

The largest nonprofit recipient of a major foundation grant in 2005 was Families in Schools, the organizational descendant of the Los Angeles Annenberg Metropolitan Project (LAAMP). The $2.2 million grant to Families in Schools from the Annenberg Foundation was designated to support the Boyle Heights Learning Collaborative—an

Table 5.1 2005 Grant Dollars by Organization Type

Organization/Institution	Total Funding
Charter management organizations, charter schools, and facilities	$16.2 million
Nonprofit service providers	$3 million
Advocacy organizations	$611,302

Source: Author's data gathered from foundation tax returns.

education reform organization focused on the Boyle Heights neighborhood in East L.A. Most of the remaining grants to nonprofit service providers focused on arts education; grantees included Inner City Arts and H.E. Art Project.

Much like major foundation grants in New York City, the grant dollars to advocacy organizations are a small share of grants overall, about 3 percent of the total grant dollars from major foundations for education in Los Angeles. A few of the grants in 2005 stem from a Gates Foundation initiative to support education organizing for high school reform in Los Angeles. Two organizations that received these grants were Alliance for a Better Community and Community Coalition. Alliance for a Better Community is a Latino advocacy organization, and Community Coalition has strong ties to the African American community in South Los Angeles. Grants to both organizations were focused on advocacy work to promote a college preparatory curriculum in Los Angeles high schools known as "A through G." Marqueece Harris-Dawson, executive director of Community Coalition, spoke positively about the Gates grant, which came about due to a "synergy between what [Gates] was trying to accomplish" and ongoing work by Community Coalition.[9] The grant funded organizing logistics to promote the "A through G" curriculum in high schools, a policy that was adopted by the board of education in 2005. Harris-Dawson added that the Gates grant was "catalytic—it helped us with other funders to get support." Nonetheless, grant dollars for advocacy organizations are minimal, compared with the millions of dollars supporting charter school expansion.

Foundation funding for CMOs in Los Angeles has stayed high since 2005, and private funding is likely to remain important for CMOs to support operations and plans for expansion. According to a recent study of CMO effectiveness:

> The average CMO relies on philanthropy for approximately 13 percent of its total operating revenues, but the number is much higher when central office revenues are isolated. Those CMOs funded by NewSchools Venture Fund report that 64 percent of their central office revenues come from philanthropy.[10]

In 2009, the Gates Foundation announced that a consortium of four CMOs in Los Angeles, known as the College Ready Promise, was selected for the foundation's new grant program focused on teacher effectiveness. The Gates Foundation selected four sites for these grants in three public school districts—Hillsborough County, Florida; Memphis, Tennessee; and Pittsburgh, Pennsylvania—in addition to the charter school consortium in Los Angeles. The four CMOs involved in the College Ready Promise include the Alliance, Green Dot, Aspire Public Schools, and Partnerships to Uplift Communities (PUC). Gates planned to provide $60 million for several teaching-related programs involving these CMOs, including training programs for new teachers and using student achievement data to evaluate and reward teachers.[11] This grant continues the pattern of major foundations funding charter schools in Los Angeles and bypassing the school district.

Charter School Expansion

The engines of charter school growth and development in Los Angeles are CMOs. Most CMOs in Los Angeles are fairly recent creations—many are scarcely a decade old. Following the passage of California's charter school legislation in 1992, the early charter schools formed in Los Angeles were conversions of existing public schools. They became autonomous charter schools, not affiliates of CMOs. The expansion of charter schools in Los Angeles accelerated considerably after 1998; in that year, new state legislation lifted the cap on charter schools, and the New Schools Venture Fund, a major investor in CMOs, was founded in the San Francisco Bay area. Two CMOs were started soon after: Aspire Public Schools and Green Dot. Starting in 2002, New Schools Venture Fund raised nearly $50 million from investors, including the Broad Foundation, Gates Foundation, and Walton Family Foundation, to support CMOs. Two additional Los Angeles–based CMOs supported by New Schools Venture Fund were founded in 2004: the Alliance and PUC. According to an official in the Charter Schools Division of LAUSD, at least eight different CMOs are petitioning to open two to four new charter schools in LAUSD each year.[12] Although LAUSD continues to approve new charter school petitions, each student attending a charter school rather than a traditional public school means fewer per pupil dollars from the state for the school district. Table 5.2 lists several of the largest CMOs in Los Angeles and the number of schools operated by each.

In addition to CMOs, another organization that independently operates several schools within LAUSD is the Partnership for Los Angeles Schools (PLAS), which Mayor Villaraigosa started after a state court judge overturned mayoral control. It manages 16 schools, mostly in East and South Los Angeles. These

Table 5.2 Schools Operated by Large CMOs in Los Angeles, 2011–2012

Charter Management Organization	*Number of Schools in Los Angeles*
Alliance for College Ready Public Schools (Alliance)	20 schools
Green Dot Public Schools (Green Dot)	18 schools (including the Locke Family of Schools)
Inner City Education Foundation (ICEF)	13 schools
Partnerships to Uplift Communities (PUC)	13 schools
Aspire Public Schools	11 schools
KIPP	7 schools

Source: Data gathered by author from CMO Web sites.

schools are not charter schools, and they "operate within the existing attendance boundaries and labor agreements."[13] Nonetheless, PLAS does resemble CMOs in other ways: PLAS has hired top leaders from charter schools and the private sector, PLAS Chief Executive Officer Marshall Tuck was previously chief operating officer of Green Dot, and PLAS Chief Operating Officer Mark Kleger-Heine had been a consultant with McKinsey & Company. Based on the 2008 tax return filed by PLAS, the Gates Foundation gave $1.2 million and the Annenberg Foundation gave $300,000 to the organization; however, the Los Angeles–based Broad Foundation did not give funds to PLAS.[14]

Within the crowded field of independent school operators in Los Angeles, many CMOs have adopted specific missions and guidelines for expansion. For example, ICEF focuses on opening schools in South Los Angeles and plans to open enough schools to graduate 2,000 students each year,[15] and PUC has also adopted a regional approach by opening schools in Northeast Los Angeles and the Northeast San Fernando Valley.[16]

The founders of the two largest CMOs in Los Angeles—Green Dot and the Alliance—have developed contrasting expansion strategies. Green Dot was started by Steve Barr, a political activist who cofounded the Rock the Vote campaign in the 1990s and has close ties to the Democratic Party. Barr's political organizing background helps guide the approach to education reform at Green Dot, which involves grassroots organizing and confrontations with the district bureaucracy and teachers' union. Meanwhile, the Alliance is essentially the organizational descendant of two previous reform efforts involving the school district: LEARN and LAAMP. The founder of the Alliance, Judy Burton, helped lead implementation of LEARN. Several board members of the Alliance, including William Ouchi, Richard Riordan, and Virgil Roberts, had ties to LEARN, LAAMP, or both. Thus, the Alliance has fairly strong insider ties to LAUSD due to its direct lineage from previous district reform efforts and has developed a less confrontational approach to expansion.

GREEN DOT

At Green Dot, political organizing and operating charter schools seem to go hand in hand. According to Dan Chang, Green Dot's former vice president of new school development, Green Dot is "a little different from most charter management organizations—equal parts new schools and political will machine."[17] Chang described Green Dot's expansion strategy as "aggressive and strategic growth." Interviewees involved in other CMOs wanted to distance themselves from Green Dot's strategy, but Green Dot embraces a more adversarial and political approach. Green Dot targeted two of the lowest performing high schools in Los Angeles—Jefferson High School and Locke High School—as sites to focus its reform efforts. In 2006, Green Dot started the Jefferson Transformation Project, opening five new charter high schools in the vicinity of Jefferson.

Locke High School represents a new role for CMOs as they continue to expand within LAUSD: the conversion of low-performing traditional public schools into charters, paired with an infusion of philanthropic funding. Green Dot is transforming this traditional large public high school into small charter schools; the Gates Foundation committed $7.9 million to the conversion effort.[18] The Locke conversion may also provide a model for ongoing CMO expansion by using existing public school facilities. According to the Gates Foundation's 2007 annual report:

> [The Locke conversion] not only paves the way for Green Dot to impact more students, it also solves one of the most difficult problems facing Green Dot and other CMOs: facilities. Charter schools in many states don't receive extra funding for facilities, and finding a place where students can engage in rigorous learning can be a serious challenge. But if these CMOs can use pre-existing facilities, then they can concentrate more fully on what they set out to do—providing the best possible education to as many students as possible.[19]

Due to California's Proposition 39, passed in 2000, school districts are required "to provide local charter schools with facilities that are sufficient and reasonably equivalent to other buildings, classrooms, or facilities in the district."[20] Nonetheless, LAUSD and Los Angeles–based charter schools have battled over the facilities requirement, and the California Charter Schools Association filed a lawsuit against LAUSD in 2010. Meanwhile, Green Dot's strategy to convert existing public schools, rather than just creating new charter schools, means the existing school building becomes part of the package.

Political strategy was a key component of Green Dot's conversion of Locke High School. According to Chang, Green Dot began holding meetings and developing relationships with groups around Locke High School prior to 2005, including teachers at Locke, the Watts Labor Community Action Committee, and local clergy. To convert the school to a charter school, 50 percent of the tenured teachers at the school would have to approve the charter. During 2006, Green Dot submitted 11 charter petitions to put pressure on the district to accept conversion of Locke. Meanwhile, Green Dot worked with allies on Locke's staff to persuade enough teachers to vote in favor of conversion. Although more than 50 percent of tenured teachers at Locke agreed to conversion in the spring of 2007, a battle with the Los Angeles Teachers' Union (UTLA) continued through the summer. The UTLA organized teachers to rescind their votes for conversion, and Green Dot organized to maintain a majority in favor of conversion. Green Dot ultimately succeeded at maintaining a majority, and the conversion was approved on September 11, 2007, although the school would not come under Green Dot's management until the following school year. The 2007–2008 school year was particularly rough at Locke, a situation that some attributed to the uncertainty of the impending conversion. A fight involving hundreds of students broke out at the school in the spring of 2008. A *Time* magazine story about the fight quotes the school's principal, Travis Kiel, explaining the situation: "There's tension between staff, students and the community around [the issue of conversion].... There's a kind of free-floating anxiety."[21]

Once Green Dot gained control of the school, transformation began on many dimensions. Foundation grants from the Gates Foundation and others helped finance these changes. According to Chang, about a third of the teachers remained at Locke, and the others were replaced. Two new small schools were established for incoming ninth-graders; continuing students were assigned to transition schools, some of which focused on helping students catch up who were behind on credits for graduation. Physically, Locke High School was spruced up, with new trees and building improvements. Yet Green Dot cannot cap enrollment at Locke as it can at its other charter schools, and it cannot rely on self-selection of "motivated parents and students who want exactly what Green Dot has to offer: safer campuses, more academic rigor."[22] According to a *Los Angeles Times* editorial, "Locke *is* the neighborhood school and educates most of the neighborhood's students"; enrollment selectivity is thus absent as a factor contributing to the success (or failure) of the school and its management organization.[23] For these reasons, the Locke High School conversion has become a closely watched experiment in education reform. Green Dot's success would demonstrate that the CMO can run the same school with the same students more effectively than the school district, acknowledging one very important difference: the CMO brings additional resources into the school, due to philanthropic support. Failure, by contrast, would add fodder to critics' claims that charter schools succeed only when they skim off the best students.

In addition to the high-profile Locke conversion, Green Dot is pursuing other strategies to spark district reform in Los Angeles, including parent and teacher organizing. Green Dot's teachers are unionized as the Asociacion de Maestros Unidos (AMU), an affiliate of the California Teachers Association. According to Chang, one goal of the AMU is to catalyze change in the UTLA. He also explained that unionizing Green Dot's teachers is essential to show that Green Dot's reforms are transferable to the fully unionized public education sector. Former UTLA president A. J. Duffy expressed regret that his union was outmaneuvered by Green Dot:

> We could have and probably should have organized the Green Dot schools. They started with one charter school, now have ten, and in short order they'll have twenty schools in Los Angeles, with all the teachers paying dues to a different union. And that's a problem.[24]

The AMU contract differs substantially from the UTLA contract. The AMU contract does not include explicit seniority preferences for layoffs or offer teacher tenure, but salaries are 10 to 15 percent higher than those earned by teachers in LAUSD. Green Dot's contract has been praised by school choice proponents who criticize UTLA for its 347-page contract, "the size of a fat phone book," compared with the 33-page AMU contract.[25]

The Los Angeles Parents Union (LAPU) was also started by Steve Barr and initially affiliated with Green Dot, although it has been reorganized and renamed Parent Revolution. Elizabeth Dill of Act4Education—an advocacy group in West L.A.—joined the board of LAPU. She explained that LAPU urged parents to use a "carrot and stick approach—go to the school and say we want these things to happen, and if they won't then we'll open a charter school."[26] In 2009, when LAPU was reorganized as Parent Revolution, this carrot-and-stick approach was made more explicit. Parent Revolution pledges that if more than half of the parents at a school sign a petition to demand improvement, Parent Revolution "will guarantee an excellent campus within three years.... If the district doesn't deliver, targeted neighborhoods could be flooded with [charter schools]."[27] Known as the "parent trigger," this approach to forcing change in a public school was enacted with a package of reforms passed by California legislators in an attempt to qualify the state for federal Race to the Top funds. If more than half of parents sign a petition in a "demonstrably failing school," the school could be turned over to a charter operator, or the entire staff could be replaced.[28]

Parent Revolution bears some resemblance to the organizing of charter school parents in New York City, particularly the efforts to organize parents in Harlem by Harlem Success Academy founder Eva Moskowitz. It is not clear whether Moskowitz modeled her approach on Barr's example, though Barr's parent organizing efforts began a few years earlier. Both Moskowitz and Barr are politically minded school reformers who have recognized that charter schools can be a vehicle for reaching parents and mobilizing them politically. Both have spawned affiliated parent organizations under new names—Harlem Parents United and Parent Revolution. Both of these organizations have been criticized as Astroturf, meaning they have the appearance of grassroots organizing, but they are backed by political elites. From the top, Parent Revolution is highly professionalized, headed by Ben Austin, a "hard-driving politico from the affluent west side of L.A." who worked in the Clinton White House and as deputy to former Los Angeles Mayor Richard Riordan; Austin also served on the California State Board of Education.[29] Parent Revolution's top organizers include parents with children who graduated from Green Dot schools.[30]

Overall, Green Dot's strategy is to "straddle the line between competition and cooperation" with the school district, says Chang.[31] So far, competition has been the more dominant strategy, which Chang attributes to "institutional inertia, lack of leadership, no push from the top [at LAUSD] to create lines of communication."[32] Green Dot's funders, including Gates and Broad, have remained supportive. According to Chang, these foundations are "pro-expansion" and they "buy into our strategy."[33] Yet while Green Dot focuses on politics, organizing, and conversion, other CMOs are working more quietly and concordantly with LAUSD.

THE ALLIANCE

Another heavyweight in the world of Los Angeles CMOs is the Alliance—the creation of veterans from LEARN and LAAMP. The Alliance maintains a relatively close relationship with LAUSD. Alliance President and CEO Judy Burton served as an outside representative on the LAUSD Board of Education Charters and Innovation Committee. This committee holds hearings on charter petitions to make recommendations to the full board of education. Furthermore, Burton formerly served as a local district superintendent within LAUSD and, later, as head of the LAUSD Office of School Reform. Compared with Green Dot, the mission of the Alliance is somewhat less focused on changing LAUSD overall. According to Kerchner and his colleagues, the Alliance "board decided it would no longer be engaged in large-scale systemic reform projects; the appetite for that had simply run out."[34] Instead, the Alliance focuses on creating charter schools drawing on aspects of the LEARN and LAAMP models, including school autonomy and small learning communities. Still, there is an expectation that the Alliance could indirectly help to drive reform of LAUSD. According to Burton, "The district is not our enemy. Our greatest hope would be that every school would have the flexibility and talent to use the strategies that are working for us."[35]

With personal connections and an expansion strategy that is less threatening to the district, the Alliance maintains a fairly cooperative relationship with LAUSD. According to the Alliance's former Chief Academic Officer David Linzey, "The Alliance works collaboratively with LAUSD and is on friendly terms. District Board members as well as district administrators visit Alliance schools, ceremonies, and have invited Alliance top officials to serve on task forces for LAUSD regional districts and projects."[36] Linzey also explained that the Alliance received a charter schools dissemination grant from the state "to share their best practices with LAUSD schools that are interested."[37] At a March 2009 meeting of the Charters and Innovation Committee, four renewal petitions from the Alliance were approved. The decisions about renewal were based on recommendations of the Charter Schools Division, which evaluates all LAUSD charter schools. These recommendations are typically laden with neutral and dense bureaucratic language and rarely go beyond cursory statements indicating whether standards were met. Yet the district's renewal documentation for the Stern Math and Science School includes a pat on the back for the Alliance beyond the usual bureaucratese: "Alliance has earned the respect of the Los Angeles community by maintaining quality schools."[38]

Nonetheless, the relationship between the Alliance and the district is not entirely cozy, particularly when conflicts over resources come to the fore. A recent dispute involved funding for special education. Charter schools in the area and LAUSD are part of the same special education local plan area (SELPA) mandated by the state. According to Linzey, "LAUSD's special education programs have encroached significantly onto the general budget, having surpassed their funding for special education.... LAUSD wants to pass these encroached costs onto the charter schools in their SELPA, which would significantly impact the charter schools budgets."[39] Meanwhile, school district leaders are frustrated at the fact that charter schools enroll fewer special education students than district schools: 11.2 percent of all LAUSD students are special education students, compared with only 7 percent in charter schools.[40]

Much like Green Dot, the Alliance expects to continue expanding and has a green light from its major funders. The Broad Foundation has committed to funding the Alliance through 2014, provided that the schools meet the foundation's internal evaluation standards. According to Alliance Chief Development Officer Jennifer Drake, the Alliance has "always gotten support to expand" from the Broad Foundation, with the goal of helping the Alliance open 20 schools.[41] The Alliance had reached the goal of opening 20 charter schools by the 2011–2012 school year.

CHARTER SCHOOLS: ASSESSING THE IMPACT

Both Green Dot and the Alliance report impressive rates of student achievement in many of their schools in comparison with nearby LAUSD schools, but overall there is a disappointing lack of rigorous evaluation of Los Angeles charter schools. The Alliance reported that eight of its high schools and four middle schools scored above the district average for the California Academic Performance Index (API) in 2010.[42] Green Dot also posts API results for its schools online.[43] Each of the CMOs tracks its performance individually, and LAUSD must gather data to assess petitions for charter renewals; however, charter schools in Los Angeles have not been evaluated with a broad randomized study similar to the Gates-funded MDRC study of small schools in New York City. Given the large foundation grants supporting CMO growth in Los Angeles, the lack of rigorous evaluation of student achievement in CMO-run schools is a striking oversight by these funders.

Although broader studies are lacking, there has been a systematic evaluation of one school—the Locke High School transformation by Green Dot—funded by the Gates Foundation.[44] This study uses student-level data to match students who enrolled in the Locke small schools operated by Green Dot to students from the same neighborhoods who enrolled in other schools. By matching on several characteristics (gender, ethnicity, parent education, poverty, etc.), the study has a quasi-experimental design, which produces a treatment group (Locke students) and a control group (students in nearby schools). The study's findings suggest that Green Dot is achieving positive results at Locke. First, the study shows that the ninth-grade students enrolling at the Green Dot Locke schools have similar socioeconomic characteristics and educational outcomes to surrounding schools. In other words, the Green Dot transformation has not significantly changed the entering student population. Second, Locke students achieved comparable or better results to the matched students at other schools based on completion of required courses and various standardized test results. Although the differences in student achievement were small for the first cohort to enroll at Locke following the transformation, the differences have grown with later cohorts. According to the study's authors, "Based on our statistical evaluation of various student outcomes—we assert that there are reasons to be optimistic with [Green Dot Locke's] progress thus far."[45] Nonetheless, the study does offer some findings that demonstrate deep and persistent challenges at Locke. For example, the Green Dot Locke schools, as well as LAUSD, lose about 30 percent of students between the fall semester of ninth grade and the fall semester of tenth grade.[46] Although Green Dot is beginning to improve student retention, the challenge remains daunting. The Locke High School transformation has been the most scrutinized charter school initiative in Los Angeles, and this study provides an important contribution toward understanding the impact of Green Dot's efforts. Nonetheless, as the charter sector continues to expand, the need for rigorous evaluation to assess the impact of CMOs on student achievement becomes more pressing.

Improving student achievement is challenging work for CMOs. Yet CMOs also face considerable challenges in their efforts to scale-up their models and negotiate the political process. Several of my informants doubted that charter schools could ever change LAUSD on their own. Raising questions about the prospects for large-scale CMO expansion, Ryan Smith of PLAS asked, "Are charter schools scalable? Can charters serve 700,000 students?"[47] Maisie Chin, cofounder of the community organization CADRE, explained that the mission of charter school proponents "was to have charter innovations trickle back to other schools, but this does not necessarily breed overall collective responsibility for kids."[48] Focusing on Green Dot's conversion of Locke High School in South L.A., Community Coalition's Marqueece Harris-Dawson pointed out that "there are eight comprehensive high schools just in South L.A. [Green Dot] has spent three years just working on Locke."[49] Both the size of LAUSD and the private resources required by CMOs to replicate their models present considerable challenges for translating charter expansion into broad district reform.

With growing numbers of charter schools in the district, there has also been increasing concern among board of education members that charter schools are not being held accountable. In a *Los Angeles Times* op-ed, board of education member Tamar Galatzan writes, "I have been extremely uncomfortable with the loose and inconsistent manner in which we consider charters for approval or renewal."[50] In an interview, former Board of Education Vice President Yolie Flores explained that she is "concerned about charters that are not enrolling the same proportion of students that are special education or English learners" compared with the numbers enrolled in district schools.[51]

Nonetheless, LAUSD is moving toward greater cooperation with charter schools, even as conflict remains prominent in the public discourse. The district's new charter school policy, adopted in 2010, acknowledges the complexity of the relationship between the district and charter schools, albeit with a positive spin: "The relationship between the District and charter schools involves cooperation, choice, and healthy competition."[52] The district is charged with authorization and oversight of charter schools, but district leaders also see charter schools as a potential source of innovation in the district. Toward this end, the charter school policy includes provisions intended to streamline data sharing and identify promising practices within charter schools. Another statement of cooperative intentions between the district and charter schools was developed in 2010 through the Quality Schools Compact, an agreement between district and charter leaders to cooperate on areas such as evaluation, principal training, and advocacy for state funding.[53] The Gates Foundation has offered funding for cities that develop district-charter compacts to support the plans for collaboration.

So far, the evidence of district-charter collaboration is more extensive on paper than it is in practice. Nonetheless, the role of charter schools in the district is growing, as LAUSD is increasingly willing to seek assistance from the nonprofit school operators, including CMOs. Although some might view the Locke High School transformation as a hostile takeover, the opposite occurred in 2011, when LAUSD sought outside intervention for a persistently failing school. The district turned over Jordan High School to undergo a transformation led by two outside entities—Green Dot and PLAS (the nonprofit started by Mayor Villaraigosa).[54] These organizations are beginning to position themselves as potential turnaround artists. Yet this strategy carries considerable risks; the story of Green Dot's efforts to turn around Locke High School demonstrates that transforming a chronically low-performing school is very challenging and costly work.[55] Nevertheless, success in schools like Locke and Jordan could make CMOs essential partners in LAUSD's future reform efforts.

The political impact of charter schools in Los Angeles has grown steadily as CMOs have opened new schools, developed new expansion strategies, and fostered political organizing. In Los Angeles, CMOs have expanded rapidly with substantial support from major foundation grants. The CMO model in Los Angeles has roots in earlier reform efforts; the pairing of limited district oversight with independent school operators resembles the decentralization and devolution of authority that LEARN and LAAMP reformers hoped to achieve in LAUSD in the 1990s. Unlike LEARN and LAAMP, however, CMOs are not a broad district-level reform effort. Their development and expansion is piecemeal and dependent on the particular strategies of each CMO, as well as CMOs' ability to negotiate school district politics. The CMO expansion has added new dimensions of conflict to education politics in Los Angeles, as charter schools seek more resources and space. Thus, it seems likely that Los Angeles would have a conflicted and divided education policy network—much like New York City. Yet results from the survey and analysis of the policy networks suggest that foundation-funded reforms have fostered very different political consequences in Los Angeles.

Diverse at the Core

In the fall of 2008 and winter of 2009, I conducted a survey of key players in the Los Angeles education policy community to assess the relationships between major foundations, CMOs, and other actors involved in Los Angeles education policy. The survey also included questions about education politics and the policy priorities of different actors.[56] The data collection approach and methods I used for the Los Angeles survey mirror the strategies I used for New York City. In Los Angeles, I focused on six key sectors of the local education policy community: LAUSD administrators, unions, nonprofit service providers, advocacy organizations, the board of education, and charter management organizations. I developed a list of survey contacts covering each of these six sectors by including all of the foundation grant recipients from 2005 and consulting with experts on Los Angeles education politics. I applied the same method I used for New York City to distinguish between nonprofit service providers and advocacy organizations.[57]

My contact list included more than 30 nonprofits and advocacy organizations. I also contacted the CMOs that received major foundation grants, the members of the board of education and their staffs, and the divisions of LAUSD most closely connected to reform efforts, such as the charter schools division. In total, I distributed the survey to 87 individuals and received 35 responses—a 40 percent response rate.[58] The respondents were relatively distributed among the six sectors of the education policy community in Los Angeles, although lower response rates from union leaders and the board of education produced fewer completed surveys from these sectors (table 5.3). I also conducted interviews with 18 individuals involved in Los Angeles education reform.

Drawing on the survey data, I used social network analysis to examine how policy information is exchanged among Los Angeles education stakeholders. Using the same questions that appeared on the New York City survey, I created two networks focusing on two types of policy information exchange. I asked each Los Angeles respondent to identify organizations and institutions that provided them with "useful data or research." Also, I asked each respondent to identify organizations and institutions that provided them with "useful information

Table 5.3 Survey Responses

Los Angeles Education Policy Sector	Survey Responses
Los Angeles Unified School District	7
Unions	2
Nonprofit service providers	6
Advocacy organizations	10
Board of education	3
Charter management organizations	7

about local community needs or preferences." These questions were designed to identify the sources of two different types of policy information. The data and research question was designed to highlight expert-oriented or research-based sources of policy knowledge. The local needs and preferences question was designed to highlight sources of grassroots or community-based policy knowledge. All of the referents named by my survey respondents are included in the networks. I used the data gathered in response to both of these questions to create visual representations of the networks with the Netdraw program available in UCINET Version 6.166.[59]

The LAUSD appears to have all the ingredients for disconnected and decentralized education politics—the district encompasses multiple diverse municipalities, more than 180 charter schools, and a host of reformers leading different initiatives with different organizations. Based on this characterization, one might expect education stakeholders in LAUSD to be dispersed, exchanging information in isolated clusters. Using social network analysis, I found that Los Angeles has an inclusive core of actors exchanging education policy information. Dense ties of information exchange link foundations, CMOs, LAUSD, and advocacy organizations, sharing both data and research and grassroots knowledge about community needs or preferences.

Figure 5.1 displays the network of information exchange of policy expertise ("useful data and research") between education policy actors in Los Angeles. I have aggregated the survey responses from individuals into their main organizational or institutional affiliation; for example, all respondents who were board members or staff for the board of education are grouped together as "Board of Education."[60] The arrows indicate the direction of information flow from source to recipient, and thicker lines indicate that more information exchange occurs between two nodes. The size of the nodes is based on the outdegree centrality of each organization; larger nodes have higher outdegree centrality.[61] Organizations with high outdegree centrality are designated sources of each type of information for many respondents in the network; organizations with low outdegree centrality were regarded as sources of information by only a few respondents.

Last, the shading of the nodes—gray or black—indicates whether the organization is a member of the network core or the periphery. Unlike New York City, there is not a clear divide in Los Angeles between recipients of major foundation grants and organizations that did not receive grants. Instead, the network more closely resembles a core-periphery structure. Social network analysis offers a technique to formalize the concept of a core-periphery structure, in which a core group of actors is densely connected and peripheral actors are relatively unconnected.[62] Actors within the highly dense core are represented with gray nodes, and actors in the less dense periphery are represented with black nodes.

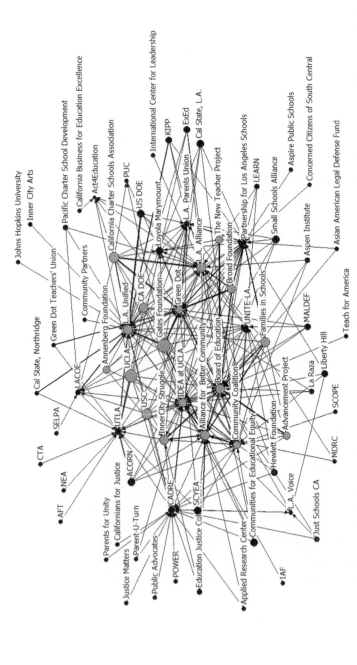

Figure 5.1 Los Angeles Policy Information Network with Core: Expertise. Node Color Guide: Gray = Core Organizations; Black = Periphery Organizations. The figure depicts a single-mode network of information exchange. Links indicate the exchange of "data or research"; arrows indicate the direction of information exchange from source to recipient.

Table 5.4 Density of Links between Core and Periphery in the Expertise Network[a]

	Core	*Periphery*
Core	0.369	0.068
n = 18		
Periphery	0.076	0.019
n = 56		

[a]Information transfer from row to column.

I used the core-periphery algorithm available in UCINET to identify core actors in the network, based on the data and research ties from the survey. The Los Angeles education policy expertise network fits the core-periphery structure very well. The density of ties within the core is much higher than the density of ties within the periphery or between the core and periphery (table 5.4). Density is the number of actual ties divided by the number of possible ties, reported on a scale from 0 to 1. Thus, actors in the core share information extensively with one another. This is quite different from the New York City expertise network, which lacked a central core; instead, New York City's network was divided between major foundation grantees and groups that did not receive major foundation grants. In Los Angeles, the network defies factional partitions; other than clusters around the community organization CADRE and around UTLA, there is no clear evidence of factions or cliques. The core of densely linked organizations in Los Angeles involves a fairly diverse set of 18 organizations and institutions, although grant makers and grantees are particularly well represented in the core.

The network core includes three of the biggest grant makers in Los Angeles—Gates, Broad, and Annenberg—as well as some of their largest grantees. These grantees include CMOs, such as Green Dot and the Alliance, and nonprofits—Families in Schools and the Advancement Project. The California Charter Schools Association is also part of the core. The public sector is represented in the core, including LAUSD (L.A. Unified), the board of education, and the California Department of Education (CA DOE). Advocacy organizations, including InnerCity Struggle, Community Coalition, and Alliance for a Better Community, are also part of the core. Universities and research institutes are part of the core, including the University of California–Los Angeles (UCLA), the University of Southern California (USC), and a research institute at UCLA known as IDEA, the Institute for Democracy, Education, and Access, which works with advocacy organizations to use research in their work. The final member of the core is the New Teacher Project, a national nonprofit organization focused on teacher quality. For actors within the core, access to information from decision makers or organizational allies is relatively straightforward. The executive director of Community Coalition regards coordination across sectors involved in Los Angeles education as a highly feasible: "We all know each other and talk on a semi-regular basis," said Harris-Dawson. "It's a phone call away."[63]

Meanwhile, some key actors are not part of the network core. Notable peripheral actors include the mayor's nonprofit, PLAS, as well as UTLA. At the time of the survey, PLAS was a relatively new organization, and it may need more time to establish broader ties of information exchange. As for the UTLA, the union's peripheral position is more likely a function of the perceived role of the union in local education politics. Twenty survey respondents—57 percent—either somewhat agreed or strongly agreed with the statement "In this district, the teachers' union obstructs efforts to reform the schools." Respondents who strongly agreed with the statement included leaders at CMOs, advocacy organizations, nonprofits, the board of education, and LAUSD. Only five survey respondents somewhat or strongly disagreed with the statement. These results contrast with New York City, where many advocacy organization leaders held a more favorable view of the teachers' union. Furthermore, the somewhat isolated position of the UTLA in the network fits with recent accounts of UTLA's declining political influence. For eight years, UTLA failed to "put a candidate on the Board of Education in a race in which another contender also had strong financial support."[64] According to one member of the board of education quoted anonymously in the Los Angeles Times, "Most of us roll our eyes when things come up with UTLA because they're less and less influential in the conversations we're having."[65] Nonetheless, UTLA has continued to fight for political influence in the district; in 2011, the union backed a school board candidate who defeated the candidate supported by Mayor Villaraigosa.[66] The relative isolation of UTLA, in contrast with the highly engaged and connected UFT in New York City, may also be a product of UTLA's hard-line stance on issues such as charter schools. The UFT has adopted a more moderate position on charter schools, even partnering with Green Dot to create a unionized charter school in New York City.

Although I have emphasized the diversity of actors in the Los Angeles network core, a core-periphery structure also implies that many actors have less access to the information exchanged among core members. Survey responses suggest that leaders of organizations in the periphery feel that they have fewer opportunities for involvement in local education politics. The survey asked for respondents' level of agreement with the statement "Community organizations and parent groups are shut out of education politics here." Responses were coded on a five-point scale: strongly disagree (–2), somewhat disagree (–1), neutral (0), somewhat agree (1), or strongly agree (2). Respondents from the core generally disagreed with this statement (–0.47; $n = 17$), but respondents in the periphery generally agreed (0.77; $n = 13$), suggesting that peripheral groups do feel excluded. The difference in means between the two groups is statistically significant ($p < 0.05$).

On other survey questions, there was no significant difference in attitudes between respondents in the core and those in the periphery, nor was there a difference between major foundation grant recipients and organizations that did not receive grants. Charter schools have been among the more divisive issues in the district, but the issue does not appear to produce distinct coalitions of supporters and opponents. Union leaders are the only sector that consistently opposes charter school expansion. Forty-eight percent of survey respondents indicated that there are "too few" charter schools in Los Angeles, and only 13 percent responded that there are "too many." The remainder either regarded the number of charters as "just right" or had no opinion. The respondents who indicated that there were "too few" charter schools included CMO leaders, advocacy organization leaders, LAUSD staff, and nonprofit leaders. There is some difference in attitudes toward charters between organizations in the network core and those in the periphery, but the difference between the groups is not statistically significant. Based on coding the responses on a three-point scale—too many charters (-1), just the right number (0), and too few charters (1)—respondents in the core generally thought there were too few charter schools (0.73; $n = 11$). Among those in the periphery, there was slightly less support for charter expansion (0.25; $n = 12$).[67]

Overall, the exchange of policy expertise and the distribution of policy attitudes in Los Angeles differ considerably from New York City. Although the Los Angeles expertise network is somewhat divided between insiders (the core) and outsiders (the periphery), the core includes a relatively diverse group of organizations. Furthermore, the division between core and periphery does not correspond with clear divisions in attitudes toward education politics and policy in Los Angeles, even on the issue of charter schools. Nonetheless, groups in the periphery do indicate concern that parents and community organizations are left out of education politics in Los Angeles.

In addition to the policy expertise network, I also created a network with the exchange of community needs or preferences information for Los Angeles (figure 5.2). As with figure 5.1, node size is based on outdegree centrality, and the color of the nodes is based on whether the organization is part of the core or the periphery in the community network. The core includes a slightly different group of organizations in the community network; it is less diverse than the policy expertise core and primarily includes advocacy organizations and nonprofits. Like the New York City community network, the Los Angeles community network is less dense than the policy expertise network; in other words, respondents indicated fewer sources of community needs or preferences information.

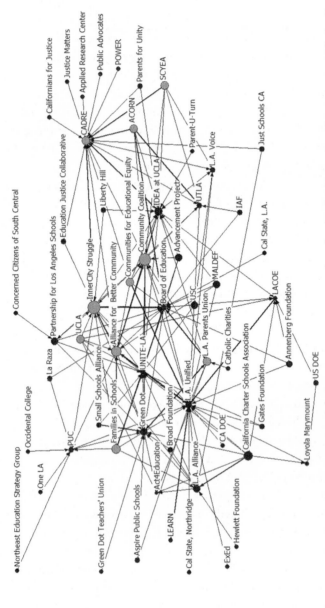

Figure 5.2 Los Angeles Policy Information Network with Core: Community. Node Color Guide: Gray = Core Organizations; Black = Periphery Organizations. The figure depicts a single-mode network of information exchange. Links indicate the exchange of "community needs or preferences"; arrows indicate the direction of information exchange from source to recipient.

Table 5.5 Top "Senders" of Policy Information

Data and Research		Local Community Needs/Preferences	
Organization	Outdegree Centrality	Organization	Outdegree Centrality
Gates Foundation	19	InnerCity Struggle	15
California Charter Schools Association	15	Community Coalition	12
UCLA	13	Alliance for a Better Community	10
Broad Foundation	12	Families in Schools	9

Unlike New York City, information about community needs or preferences is more widely distributed in Los Angeles.[68] The LAUSD, the board of education, and CMOs such as Green Dot and PUC mentioned several local advocacy organizations as sources of information, including InnerCity Struggle, Community Coalition, Alliance for a Better Community, and L.A. Voice. Interestingly, UTLA was only mentioned once—by one administrator at LAUSD—as a source of community needs or preferences information. None of the respondents from other sectors—including the board of education and local advocacy organizations—indicated UTLA as a source of information. Once again, this points to the political isolation of UTLA.

The fact that CMO leaders recognized and indicated local advocacy organizations as sources of useful information shows an important distinction between CMOs as school operators in Los Angeles and some of New York City's nonprofit school operators. In New York City, respondents from nonprofit school operators such as New Visions and Replications Inc. did not indicate any sources of local needs and preferences information. The CMOs in Los Angeles appear to be more aware of and more closely linked to local advocacy organizations. This could be a consequence of the competitive relationship between CMOs and the school district in Los Angeles, in contrast to the more collaborative relationship between nonprofit school operators in New York City and the school district. In Los Angeles, CMOs need to compete to attract students and establish a base in the communities where they operate schools. This may provide them with a stronger incentive to broker relationships with organizations on their own, rather than relying on their relationship with the district administration for political cover and support.

A comparison of the expertise and community networks for Los Angeles shows that very different sets of organizations are dominant sources of each type of information. Table 5.5 lists the organizations that have the highest outdegree centrality for each type of information. Two of the major foundations—Gates and Broad—are very prominent as sources of data and research in Los Angeles. In fact, more than half of the respondents mentioned the Gates Foundation as a source of useful data and research. This is also a contrast with the New York City network, where the foundations were less visible as direct sources of information. It is also a bit surprising—the Gates Foundation is a source of funding for numerous organizations that produce data and research, but the foundation itself is certainly not a think tank. Nonetheless, foundations often help to publicize the work of grantees through press releases, speeches, and events, which may explain the prominence of Gates and Broad as sources of data and research. The centrality of the California Charter Schools Association is indicative of the importance of CMOs in Los Angeles, and UCLA, as a major research university, is an obvious source of data and research. The district administration—LAUSD—is surprisingly absent among the top providers of data and research.

Meanwhile, an entirely different set of organizations serves as the main source of information about local community needs or preferences. The top organization—InnerCity Struggle—is an advocacy organization based in East Los Angeles, a predominantly Latino area. InnerCity Struggle has worked to mobilize students in East L.A. high schools. Community Coalition, based in South L.A., has ties to African American political leaders, and Alliance for a Better Community focuses on Latino advocacy. Families in Schools is the nonprofit descendent of LAAMP. The most central organizations for community information represent different parts of the city and different racial and ethnic groups.

In Los Angeles, the diverse network core—particularly in the data and research network—suggests that policy expertise is more widely shared among stakeholders in Los Angeles than in New York City. Major foundations have a highly visible role as providers of data and research; they are more prominent in Los Angeles in this respect, and they are linked to a wide range of actors in the policy network. Additionally, several local advocacy organizations stand out as sources of knowledge about local community needs or preferences. Peripheral organizations do find local education politics less accessible, and the core is not inclusive enough to involve certain key groups, such as the UTLA.

Foundation grant-making strategy in Los Angeles has not fostered a policy network divided between philanthropically supported charter schools and interests tied to traditional public schools. Instead, major foundation grantees participate in a high level of informal information exchange among stakeholders. This does not mean that these relationships or exchanges are always collaborative. Nonetheless, the networks suggest that interest groups and organizations in Los Angeles have oriented themselves around multiple centers of policy making in the district, and there is mutual exchange of information between the district administration, CMOs, and many local advocacy groups. Rather than remaining isolated, some CMOs in Los Angeles are well connected and engaged with key political actors and constituencies.

As LAUSD, CMOs, and PLAS each vie for influence and control over Los Angeles schools, education policy in Los Angeles could be headed toward incoherence. Month-to-month accounts of politics and policy in LAUSD often appear haphazard—one month the district is handing off schools to outside operators; a few months later, district leaders are trying to limit charter school expansion. Nonetheless, the relationships shown in the Los Angeles education policy networks suggest a configuration that could build long-term support for decentralization. Recent policy changes in LAUSD—including the public school choice policy and the new MOU between UTLA and LAUSD—indicate that the district is moving toward more radical decentralization and extending charterlike autonomy to public schools. Yet the future of these policies depends on continuing political mobilization by constituencies invested in school-level autonomy.

The Public School Choice Policy

Reform efforts within LAUSD during the last decade have often appeared disjointed and were sometimes abandoned before completion. If there is a reform happening nationally—small schools, pilot schools, school autonomy, mayoral control—it was attempted or it can be found in some form in LAUSD. Yet these reforms were often implemented by tiny district offices with short bureaucratic life spans. A lack of stable leadership has not helped matters; the district has had three superintendents since 2006. Despite this pattern of inconsistent reforms, there is a discernible trajectory toward decentralization of LAUSD, involving increasing autonomy for many schools and partnerships that grant outside organizations a large role in operating schools.[69] The Public School Choice Motion, adopted in 2009, was a particularly bold step toward decentralization. According to Charles Kerchner, LAUSD was beginning to "look more like a modern network-style organization and less like an early 20th century hierarchy," in part because "more than a quarter of the schools in Los Angeles operate outside the traditional hierarchy or under special rules."[70] Several previous policies have moved LAUSD toward decentralization, though the public school choice policy created a more formalized and transparent process.

An important backdrop for the adoption of the public school choice policy was LAUSD's $20 billion school construction program, which planned to add 131 newly built schools to the district. Due to severe overcrowding, almost half of LAUSD students were attending schools on multitrack year-round schedules to accommodate more students.[71] With dozens of new schools slated to open each year as construction is completed, local interests and CMO allies—including Eli Broad, Parent Revolution, and the Southeast Cities Schools Coalition—argued that some of the new schools should be opened as charter schools.[72] Yet these were often particularized interests: Eli Broad hoped to see the new High School for the Visual and Performing Arts, which had received $5 million from Broad, become a charter school; the Southeast Cities Schools Coalition was focused on newly opening schools in their section of the district. Politically, the notion of transforming more than 100 newly constructed school buildings throughout the district into charter schools was hardly feasible.

The Public School Choice Motion, which was introduced by former Board of Education Vice President Yolie Flores in July 2009, allowed nonprofit organizations, including CMOs, to offer competing bids to operate newly opening and low-performing LAUSD schools. Flores, who has been described as a "Latina Saul Alinsky," represented part of East Los Angeles and several small cities in the southeastern portion of the district.[73] She was one of the board of education members supported by Mayor Villaraigosa's political organization, Partnership for Better Schools, in her 2007 election bid. After the mayor's failed attempt at mayoral control, he channeled $3.5 million in campaign donations to elect allies to the board of education and successfully won a four-member majority on the board.[74]

Once she began her term on the board, Flores heard from groups such as Parent Revolution and the Southeast Cities Schools Coalition, which supported converting new school buildings to charter schools. Yet she also heard from constituents who were not "enamored with charters."[75] Flores explained that she wanted the public school choice policy to use "competition as the lever for change."[76] Mayor Villaraigosa, CMOs, and some local advocacy organizations supported the proposal; UTLA opposed it. The Public School Choice Motion passed by a board vote of 6–1. Marguerite LaMotte, the only African American member of the board of education, voted against it. According to the motion passed by the board:

> Los Angeles Unified School District will invite operational and instructional plans from internal and external stakeholders, such as school planning teams, local communities, pilot school operators, labor partners, charters, and others who are interested in collaborating with the District to operate the District's new schools and PI 3+ schools (as identified by the Superintendent and authorized under NCLB, beginning with PI 5+), in an effort to create more schools of choice and educational options for the District's students and families.[77]

Schools designated as PI 3+ or higher are schools facing corrective action because they have not made adequate yearly progress for five years or more, as defined by NCLB. By adding low-performing schools to those eligible for out-side bids, the board considerably increased the number of LAUSD schools that could someday be operated by outside organizations. In the fall of 2009, LAUSD Superintendent Cortines began work to implement the new policy.

In the first round of bidding, which began in November 2009, 24 newly open-ing schools and 12 low-performing schools were opened to outside operators, and 80 bids were submitted to run these schools. Although charter school sup-porters had championed the new policy, CMOs ultimately submitted relatively few bids for schools. As reported by Fuller, "Charter firms, including Aspire, Green Dot, Alliance for College-Ready Public Schools, and smaller charter operators, put forward one-quarter of the takeover plans, but only one plan was aimed at turning around a chronically low-performing focus school."[78] Most of the bids for low-performing schools came from groups of teachers in the district, often supported by UTLA. The nonprofit started by Mayor Villaraigosa, PLAS, submitted bids for four schools.

The public school choice policy was implemented with a relatively high level of transparency. All of the proposals submitted for school takeovers were posted on the LAUSD Web site. The process was also designed to elicit public input, and "advisory votes" were held on each of the proposals, including participa-tion from parents, employees, community members, and high school students. Flores had mixed feelings about the implementation of the public engagement process. "It got very politicized. The teachers' union played a very strong role in creating a lot of misinformation…. On the other hand, one thing I was really pleased with was the amount of engagement and parents coming out and getting in line to vote," Flores explained.[79] In most of the advisory votes, the plans sub-mitted by groups of teachers garnered substantially more votes than the plans submitted by CMOs. Ultimately, the board of education voted to award only four schools to charter groups, over the objections of Flores.

At the beginning of the 2010–2011 school year, the process for Public School Choice 2.0 got started with 10 new schools and 3 low-performing schools avail-able for bids. Although CMOs largely came away empty-handed after the first round, several CMOs—including Green Dot, Aspire Public Schools, ICEF, and the Alliance—submitted proposals in the new round. By supporting several teacher-formulated bids, UTLA also participated. In March 2011, the board of education voted for eight of the bids submitted by charter schools; the remain-ing schools were awarded to internal district-led and teacher-led groups. The board meeting had several heated moments because a majority of board mem-bers opted for charter school operators for some schools against the recommen-dations of Superintendent Cortines.[80]

Although the public school choice policy was initiated locally, without external funding or support, LAUSD received a boost for the policy from the federal Department of Education and was awarded one of 49 federal grants in the Investing in Innovation (I3) grant competition for its proposal, titled "L.A.'s Bold Competition." The proposal requested $4.8 million to help the district "create a rich portfolio of high-performing schools that are tailored to and supported by the local community."[81] Thus, in late 2010, public school choice was receiving national recognition as an innovative policy. Nonetheless, soon after the announcement of the I3 grant, the political foundations for the policy grew shaky.

Several events in 2011 altered the political landscape in LAUSD. Flores resigned from her seat on the board to become CEO of an organization funded by the Gates Foundation—Communities for Teaching Excellence—that is focused on public awareness and community engagement concerning teacher quality.[82] Los Angeles is one of four sites that received Gates grants focused on teacher effectiveness initiatives, and Communities for Teaching Excellence works in all four sites. Two candidates contested the board seat formerly occupied by Flores—one backed by UTLA and another backed by Villaraigosa—and the UTLA-backed candidate won. In addition to the shift on the board of education, there was growing backlash, particularly from UTLA, over the number of schools relinquished to charter operators through public school choice and for school turnarounds. Furthermore, the three-year teacher contract expired in June 2011, opening contract negotiations between the district and the union. Meanwhile, in the fall of 2011, public school choice would enter its third round, with a large number of schools available for bids—15 newly constructed schools and 22 existing low-performing schools.

Last, a new superintendent, John Deasy, took the reins in LAUSD in April 2011. Deasy previously served as deputy director for education at the Gates Foundation, and he was formerly superintendent of Prince George's County Public Schools.[83] Also, Deasy is a graduate of the Broad Superintendents Academy, which was started by the Broad Foundation to recruit and train urban school district superintendents.[84] Deasy's former position at the Gates Foundation and his participation in the Broad Academy led many to assume that his agenda would be influenced by these foundations' priorities. Although Deasy was supportive of the public school choice policy, school district superintendents are not known for carrying out their predecessor's policies without revision.

Thus, after two years of the radical decentralization enabled by public school choice, the shifting political winds gave district leaders an opportunity to revise their approach. First, in August 2011, the board of education voted unanimously to give first consideration to applicants from within the district (i.e., groups of teachers) in the public school choice process, contingent on the negotiation of a new labor agreement by November 1.[85] This would effectively exclude outside operators (i.e., CMOs and other nonprofits) from the third round of public school choice. Some observers saw this as a move by the board to encourage UTLA to agree to broader districtwide reform in the new contract.[86] Second, Deasy negotiated a new MOU with UTLA, which undercut the competitive approach of public school choice. According to the new agreement, known as the LAUSD-UTLA Local Stabilization and Empowerment Initiative, outside applicants will be excluded from the public school choice process until 2014.[87]

Although the MOU substantially altered public school choice, it also created a new platform for decentralization and school-level autonomy in LAUSD. According to the MOU, schools can be "granted automatic waivers from central-District controls and from parts of the District-UTLA Agreement as needed to implement various matters that are subject to local determination."[88] Waivers could cover areas such as curriculum, assessments, schedule, school organization, professional development, budget, and hiring. The reaction to the MOU varied widely. Many charter school leaders were very disappointed, arguing that Deasy discarded public school choice without adequate concessions from the union. According to Burton, who heads the Alliance, "I think [the district] gave up too much for what they got. There should be more accountability for performance."[89] Flores, the originator of public school choice, was very critical of the agreement: "It eradicates the entire intent and purpose of [public school choice] which is to use choice and competition as a powerful lever."[90] Yet the response from many advocates for teachers was quite positive, including organizations representing teachers who favor substantial reforms to existing labor agreements. Ama Nyamakye, executive director of Educators 4 Excellence in Los Angeles, wrote about the agreement on the *Huffington Post*:

> This type of teacher-led change is exactly what Educators 4 Excellence has been fighting for over the past few years. With more than 3,500 members nationwide, E4E elevates the voices of teachers in the policy decisions that shape our classrooms and careers. Our members in California were clamoring for teacher-created change, which was the catalyst for the launch of E4E's chapter in Los Angeles.[91]

Superintendent Deasy also defended the agreement and the concessions he gained from the union: "Deasy said the agreement with the teachers union could give all district schools the advantages of charters. Any school could opt out of provisions of the union contract as well as district policy, gaining new freedoms."[92] The UTLA members voted to ratify the MOU, with 70 percent voting in favor of the agreement.

The new MOU does offer a path for public schools in Los Angeles to acquire the freedom and autonomy currently reserved for charter schools. Yet the implementation of this path will depend on politics. Policy making in LAUSD sometimes appears aimless and erratic. Nonetheless, the expansion of CMOs, the public school choice policy, and the MOU have fueled political momentum for decentralization and school-level autonomy among a widening set of constituencies. There is no guarantee that this political momentum will lead to sustainable policy change in Los Angeles. The erosion of public school choice clearly demonstrates the political vulnerability of reform in the district. Yet public school choice was not an isolated policy—it is part of a broader set of changes in LAUSD involving a diverse and closely linked set of policy makers and organizations. While these groups remain active in education politics and policy, it is certain that their mobilization will shape the future direction of the district.

Policy Feedback

Charter school expansion in Los Angeles has been extensive. Yet charter schools are a policy based more strongly on "exit" than "voice"; attending a charter school means opting out of a traditional public school.[93] Even as some charter operators undertake public school turnarounds, charter school expansion alone is unlikely to foster broader political mobilization for district-level reforms. Public school choice and the new MOU are built on voice for district-wide change. In its original form, public school choice allowed CMOs, nonprofits, and groups of teachers to offer bids to operate schools. With this reform, a diverse set of groups found reasons to invest in public school autonomy and decentralization. Furthermore, the negotiations over the new MOU—a process that is typically the epitome of backroom politics—spurred the formation of a broad citywide coalition involving nearly two dozen advocacy organizations, civil rights groups, and nonprofits. Members of the coalition included InnerCity Struggle, Community Coalition, Alliance for a Better Community, Families in Schools, Families That Can, and Parent Revolution, as well as major nonprofits like the United Way and Los Angeles Urban League. The coalition, known as "Don't Hold Us Back," developed a set of policy priorities to try to influence the contract negotiations.[94] The coalition's priorities included expansion of school-level autonomy by devolving greater authority over hiring and work rules to individual schools and increasing parent involvement in school site decisions.

It is still too early to assess the policy feedback process following the adoption of the public school choice policy and the MOU. Nonetheless, the initial political mobilizations tied to these policies offer some clues. According to Patashnik, two important elements of positive policy feedback are investments and reconfiguration.[95] Groups invest in the new policy by committing resources or developing capacity specifically geared toward the new policy. Reconfiguration involves "[transformation] of group identities, incentives, and coalition alignments";

through reconfiguration, new constituencies may emerge as supporters of the reform while opponents are weakened.[96]

In fact, some reconfiguration of the relationships between local advocacy organizations and CMOs was under way prior to the adoption of the public school choice policy. According to Julie Flapan of UCLA IDEA:

> Groups have taken the charters as an opportunity to become more influential in ways they couldn't in the school system.... Over the last year, some groups have said, we haven't been successful in the existing structure—the only option is to give charters a try.[97]

In South L.A., Community Coalition developed a working relationship with Green Dot. One of Green Dot's new small schools at Locke High School is an Architecture, Construction, and Engineering Academy, started in response to a multiyear campaign led by Community Coalition for new trade and career academies in South L.A. public high schools.[98] South L.A. neighborhoods now have schools operated by a broad array of groups, including multiple CMOs and PLAS. According to Community Coalition's executive director, these alternative school operators can be better partners than the district: "Everybody is more accessible and easier to work with than the district," said Harris-Dawson.[99]

The public school choice policy reshaped the relationship between LAUSD, CMOs, and advocacy organizations. Based on the original formulation of the public school choice policy, advocacy organizations could have a greater role in supporting, developing, or implementing particular reform models, rather than trying to influence LAUSD or CMOs from the outside. Advocacy organizations could compete to operate their own school or choose to support a particular operator. Furthermore, advocacy organizations could find themselves in competition with CMOs over particular schools.

In East L.A., InnerCity Struggle has invested resources and capacity in the public school choice policy. The executive director of InnerCity Struggle is Maria Brenes, who also helped to organize the East Los Angeles Education Collaborative. The collaborative includes other local nonprofits such as Families in Schools and Alliance for a Better Community. InnerCity Struggle cut its teeth in education organizing by focusing on Garfield High School, a severely overcrowded school in East L.A. built for 1,500 students. Garfield enrolled more than 5,000 students in the early 2000s, and InnerCity Struggle organized a campaign to demand new schools for East L.A.[100] The new Esteban Torres High School campus, which opened in 2010, was the first new high school in East L.A. in more than 85 years. Yet due to the newly adopted public school choice policy, the management of the school was opened up for competitive bids in 2009. Two CMOs—the Alliance and Green Dot—each submitted proposals to open small schools on the

Esteban Torres campus. Meanwhile, InnerCity Struggle and the East Los Angeles Education Collaborative mobilized the community around a plan for five pilot schools on the campus, based on proposals submitted by groups of teachers.[101] Pilot schools are granted greater autonomy from the district and use a "thin" labor contract for teachers. Although Superintendent Cortines recommended awarding one small school each to the Alliance and Green Dot and awarding the three remaining schools to pilot applicants, the board of education voted to accept all five of the pilot school proposals. This was a victory for InnerCity Struggle, but it was a defeat for two of the city's most prominent CMOs.

The UTLA was the primary opponent of public school choice, but the policy also created conflicting currents within UTLA. The official position of the union's leadership has been outright opposition to the policy. In December 2009, UTLA filed a lawsuit to block the district from using the public school choice policy to transfer schools to CMOs.[102] Nonetheless, UTLA participated in the public school choice implementation process by supporting groups of teachers who submit bids for schools. According to Fuller, "The UTLA's sudden enthusiasm for innovative school management is breathtaking, and largely the work of a young generation of impatient members."[103] Teachers have started new organizations that offer counterweights to the union's power, such as Educators4Excellence. In addition, a group of teachers formed an alternative organization within UTLA, known as NewTLA, which supports changing policies long supported by the union, such as seniority-based layoffs.[104] In 2011, UTLA held elections for a new president, and the underdog candidate backed by NewTLA won the election.[105] NewTLA did not have a stated position on public school choice, but the organization is critical of UTLA leadership for obstructionism, favoring a "pro-active and progressive role in the deliberation and development of educational policy."[106] The divisions within UTLA show how policy change can affect group identities. Some teachers found that the opportunity to propose their own reform models for schools was more attractive than backing the union leadership in opposing the policy.

A startling sign of shifting identities involving the union occurred in the fall of 2011, when former UTLA president A. J. Duffy announced the formation of a charter school network—Apple Academy Charter Public Schools.[107] Reporters covering Duffy's new affiliation could scarcely conceal their astonishment. According to *Los Angeles Times* columnist Steve Lopez, Duffy "pulled off a flip so incredible, he could have joined Cirque du Soleil."[108] Furthermore, the board of Apple Academy includes Caprice Young, former president of the LAUSD Board of Education and former head of the California Charter Schools Association. Not only is Duffy leading a charter school network but also he has partnered with one of his former political enemies. The LAUSD has approved a charter for Apple Academy, and the first school will open for the 2012–2013 school year.

Within just two years, public school choice was beginning to influence the political alignments of both advocacy organizations and teachers. The revisions to the policy have cast uncertainty on these political changes. Nonetheless, some of the seeds planted by public school choice may have found a new outlet in the UTLA contract negotiations. The focus on the teacher contract negotiations was partially spurred by a 2011 report, "Teacher Quality Roadmap: Improving Policies and Practices in LAUSD," commissioned by the United Way of Greater Los Angeles, with support from several community organizations (including Families in Schools and Alliance for a Better Community) and funded by the Gates Foundation.[109] The report argued in favor of new practices in teacher hiring, as well as a comprehensive teacher evaluation system. The Don't Hold Us Back coalition involved the groups behind the report and more than a dozen other organizations, including many grassroots organizing groups.

The formation of the coalition signaled a shift in the relationship between many advocacy organizations and the UTLA. According to coverage in *LA Weekly*, many Don't Hold Us Back coalition members were "Democrat heavy organizations, traditionally reluctant to criticize UTLA, their political ally."[110] The executive director of Alliance for a Better Community, Angelica Solis, explained, "Many, if not most, of the coalition members have been strong allies of labor groups, including UTLA. To stand up and say we wanted certain changes was new. In a sense, we were really challenging the status quo amongst our allies and that really surprised some people."[111] As Kerchner commented, the coalition was trying to bring a "third chair to the bargaining table…attempting to influence both labor and management."[112] The positions supported by Don't Hold Us Back suggested that the third chair was positioned closer to Superintendent Deasy's chair than to UTLA's chair. The coalition's platform included support for more autonomous schools, more comprehensive teacher evaluation, and continuing public school choice.[113]

The Don't Hold Us Back coalition engaged in a wide range of mobilization tactics. According to Brenes, executive director of InnerCity Struggle and member of the coalition, these approaches included "board room mobilizations, petition gathering, meeting with individual board members, meeting with UTLA leadership, and media strategy."[114] The coalition purchased full-page ads in the *Los Angeles Times, Daily News,* and *La Opinion.* Leaders of the organizations involved in the coalition spoke to the board of education. Grassroots organizations like InnerCity Struggle organized parents by "informing and educating parents on complex issues, assisting them in connecting the solutions to their own lived experiences and challenges, and empowering them to speak to decision-makers and demand the changes."[115] In many respects, the broad-based coalition involved in the Don't Hold Us Back campaign has the basic ingredients of civic capacity; the stakeholders are diverse, the coalition is formalized, and the agenda is clearly articulated.

Nonetheless, the MOU that resulted from the contract negotiations did not salvage the original form of public school choice. The provisions in the MOU that could enable school-level autonomy throughout the district are far-reaching, but implementation is highly dependent on continuing activism and engagement by supporters of autonomy and decentralization. According to Solis, Alliance for a Better Community plans to remain highly engaged with the coalition partners and with monitoring the implementation of public school choice and the MOU: "We were really invested in Public School Choice from the very beginning and given what is happening now, we are still really committed. We're going to be working to build awareness of the MOU and Public School Choice . . . by engaging parents, continuing to work with the school district, and partnering with other community based organizations also doing work with parents."[116] Solis added that a challenge for advocacy organizations would be finding the resources to maintain the work they have started. Nonetheless, these groups have developed strong partnerships and expect to continue working together in the future.

The difficult question is whether the coalition signals a long-term transformation of Los Angeles education politics. According to Kerchner, there is compelling evidence of transformation: "The increasingly bold and strident parent and community voice, amplified and modulated with foundation money, changes the politics of collective bargaining and challenges the union's historic claim on parent loyalty."[117] Kerchner offers an important observation about the role of philanthropy in the political changes in Los Angeles. Philanthropic money has "amplified and modulated," but local organizations and parents are the voices. Philanthropy provided substantial funding for CMOs in Los Angeles. More recently, the Gates Foundation has committed resources to research and parent organizing on teacher quality in Los Angeles, and its presence in Los Angeles may grow more dominant in the future. In spite of a philanthropic reform strategy based largely on exit through charter school expansion, a growing movement of voice—partially inspired by charter school autonomies—has developed in Los Angeles. Yet local political transformation requires initiative, investment, and continuing engagement from the groups that will live with the consequences of reform. In the future, a philanthropic strategy of circumspect support—rather than heavy-handed or top-down policy engagement—may be required to allow these local investments to flourish.

Conclusion

The visibility of major foundations in Los Angeles education politics—as funders of CMOs and as sources of policy information—is substantial. Rather than working in alliance with powerful central leadership in the district, as they do in New York City, major foundations involved in education reform in

Los Angeles are part of a broader mix of groups developing and implementing reforms. By facilitating rapid growth of CMOs, major foundations have spurred competition for LAUSD. The CMOs have also aspired to shape reform within LAUSD, through direct political advocacy, through insider relationships, and by leading public school turnaround efforts.

In both Los Angeles and New York City, education reform has been influenced by the Boardroom Progressive agenda and the involvement of foundations. Yet the promotion of reforms in Los Angeles has occurred by very different means than in New York City. The emerging evidence of positive policy feedback in Los Angeles highlights some important aspects of the policy-making process that are not present in New York City. In Los Angeles, mechanisms for public participation and oversight have remained in place, even as the school district has been opened up to dozens of new private operators of public schools. With an elected school board and a well-organized sector of advocacy groups, Los Angeles has multiple ways for parents and community members to respond to changes happening in the district. In New York City, there is little transparency in contracting with nonprofits, and institutions for public engagement have been eliminated or sidelined. Reformers in New York City tended to view public engagement as a roadblock to rapidly implementing reforms; in Los Angeles, public engagement has shaped the district's approach to decentralization. Community involvement was integral to the public school choice policy and was carried forward during the negotiations over the MOU. Even after a reform loss—the rollback of public school choice—community organizations in Los Angeles remained invested enough to fight a new battle. In New York City, despite a massive investment of private funding to develop and implement Children First, the local political investments in these reforms remain narrow. Foundations have given less financially to support education reforms in Los Angeles, but the local political investments are stronger in Los Angeles than they are in New York City.

If the emerging process of positive policy feedback continues in Los Angeles, the next 15 to 20 years could see schools in Los Angeles managed by a linked network of school operators, including CMOs, other nonprofits, and groups of teachers running autonomous schools. The end point could lead Los Angeles to a radical departure from the traditional hierarchical design of public school districts. In New York City, the extensive foundation-funded reform agenda undertaken by Bloomberg and Klein relies on a strong central office and top-down leadership; New York City still retains characteristics of Progressive Era corporate management, although middle layers of the bureaucracy have been stripped away or replaced with nonprofit contractors.[118] Based on the road maps for school autonomy contained in public school choice and the new MOU, Los Angeles may no longer resemble a traditional urban school district in the form that developed a century ago.

Conclusions and Implications

The Boardroom Progressives have achieved significant educational policy change in New York City and Los Angeles. Major policy change has also occurred in several other districts that received large targeted investments from major foundations, such as Chicago, New Orleans, Oakland, and Washington, D.C.[1] These districts house hundreds of new schools—often operated by private organizations—and a range of market-based and accountability reform efforts, such as public school choice, charter schools, and teacher merit pay. As their role in education policy has grown more visible, the Boardroom Progressives—particularly the major foundations—have faced greater scrutiny in the media. Several recent news reports have documented the "behind the scenes influence" of philanthropists in education policy, both nationally and locally.[2] These articles reflect a growing public perception that major foundations are powerful actors, able to shape the direction of education reform.

This book reveals the mechanisms behind growing foundation influence in urban school districts by showing how major foundations change urban education policy and politics. First, major foundations have targeted grants dollars to school districts with political characteristics that enable greater foundation influence—particularly in the short term. In school districts with mayoral or state control, like New York City, district leaders are often able to act more quickly, with fewer veto points and limited public engagement. Combined with private dollars to support new initiatives, this arrangement can produce rapid policy change. Second, foundation funding can change the set of organizations that are influential in urban districts. Foundation involvement raises the prominence of charter schools and insider nonprofits—sometimes at the expense of traditional stakeholders such as parent organizations and unions. The convergence of major foundation funding to similar organizations and a targeted set of school districts has helped to harden the distinction between the people, places, and organizations in the education "reform" camp and those outside it. Foundation leaders, the media, and the secretary of education have highlighted districts such as New York City as national models of education reform—combining top-down governance, swift policy change, substantial foundation investments, and market-based policies. Districts that lack these characteristics typically receive little national attention or external resources. Yet New York City's national prominence as a site of reform has not ensured broad support for reforms locally. Instead, deep divisions characterize New York City education politics.

This book also shows how foundations became important policy entrepreneurs in elementary and secondary education. Foundations benefited from major policy changes—including No Child Left Behind and state-level charter school legislation—that undermined the legitimacy of traditional urban school district leaders and offered new levers for involvement in urban schools. These changes provided a window of opportunity for foundations to become more influential in urban school districts. Philanthropists also changed their investment strategies—giving less money to public-sector organizations and more to the private sector, targeting grants to fewer districts, and taking on a more visible role in policy advocacy.

Although major foundations are becoming more influential in many urban school districts, this does not ensure the sustainability of Boardroom Progressive policy changes in specific school districts. By focusing resources on districts with mayoral or state control, rather than districts with elected boards, major foundations and their partners may be achieving short-term evidence of policy impact at the expense of long-term policy durability. The New York City case shows that rapid top-down policy implementation can achieve significant changes in the short run, but it could leave policies vulnerable to erosion or reversal in the longer term. Policy reforms in New York City have been entrenched by Mayor Bloomberg and district leaders, but these policies lack support and investment from diverse stakeholders. The Los Angeles case demonstrates how a more open process of implementation offers opportunities for a diverse set of stakeholders to become invested in new polices. This may lead to complications and disruptions as policies are developed and implemented, but it could also provide the groundwork for longer term policy sustainability.

Admittedly, it is difficult to generalize from two cases. The findings presented in this book are limited by the unique characteristics of the cases. New York City and Los Angeles are the nation's two largest school districts, and they are located in the nation's two largest cities. They are the only U.S. school districts with more than half a million students. The size and prominence of these districts makes them a magnet for attention, including philanthropic attention. Although many districts with fewer than 100,000 students—such as Austin, Newark, Oakland, and Boston—have attracted substantial philanthropic investments, most urban districts will never receive major foundation investments of this magnitude. Meanwhile, the political complexity of these school districts also sets them apart. Managing a school district with hundreds of thousands of students involves massive budgets and large bureaucracies. Political constituencies in New York City and Los Angeles are diverse, numerous, and tied to dozens of geographic, racial, ethnic, and issue-based identities. These qualities make both places complex and fascinating to study. Yet these qualities also set New York City and Los Angeles apart from smaller urban districts.

Nonetheless, the New York City and Los Angeles cases do offer important lessons about the challenge of sustainable reform and the tensions that may arise between outside philanthropists and local advocates. The New York City case shares many characteristics with other districts that have top-down governance systems and large philanthropic investments. For example, districts with mayoral or state control, such as Washington, D.C., and Oakland, also demonstrate how foundation-funded reforms can become politically vulnerable. Meanwhile, the expansion of market-based reforms in Los Angeles through a relatively open political process shows how greater democracy and transparency might enhance the durability of foundation-funded reforms in the long term.

Implications for Theory

Urban school districts were long known for their political insulation or "the cocoon of localism."[3] Major philanthropies are outsiders in urban education politics: they lack a constituency to represent, and their policy preferences are usually defined on a national scale. Yet these organizations have become highly influential in many urban districts. For scholars, the increasing openness of urban school districts to influence from national philanthropies and organizations challenges existing approaches to the study of urban education politics. Scholars cannot assume that elected school boards, teachers' unions, administrators, and organized parents are the key actors in urban education. Foundations and other external organizations—often, foundation grantees—have become powerful actors in many large urban school districts. These actors receive little notice in the existing literature on urban education politics and policy, as well as the broader literature on public policy.

The public policy literature has devoted increasing attention to the concept of policy feedback, emphasizing the political consequences of policy change. Scholarly work on policy feedback has shown how policies ranging from Social Security to airline deregulation affect mass political behavior, as well as the mobilization and strategies of interest groups and businesses.[4] As Patashnik argues, the political consequences of policies also affect the likelihood of reform survival in the long term.[5] Many of the important contributions in this field have focused on federal policy making; there is less attention to policy feedback in state and local politics. Yet policy feedback can also occur locally, shaped by the design of city, county, or school district policies, as well as the characteristics of local institutions and organizations.[6] This study adds to our understanding of the policy feedback process, emphasizing the importance of variation in the structure of the local policy-making process.

FOUNDATIONS AS POLITICAL ACTORS

Foundations differ significantly from traditional political actors. Scholars must account for these differences in designing research and developing theories to understand the role of foundations in politics and policy. Lacking a public constituency to represent, the priorities of foundations are defined by their founders and/or professional staff. More traditional political organizations are tied to a particular constituency—such as a neighborhood, a racial or ethnic group, an occupation, or a common interest. For foundations seeking to influence policy, the lack of a constituency is both a challenge and an opportunity for substantial flexibility. The challenge for foundations is finding ways to develop an affiliated constituency beyond their grant recipients. "Buying" supporters attracts considerable suspicion in the political arena, but grant making is the primary tool available to foundations for developing new partnerships.

Nevertheless, lacking a permanent affiliated constituency gives foundations considerable leeway. Unless the founder provided a highly specific mission for the foundation, most foundations can change their priorities quickly. Old grantees might object, but the foundation can find new grantees that are eager to accept funding for new initiatives. Foundations can cut loose programs regarded as failures and follow new ideas in response to changing conditions. For example, in 2008, the Gates Foundation shifted from an agenda focused on small schools to a focus on teacher effectiveness. Districts with Gates-supported small schools have had to choose whether to maintain these schools, which are more expensive to operate, with public funds. Meanwhile, Gates money is flowing for organizations and researchers working on strategies for teacher evaluation and development.[7]

Nonetheless, flexibility has also brought criticism to foundations. Philanthropists are frequently branded as fickle or susceptible to fads. Many grantees are justifiably wary that their benefactor will change course before there is an opportunity to fully develop programs. Fickle foundation behavior may also be a consequence of the growing emphasis on measurable outcomes and results among philanthropists. This approach can be problematic if foundations do not allow adequate time for projects to develop and begin producing measurable outcomes. Furthermore, when foundations do not maintain a consistent agenda over the long term, their approach to the political process is affected. Outcomes in politics are often slow to develop; the American political system is crowded with veto points, divided authorities, and advocacy groups. The enactment of a policy is often only the beginning of a long process of implementation and further contestation. Foundation time horizons rarely match up with this grinding process.[8] As I demonstrate, foundations have been particularly attracted to political systems—such as mayoral or state-controlled school districts—that minimize these common characteristics of American democracy. In combination, these factors—the lack of a constituency, agenda flexibility and fickleness, and a strong emphasis on short-term results—tend to distinguish foundations from more traditional political organizations or policy advocates.

POLICY FEEDBACK

Applying the concept of policy feedback, I show that a school district with a highly centralized noninclusive policy process can produce political dynamics that can jeopardize policy reforms in the long term. Meanwhile, a district with greater political openness and public engagement can spur a process of involvement and investment by diverse constituencies that may improve the prospects for reform longevity. These conclusions are based on my New York City and Los Angeles case studies. Given that the policy feedback process develops over many years, if not decades, policy feedback from foundation-funded reforms in both districts is likely to continue evolving for many years. Nonetheless, the political consequences of policy reforms in each district already differ considerably.

Many scholars applying the concept of policy feedback have emphasized the importance of policy design for understanding political consequences.[9] This approach focuses attention on the specific costs and rewards included in a given policy, as well as the distribution of these costs and rewards to different constituencies. My findings show that the political consequences of policy change are not only the result of policy design; political consequences are also shaped by the structure of the policy-making process. The policies supported with foundation grant dollars in New York City and Los Angeles shared many characteristics. Both funded the development of new schools operated by nonprofit partners, and both involved some degree of school choice. Both had roots in reforms started during the Annenberg Challenge. Both distributed rewards, including grants, to nonprofit partners. Costs, including increased competition for students and space, were largely borne by traditional public schools in both districts. The policies were not identical: in New York City, the new schools are small public high schools; in Los Angeles, they are charter schools.

Yet differences in the structure of the policy process, including the characteristics of governing institutions and the exclusion or incorporation of outside interests, shaped the development and implementation of policies in each district. New York City's district leadership focused on speed—involving few constituencies and working closely with insider nonprofits; due to mayoral control, governing institutions for New York City schools were well suited for fast action. In Los Angeles, institutions were not designed to facilitate rapid policy change. Policies developed slowly and from different directions, but they have increasingly converged around an agenda of decentralization and public school autonomy.

My analysis of the political consequences of policy reforms in each district suggests that there is a trade-off between speed and the development of broad support for reforms. The institutions that facilitated rapid reform development and implementation in New York City restricted opportunities to foster engagement and investment from more diverse groups. Meanwhile, through more open political institutions in Los Angeles, a wider range of groups had opportunities to shape policy development. There is still conflict in Los Angeles over charter school expansion and the extent of market-based reforms, but diverse groups— including many advocacy organizations, some teachers, and key elected officials—have become invested in extending charterlike autonomy to public schools. Thus, in addition to policy design, the structure of the policy-making process can have important implications for policy feedback.

Furthermore, I show how social network analysis has useful applications for studies involving policy feedback. Using social network analysis allowed me to identify relationships—or the lack of relationships—between leaders of policy reforms and various constituencies. This type of analysis is particularly well suited for studies of policy feedback in dense organizational environments. Following an important policy change, the policy feedback process can involve new alliances, new coalitions, or sidelining of traditionally powerful groups. Social network analysis makes it possible to quantify and visualize these relationships between groups. This technique could further contribute to our understanding of the mechanisms and intergroup dynamics that underlie policy feedback in different contexts.

Implications for Practice

Additionally, my findings point to important implications for local political actors and district leaders in urban school districts, as well as for grant makers. District leaders may see much to gain from foundation involvement in their district—an infusion of new resources, endorsement by powerful external actors, and the potential for a public profile as a "reformer." As foundation grant making has become more targeted, this is increasingly an all-or-nothing scenario: a small group of districts receive the bulk of major foundation resources; the remainder receive little or none. Nonetheless, district leaders would be mistaken to assume that philanthropic support and prominence on a national scale will translate into political support for new policies at the local level. Private funding can enable considerable policy change with fewer public resources, and funding may even be devoted to communications strategies and outreach to inform the public. Yet these resources are not a substitute for the processes of political persuasion and bargaining that can support sustainable policy reform. National philanthropies may remove their investments and depart for greener pastures; investments from core local constituencies may have lower dollar values, but they are considerably more rooted and politically essential.

Furthermore, the opportunity to develop and implement reforms quickly, with limited public involvement, could be very attractive to district leaders. A slower process that allows for more public input means that proposals are likely to be revised and watered down. Political conditions can change because of elections or new appointments, and leaders may want to take advantage of particularly favorable circumstances for sweeping reforms. Yet these short-term calculations for acting quickly may underestimate the importance of actions that pay off in the long term. Failing to make investments in engaging key constituencies, even if it slows down reforms, can create challenges for reform durability in the future.

Despite these potential shortcomings, other urban districts have followed a reform model similar to New York City, including a heavy reliance on external sources of support and a rapid noninclusive process of policy development. In 2006, the future mayor of Washington, D.C., Adrian Fenty, visited Mayor Bloomberg in New York City to learn about Bloomberg's approach to education reform. "After meeting with Bloomberg and schools Chancellor Joel Klein, Fenty said he would borrow heavily from the New York model."[10] In 2007, Fenty gained control of the D.C. schools, and he selected Michelle Rhee as the new chancellor of the D.C. public schools.

Rhee attracted funding from major national foundations, but she had difficulty gaining support from local constituents. Based on a report in Washington's independent weekly, the *Washington City Paper*, Rhee had contacts with several foundations as chancellor: "Rhee has become part of a vast network of education-oriented charities, think tanks, business interests, and 'venture philanthropists.'"[11] An examination of her official schedule found that Rhee had 10 contacts with the Gates Foundation since June 2007; "at least 11 contacts" with the Broad Foundation since September 2007, including one meeting with Eli Broad; and 4 contacts with the Walton Family Foundation since January 2009.[12] Although Rhee courted support from national philanthropies and received considerable attention in the national media, her base of support among local constituencies remained shaky. Rhee's primary opponent in the district was the teachers' union, but some parents and community organizations objected to Rhee's tactics. An organization called Save Our Schools fought school closures and expansion of charter schools in the district.[13] Among African Americans, approval of Rhee fell precipitously, from 50 percent approval in January 2008 to 27 percent in September 2010.[14]

Disgruntlement with Rhee may have contributed to Mayor Fenty's electoral loss in September 2010.[15] The combination of mayoral control and strong philanthropic support for education reform in Washington, D.C., shares many similarities with New York City. Rhee's reforms were balanced on a narrow base of local support, although she enjoyed considerable prominence nationally. The key difference is that Fenty lost his reelection battle, creating greater uncertainty about the future of Rhee's reforms, but Bloomberg has remained in office, able to support entrenchment of Klein's reforms.

Similarly, recent reforms in the Oakland Unified School District combined philanthropic support and a system of top-down governance—state control. The 2003 state takeover of Oakland Unified, in response to the district's budget deficit, prompted large-scale investment from major foundations in a new reform plan called "Expect Success."[16] The Expect Success plan combined small schools reform with reorganization of the district administration. Although the small schools reform in Oakland began with a grassroots organizing movement prior to state takeover, it accelerated considerably following the state takeover and infusion of funding from the Gates Foundation and the Broad Foundation. With foundation dollars and state control, rapid implementation became a top priority among the leaders of the reform effort in the district and in the philanthropic community. Kevin Hall of the Broad Foundation explained, "Speed was important.... We felt that if this happened slowly, you would give the forces of opposition too many opportunities to stop it in its tracks."[17] Yet this course of action did not facilitate engagement with community organizations or local political leaders.[18] Some community organizations that were active in the small schools movement remained engaged and involved in the broader district reform efforts. Yet African American community leaders, the teachers' union, and members of the board of education—who remained in office during the state takeover—were largely sidelined. The reformers in Oakland may have "reaped some advantages by avoiding the typically slow and deliberative political process. Yet by failing to establish alliances with key political constituencies, they also jeopardized the long-term success of their reform agenda."[19]

State takeover occurred in Oakland to address a budget crisis, but the district returned to local control in 2009 with a projected budget deficit.[20] The board of education regained authority over the district, including the power to select the superintendent. The future of the reforms implemented during the state takeover now depends on officeholders who were largely excluded from decision making for six years. Additionally, some of Oakland's small schools face an uncertain fate since the Gates Foundation has shifted away from funding for small schools. With declining enrollment and a growing deficit, the board of education has closed some small schools and has considered closing or merging others.[21] Local organizing to maintain support for reforms has developed, including the Great Oakland Public Schools organization.[22] Yet the period of state takeover and infusion of foundation funds appears disconnected from the current fiscal and political realities in the district. Without continuing investment from external sources—including philanthropic funding and state leadership—it is not clear whether Oakland will generate the local resources necessary to continue the Expect Success agenda.

LESSONS FROM LOS ANGELES

Due to the larger investments by major foundations in districts with mayoral or state control, Los Angeles is a more exceptional case. Although it is difficult to generalize from the particular political dynamics of Los Angeles, the case does suggest some lessons for would-be reformers in urban school districts. Furthermore, these lessons are not necessarily contingent on the governing system of a school district—district leaders and local organizations could apply these strategies in a district with mayoral or state control, as well as a district with an elected board. Instead, these lessons show how funders, grantees, and others involved in promoting education policy reform could account for the political consequences of their strategies.

First, in Los Angeles, the organizations that received major foundation funding to implement reforms—primarily charter management organizations—developed direct relationships with local advocacy organizations and constituents. This strategy applies not only to charter school operators but also to any organizations that receive external foundation support to develop and implement local reforms. For organizations working to shape education policy, locally generated political support and investment in a shared agenda is a resource that cannot be bought with external funds. Investment from diverse constituencies requires persistent engagement with local groups and willingness to seriously address local concerns—not just "outreach" or "communication strategies."

Second, the benefits of rapid policy development and implementation must be weighed against the cost of future political backlash. Reformers often feel a great sense of urgency to act quickly so more children will not face the costs of a failing school system. Yet these children also face costs when policies are changed and reversed, creating turmoil in their schools and classrooms. Avoiding political bargaining in the short run does not exempt reformers from dealing with political realities at a later date. In Los Angeles, reforms such as charter schools and the public school choice policy developed through fairly traditional processes of public debate, deliberation, community organizing, and electoral politics. There is not universal support for these policies, and public school choice has already been revised from its original form. Additionally, there is still considerable uncertainty about the new MOU with UTLA and the implementation of school-level autonomy for all schools. Yet these reforms in Los Angeles have backing from board of education members, the mayor, several local advocacy organizations, charter school supporters, and many public school teachers. Los Angeles has moved toward the development of civic capacity, with diverse stakeholders becoming invested in a shared agenda. For an outside philanthropist concerned with long-term sustainability, supporting this type of political alignment should be more attractive than seeking out the next Michelle Rhee.

Interestingly, very similar lessons were reported by a philanthropy involved with education reform nearly two decades ago. The Annie E. Casey Foundation published *The Path of Most Resistance* in 1993 to analyze the foundation's New Futures Initiative. The initiative focused on services for youth, including education, in five midsize cities. The report describes eight lessons from Casey's experience, such as "Comprehensive Reforms Are Very Difficult," "It Takes Time," "Building Local Ownership Is No Simple Matter," and "Communicate." The section on local ownership offers a lesson that is particularly salient in light of the recent strategies of major foundations:

> Foundations, universities, advocates, and business interests can serve a crucial role—providing ideas, expertise, money, reassurance, advice— and cover for risk-taking. However, if the role of the outsider is not done carefully and deferentially, its presence can become an obstacle to local ownership and local political control of the agenda. Because system change ultimately requires the political reassignment of local public dollars and public functions, it absolutely demands local ownership. When a project becomes known as the Casey project after the third year, the project is in trouble.[23]

The issue of local ownership speaks directly to the factors that distinguish Los Angeles from New York City and other districts that followed the New York model. Local ownership of reform is developing in Los Angeles, through investments from diverse constituencies. In New York City, ownership of reforms has remained more limited and often overly identified with philanthropies, Joel Klein, and Mayor Bloomberg. The issue of ownership is challenging for philanthropies, which have a very large stake in their investments, but it is among the most important political hurdles that a foundation must overcome to support sustainable policy reforms.

An Emerging National Agenda

My analysis of foundation grant making shows that foundation strategies are converging; foundations are supporting a smaller group of school districts and targeting funds to similar types of organizations. Within New York City and Los Angeles, there is increasing overlap in grant making among major funders, with grants from multiple foundations supporting the same organizations or organizations of the same type. Convergent grant making can provide greater leverage to support the shared policy objectives of funders. By working concurrently, major foundations have supported Boardroom Progressive policy reforms in large urban districts.

Yet funders are not only combining efforts to influence policy locally; coordination among major philanthropies is also occurring on a national scale.[24] Convergent grant making to D.C.-based think tanks, advocacy groups, and organizations of public officials has grown since 2000. The role of philanthropists in national education policy has become increasingly visible under the Obama administration, which has adopted many of the policy priorities favored by the Boardroom Progressives. In some respects, major foundations appear to be leading the way on this agenda, as the federal government draws talent and ideas from the philanthropic sector. Simultaneously, the Department of Education is relying on foundations as partners and supporters to advance aspects of the administration's agenda. Whether as leaders or as partners, the agenda of major foundations increasingly overlaps with the federal education agenda. Thus, elements of the reforms that have already occurred in New York City and Los Angeles are becoming part of an emerging national education agenda led by public and private actors.

Soon after his selection by President Obama, philanthropists recognized a close ally in Education Secretary Arne Duncan. The Broad Foundation's 2009–2010 annual report glowingly commented on Duncan and his agenda:

> The election of President Barack Obama and his appointment of Arne Duncan, former CEO of Chicago Public Schools, as the U.S. secretary of education, marked the pinnacle of hope for our work in education reform. In many ways, we feel the stars have finally aligned. With an agenda that echoes our decade of investments—charter schools, performance pay for teachers, accountability, expanded learning time and national standards—the Obama administration is poised to cultivate and bring to fruition the seeds we and other reformers have planted.[25]

Duncan selected top staff members with ties to major foundations, including three former employees of the Gates Foundation. One key appointment was former Gates program officer, Jim Shelton, who now leads the Office of Innovation and Improvement.[26] At the 2009 New Schools Venture Fund summit, Duncan announced via video conference that Chief Operating Officer Joanne Weiss of New Schools Venture Fund would oversee the Department of Education's multibillion-dollar Race to the Top program. Duncan explained that his choice represented a strategy to bring new nontraditional actors into the bureaucracy: "Recruiting successful professionals from the entrepreneurial community is one way we will change the culture and our way of doing business at the Department of Education."[27]

In addition to personnel, the education policy agenda of the Obama administration has included funding and incentives geared toward top Boardroom Progressive priorities. Duncan's first few months as secretary of education showed strong evidence of a convergence between the education reform agendas of the administration and major foundations. Duncan spoke out in favor of maintaining mayoral control in New York City and stated that if the number of mayors in control of schools did not increase during his term as secretary, he "will have failed."[28] Duncan's first edition of the Department of Education's monthly television broadcast was "Charter Schools: School Reform That Works."[29] The Office of Innovation and Improvement (OII), headed by Jim Shelton, was configured to resemble a foundation; according to Mike Petrilli of the Thomas B. Fordham Institute, "I was fortunate to get to play a role in creating OII, and those of us that got it off the ground consciously tried to model it after Gates and other 'venture' philanthropies."[30] Based on these policy positions and key staff selections, the administration signaled a close affiliation with the Boardroom Progressive agenda.

Two competitive education grant programs have formed the backbone of the Obama administration's education policy—Race to the Top and the Investing in Innovation Fund. The American Recovery and Reinvestment Act (also known as "the stimulus") created and funded these new programs. Race to the Top (RTT) was the larger program, offering $4.35 billion in competitive funding for states. The Investing in Innovation Fund (I3) was a $650 million program intended to fund "innovative practices" that are demonstrated to improve student achievement. Local districts, charter schools, and nonprofits were eligible to apply for I3. Both programs were led by individuals with backgrounds in education philanthropy—Joanne Weiss and Jim Shelton. These grants represent "the largest pot of discretionary funds ever put at the disposal of a U.S. secretary of education."[31] The design of these programs—focused on rewarding places that have advanced toward adopting preferred reforms, rather than categorically distributing funds based on need or population—is closer to the model of grant distribution used by major foundations, rather than a typical federal government program.

During the implementation of RTT and I3, several major philanthropies acted as partners, facilitating the federal government's efforts. The Gates Foundation became directly involved in the application process for RTT by providing funding to some states to support their application development. Gates initially selected 15 states to receive up to $250,000 each for grant proposal preparation.[32] These selections raised concerns among other state officials that Gates was handpicking winners of the competition. Responding to this criticism, Gates offered the funding to all states that "can prove they share the foundation's views about education reform by signing an eight-point checklist."[33] Ultimately, Gates provided funding to 24 states. Among the 12 states that won the RTT competition, 9 had received funding from Gates for their applications.

The I3 program required a 20 percent private grant match for any federal funds awarded. To facilitate matching, the Department of Education coordinated directly with philanthropies for funding the I3 program. Initially, 12 foundations—including Gates, Carnegie, Ford, Wallace, and Walton—committed $500 million to "aligned investments" with the I3 program.[34] These foundations created an online Foundation Registry for the I3 program, which grew to 40 participating foundations. All of the applicants selected by the Department of Education for I3 grants were able to secure private matching funds.

The prospects for continuing philanthropic influence in national education politics appear strong. Following difficult budget negotiations in the spring of 2011—involving a Republican House majority and growing concerns about the federal deficit—both RTT and I3 were funded for another year. Thus, the administration has continued to pursue an incentive-based strategy for education reform using competitive grants. Major foundations have remained aligned with the Obama administration's education agenda. With increasing funding for advocacy organizations and think tanks, major foundations are focusing on policy reform in Washington, D.C., as well as state capitals.[35]

Combined, the converging agendas of major foundations and federal officials could be a powerful force to nationalize education reform. The hyperlocal character of education politics and policy has been the norm for much of the nation's history. In the positive sense, increasing nationalization of education reform could indicate a desirable breaking down of bastions of parochialism and facilitate the spread of innovations and best practices. Yet philanthropy has often supported projects considered too controversial or experimental for public funding. If major foundations are steering the national agenda, rather than challenging or critiquing it, private and public funding will be concentrated on a narrower set of priorities. Furthermore, if significant private and federal resources begin guiding education governance reform in a market-oriented direction with competitive grant making, local districts have little incentive to explore legitimate alternatives.[36]

Challenges

Although the Boardroom Progressives have achieved a broad alignment of federal and private resources to support their agenda, there are major fiscal challenges on the horizon for actors hoping to make changes in K-12 education. Both philanthropic and federal grants are a tiny proportion of overall funding for K-12 education in the United States. Most education funding comes from state and local sources. State and local governments have been facing growing deficits; as a major area of public spending, K-12 education frequently suffers during times of retrenchment. These funding cuts have already been felt in urban school districts, where teacher layoffs, growing class sizes, and program elimination are becoming commonplace. Fiscal austerity may make some districts less open to new policies, as they focus on salvaging existing programs. Alternatively, as districts face increasing resource constraints, philanthropists may find that their grants have even greater leverage for shaping policy. In either case, school districts will be struggling to achieve greater gains with fewer resources than they had in the past.

A second challenge for Boardroom Progressive reformers is the challenge of scale. Many of the policy successes that Boardroom Progressives have achieved remain small in relation to the massive scale of the U.S. elementary and secondary education system. For example, consider the case of charter schools. By the 2009–2010 school year, the share of K-12 students nationally enrolled in charter schools was only 3 percent.[37] This percentage is much higher is some large urban districts, such as Los Angeles, New Orleans, Detroit, and Washington, D.C. Yet these districts represent only a handful among hundreds of urban school districts nationally. Furthermore, in districts that do house dozens of charter schools, there is substantial variation in quality, and many charter schools do not achieve results that are significantly better than traditional public schools. From this perspective, even the most successful examples of schoolwide or districtwide improvement are pilots—isolated cases that can be extremely difficult to replicate or expand. The stars may have finally aligned for Boardroom Progressives—linking philanthropists to strong allies in Washington—but the scale of their challenge remains daunting.

Third, there is the challenge posed by the very act of reforming education. Frederick Hess coined the phrase "spinning wheels" to characterize the perpetual state of reform in education policy, noting: "Reform is the status quo."[38] The Boardroom Progressives are part of a long tradition of well-meaning advocates using the tools of public policy—such as new incentive structures, new rules, institutional changes, and pilot programs—to improve student achievement. Currently, school districts are managing the varying demands of No Child Left Behind, state-level policies, new expectations for teacher evaluation and incentive systems, and layers of past reforms—involving technology, curriculum, and a host of other program areas. Evaluating the success of a new program can be particularly challenging when multiple initiatives intersect in the same school or district. Often, reformers proclaim the intention to sweep away the old practices and institutions, but they rarely succeed. A question that is seldom asked is: Can there be too much reform? The Boardroom Progressives, like many of their education reform predecessors, may simply add their new layers of rules, institutions, and incentives on top of the old.

Philanthropy and Accountability

There are several important implications from the findings presented in this book for our understanding of philanthropic influence in a democratic political system. Major foundations are currently highly influential organizations in education policy in several major cities and nationally, but they are politically unaccountable. The public often does not know which specific initiatives or organizations are supported by private funding, nor does the public know which foundations are involved in supporting these programs. Sometimes, foundation funding directly compensates public officials; top district officials in Detroit and Los Angeles have received salaries supplemented by philanthropic dollars.[39] The relative lack of oversight of private philanthropy in the United States is not entirely negative; by incentivizing philanthropy with the tax code and requiring little oversight, foundations operate with extraordinary resources and freedom to experiment with new initiatives and support our diverse civil society.[40] As calls for transparency and accountability grow louder, philanthropists may respond with greater openness to preempt increased public oversight. In the meantime, the most promising efforts to improve philanthropic accountability are likely to begin with reporters, scholars, and activists who expose philanthropic strategies and evaluate their impact.

More important, the policy feedback argument presented in this book shows that foundations should be more attentive to the political consequences of their investments. Greater transparency and public engagement in the implementation of policy reform are key components of positive policy feedback. These democratic aspects of policy implementation are particularly essential for market-based reforms. The development of a new market for services in an urban district relies on significant investments from local organizations, which will become the market's innovators and entrepreneurs. Additionally, markets require transparency so providers and consumers can make informed choices.

In the contentious political environment of an urban school district, major policy reforms are unlikely to take hold without political investments and support from diverse communities. The majority of students in large urban districts are African American or Latino children from low-income households. For public school parents, traditional political channels—voting, PTAs, neighborhood organizing—are the primary vehicles for involvement in policy decisions that affect their children's education. Teachers' unions are often extremely influential in urban education politics, and they are frequently cited as the primary opponents of the Boardroom Progressives. Unions have considerably more inside channels for influence than parents. Citing the substantial influence of teachers' unions, some Boardroom Progressive reformers and foundation leaders have argued that policy change must happen swiftly, by avoiding consultation with "special interests" and public debate. This strategy often depends on strong centralized leadership, large-scale private funding, and the expectation that the public can be persuaded after the fact. Yet this insider political strategy means reformers lose the opportunity to build a diverse coalition. In addition to avoiding compromise with union leaders, the insider reform strategy also removes the political channels available to public school parents and other less powerful local interests.

Using inside-the-beltway parlance, the image of wealthy white foundation heads coordinating policy for minority school children through elite channels is not just bad optics. Promoting policy reforms "to" a community rather than "with" a community also has important political consequences, and leaders who ignore these consequences often pay the price at the ballot box. In the long term, political success achieved through a more transparent and democratic process can cultivate the investments from the diverse local constituencies that are necessary for lasting policy change. Foundation-funded reforms will have greater staying power if they can prosper with transparency and lively democratic politics.

Appendix A

TOP 15 GRANT MAKERS TO K-12 EDUCATION, 2000 AND 2005

LARGEST DONORS[1] TO K-12 EDUCATION IN 2000:

1. Bill and Melinda Gates Foundation
2. The Annenberg Foundation
3. Walton Family Foundation, Inc.
4. J. A. and Kathryn Albertson Foundation, Inc.
5. The Ford Foundation
6. Wallace–Reader's Digest Funds
7. Lilly Endowment, Inc.
8. The Joyce Foundation
9. Ross Family Charitable Foundation[2]
10. The Brown Foundation, Inc.
11. Carnegie Corporation of New York
12. The William and Flora Hewlett Foundation
13. The Skillman Foundation
14. Bank of America Foundation, Inc.
15. W. K. Kellogg Foundation

LARGEST DONORS TO K-12 EDUCATION IN 2005:

1. Bill and Melinda Gates Foundation
2. Walton Family Foundation, Inc.
3. Lilly Endowment, Inc.
4. The Wallace Foundation
5. The Annenberg Foundation
6. The Eli and Edythe Broad Foundation
7. The Ford Foundation

8. Oberkotter Foundation
9. The William and Flora Hewlett Foundation
10. H. N. and Frances C. Berger Foundation
11. Daniels Fund
12. J. A. and Kathryn Albertson Foundation, Inc.
13. The Starr Foundation
14. Carnegie Corporation of New York
15. Community Foundation Silicon Valley

Appendix B

GRANT RECIPIENT CATEGORIES

- School district
- Public school
- Charter school
- Private school
- Charter school network
- Scholarship fund
- State department of education
- Data analysis center
- University/community college
- Publicity/media
- Local advocacy/research nonprofit
- State advocacy/research nonprofit
- National advocacy/research nonprofit
- Teacher training/recruitment
- School leadership training/recruitment
- Union/collective bargaining reform
- Association of elected/school officials
- Business constituency group
- Racial/ethnic group
- Local public education foundation
- Community organizer
- Arts education
- Disabled education
- Consultant
- After-school program
- Literacy
- Venture capital
- U.S. Department of Education

- Testing organization
- Philanthropic association
- Science/math education
- Parent Teacher Association
- Home schooling
- State education foundation
- College access promotion
- Public school network operator
- School volunteer/mentor program
- Library education
- Other student enrichment
- Civic education
- Community developer
- Legal advocacy
- Other curriculum resources
- Professional association
- Regional research/advocacy nonprofit
- School supplies/clothing

Appendix C

EXPLANATION OF DATA

I gathered data on characteristics of the 100 largest school districts from the National Center for Education Statistics, including school district enrollment and the poverty rate of 5- to 17-year-olds. I excluded one of the 100 largest districts, the Hawaii Department of Education, because the district encompasses the entire state. I gathered data for the 2004–2005 school year to pair with the 2005 grant data. In 2008, comparable data on district graduation rates were released online by the Editorial Projects in Education Research Center.[1] Drawn from a single federal data set from 2003–2004, these data provide estimates of the probability that a ninth-grader in a district will complete high school in four years with a regular diploma. Using this source, I collected data on the graduation rate for the 100 largest school districts for 2003–2004.

I also collected data on civic and political variables. Two of these variables serve as indicators of the local capacity to support nonprofit organizations to provide expertise and services in the school district: nonprofit advocacy organization density and the percent of individuals with postgraduate degrees. From the 2002 economic censuses, I gathered data on the number of social advocacy organizations per 100,000 residents within a metropolitan statistical area (MSA). I excluded five school districts in the Washington, D.C., MSA (including the District of Columbia, Fairfax County, Montgomery County, Prince George's County, and Prince William County) because the organizational density for this area is inflated by the large number of organizations that lobby the federal government. Thus, these data would not be representative of the density of local nonprofit organizations. Excluding these cases does not substantively alter the results. I will refer to this measure as *nonprofit advocacy density*. These data are available only for metropolitan statistical areas, which typically are larger than school districts. I matched each MSA with the school districts that were within the MSA boundaries. (I found no instances of school districts that encompass multiple MSAs.) Some MSAs do contain multiple school districts; as a result, I have data for 60 metropolitan areas to encompass all of the school districts in my data set. The percent of individuals with postgraduate degrees (i.e., graduate or professional degree) within the city or county where the school district is located was gathered from the 2000 Census (U.S. Census Bureau, 2000).

To assess the impact of the political system on grant dollars, I investigated how each of the 100 largest school districts was governed in 2005 based on school district Web sites and scholarly literature.[2] I created a dichotomous variable to indicate whether a school district was governed by an elected school board (0) or whether control rested with the mayor or the state (1). For one of the cases, Washington, D.C., the mayor had only partial control of the school system until 2007, meaning the mayor could appoint some school board members, and others were elected. I did not code this case as an instance of mayoral control in 2005 because the majority of the school board was elected.

I identified sources of data for additional variables to test alternative hypotheses. I gathered data from a recent report on the flexibility of teacher labor agreements in the 50 largest school districts.[3] For the purposes here, I use the scores to assess whether foundation dollars were more likely to flow to districts with less restrictive labor contracts. Data on urban superintendents with professional experience outside education was gathered from a study by Eisinger and Hula, which identifies each of the nontraditional school district leaders among the 100 largest school districts.[4] To assess whether foundations give more frequently in their immediate vicinity, I counted the number of foundations among the 15 largest education grant makers that are in the same metropolitan region as each of the school districts in the data set. For example, the William and Flora Hewlett Foundation and the Community Foundation Silicon Valley were among the top 15 grant makers in 2005, and both are located in the San Francisco Bay area. Thus, I counted two major foundations in the same metropolitan region as the San Francisco Unified School District and the Oakland Unified School District. With only 15 major foundations in my data set, largely concentrated on the East or West Coast, this variable is zero for most school districts.

Appendix D

SURVEYS

1. Please list all of your organizational affiliations that are relevant to K-12 education in New York City (i.e., employer, civic, political, and volunteer organizations):

2. Primary affiliation:

3. What is your title or role?

* * *

4. In your opinion, is this school district improving, staying about the same, or getting worse?
Please circle one:
A. Improving   B. Staying about the same   C. Getting worse

5. Which of the following aspects of local education are you **most** involved with? Please check all that apply.
   ___ Monitoring and assessing progress of district-level reforms
   ___ Monitoring and assessing progress of school-level reforms
   ___ Setting the policy direction for the district
   ___ Implementing new procedures for the central district administration
   ___ Creating and supporting new public schools
   ___ Creating and supporting new charter schools
   ___ Providing funding to support district reforms
   ___ Recruiting/training new principals and/or district administrators
   ___ Recruiting/training new teachers
   ___ Supporting principal professional development
   ___ Supporting teacher professional development
   ___ Facilitating partnerships between the district and nonprofit organizations

___ Analyzing student achievement data
___ Training school- or district-level personnel to use student achievement data
___ Curriculum selection and/or development
___ District support services (facilities maintenance, transportation, etc.)
___ Additional support services for students (after-school, health, mentoring)
___ Raising funds/development/grant writing
___ Engaging with parents and community organizations about local education
___ Involving business leaders in local education
___ Organizing and mobilizing parents
___ Organizing and mobilizing students

If the aspect of local education that you are **most** involved with is not included in the list, please write it here:

6. What specific roadblocks make it difficult to carry out your objectives for this school district? Please explain.

7. Do you think this school district has too many charter schools, too few charter schools, or just the right number?
___ *Too many*
___ *Too few*
___ *Just right*

8. Which of the following best describes the role of philanthropic foundations in school reform in this district?
___ Philanthropies do not have a very important role in school reform here.
___ Philanthropies provide an important source of funding, but they do not set the direction for school reform here.

___ Philanthropies provide an important source of funding, and they help set the direction for school reform here.

The next question asks you to look at a list of possible reform strategies.

9. Please choose **your three top priorities** from this list.

_____Pay teachers more

_____Recruit more high-quality teachers for high-need schools

_____Reduce the size of classes

_____Reward teachers who improve student achievement with a bonus

_____District administration hold all schools accountable for high academic standards.

_____Devolve decisions about the budget for individual schools from the administration to the schools

_____Devolve decisions about hiring for individual schools from the administration to the schools

_____Devolve decisions about curriculum for individual schools from the administration to the schools

_____Schools should better reflect the values of their local community

_____Increase parent role in school site decisions

_____Increase opportunities for parent choice among schools in the district

_____Grant greater autonomy to highly successful "model schools" and encourage diffusion of their innovations

_____Principals must serve as instructional leaders

_____Involve more nonprofit partners in supporting schools

_____Apply for more outside funding from philanthropies

10. Who do you currently regard as a *frequent and reliable collaborator* on local education issues? Please list individuals and their organizational or institutional affiliation.

11. Have any of the following organizations or institutions provided you with **useful data or research**? Please check all that apply.

____ Academy for Educational Development

____ Achievement First

____ Advocates for Children of New York

____ Alliance for Quality Education

____ Annenberg Institute for School Reform
____ Asia Society
____ Asian American Legal Defense and Education Fund
____ Aspen Institute
____ Bard College
____ Bill and Melinda Gates Foundation
____ Broad Foundation
____ Brooklyn ACORN
____ Brooklyn Education Collaborative
____ Brooklyn-Queens 4 Education
____ Campaign for Fiscal Equity
____ Carnegie Corporation of New York
____ Center for Educational Innovation-Public Education Association (CEI-PEA)
____ Center for Immigrant Families
____ Children's Aid Society
____ Citizens Budget Commission
____ City University of New York
____ Class Size Matters
____ Columbia University
____ Community Collaborative to Improve Bronx Schools (CCB, formerly CC9)
____ Community Education Councils
____ Community Service Society of New York
____ Council of Supervisors and Administrators
____ Cypress Hills Advocates for Education
____ Desis Rising Up and Moving (DRUM)
____ Ford Foundation
____ Fordham University
____ Future of Tomorrow
____ Harlem Children's Zone
____ Institute for Student Achievement
____ Make the Road New York
____ Manhattan Institute
____ MDRC
____ Metro IAF
____ Mercy College
____ Mothers on the Move
____ New Settlement Apartments Parent Action Committee
____ New Visions for Public Schools
____ New York City Center for Charter School Excellence

_____ New York City Coalition for Educational Justice

_____ New York City Department of Education

_____ New York City Mayor's Office

_____ New York Civic Participation Project

_____ New York State Department of Education

_____ New York University

_____ Northwest Bronx Community and Clergy Coalition

_____ Public Agenda Foundation

_____ Replications Inc.

_____ Sistas and Brothas United

_____ South Bronx ACORN

_____ South Bronx Churches

_____ The After School Corporation

_____ The New School

_____ The New Teacher Project

_____ Time Out from Testing

_____ United Federation of Teachers

_____ Urban Assembly

_____ Urban Youth Collaborative

_____ U.S. Department of Education

_____ Wallace Foundation

_____ Young Women's Leadership Foundation

_____ Youth on the Move

If any organizations or institutions that have provided you with **useful data or research** are **NOT** included in the list, please list them here:

12. Have any of the following organizations or institutions provided you with useful information about **local community needs or preferences**? Please check all that apply.

_____ Academy for Educational Development

_____ Achievement First

_____ Advocates for Children of New York

_____ Alliance for Quality Education

_____ Annenberg Institute for School Reform

_____ Asia Society

_____ Asian American Legal Defense and Education Fund

_____ Aspen Institute

_____ Bard College

_____ Bill and Melinda Gates Foundation

_____ Broad Foundation

____ Brooklyn ACORN

____ Brooklyn Education Collaborative

____ Brooklyn-Queens 4 Education

____ Campaign for Fiscal Equity

____ Carnegie Corporation of New York

____ Center for Educational Innovation-Public Education Association (CEI-PEA)

____ Center for Immigrant Families

____ Children's Aid Society

____ Citizens Budget Commission

____ City University of New York

____ Class Size Matters

____ Columbia University

____ Community Collaborative to Improve Bronx Schools (CCB, formerly CC9)

____ Community Education Councils

____ Community Service Society of New York

____ Council of Supervisors and Administrators

____ Cypress Hills Advocates for Education

____ Desis Rising Up and Moving (DRUM)

____ Ford Foundation

____ Fordham University

____ Future of Tomorrow

____ Harlem Children's Zone

____ Institute for Student Achievement

____ Make the Road New York

____ Manhattan Institute

____ MDRC

____ Mercy College

____ Metro IAF

____ Mothers on the Move

____ New Settlement Apartments Parent Action Committee

____ New Visions for Public Schools

____ New York City Center for Charter School Excellence

____ New York City Coalition for Educational Justice

____ New York City Department of Education

____ New York City Mayor's Office

____ New York Civic Participation Project

____ New York State Department of Education

____ New York University

____ Northwest Bronx Community and Clergy Coalition

____ Public Agenda Foundation
____ Replications Inc.
____ Sistas and Brothas United
____ South Bronx ACORN
____ South Bronx Churches
____ The After School Corporation
____ The New School
____ The New Teacher Project
____ Time Out from Testing
____ United Federation of Teachers
____ Urban Assembly
____ Urban Youth Collaborative
____ U.S. Department of Education
____ Wallace Foundation
____ Young Women's Leadership Foundation
____ Youth on the Move

If any organizations or institutions that have provided you with useful information about **local community needs or preferences** are **NOT** included in the list, please list here:

Leadership: The next set of questions asks you to think of individuals or organizations that are playing important leadership roles in local education.

13. Are there individuals or organizations involved in local education that you regard as change agents? In other words, have any leaders been particularly influential by mobilizing new resources or developing new strategies to improve education?
If so, please list below (please be as specific as possible).

14. Are there individuals or organizations involved in local education that you regard as honest brokers or mediators? In other words, have any leaders played an important role in mediating conflict or building bridges between different groups?

If so, please list below (please be as specific as possible).

15. Are there individuals or organizations involved in local education that you regard as operational leaders? In other words, do any leaders play a key role by operating efficiently in a complex environment?
    If so, please list below (please be as specific as possible).

16. Are there individuals or organizations involved in local education that you regard as gatekeepers or veto players? In other words, are there any leaders who must be on board with a decision for change to occur?
    If so, please list below (please be as specific as possible).

For the next three questions, please circle the option that most closely reflects your opinion.

17. "Philanthropies are too influential in this district."

| Strongly | Somewhat | Neutral | Somewhat | Strongly |
| disagree_____ | disagree_____ | | agree_____ | agree |

18. "In this district, the teacher's union obstructs efforts to reform the schools."

| Strongly | Somewhat | Neutral | Somewhat | Strongly |
| disagree_____ | disagree_____ | | agree_____ | agree |

19. "Community organizations and parent groups are shut out of education politics here."

| Strongly | Somewhat | Neutral | Somewhat | Strongly |
| disagree_____ | disagree_____ | | agree_____ | agree |

For the following questions, please indicate **the level of influence** (on a scale from 1 to 5) of each individual, organization, or institution on **school district policy**.

20. The Chancellor

5	4	3	2	1
Very		Somewhat		Not at all
Influential_____		Influential_____		Influential

21. The Mayor

5	4	3	2	1
Very		Somewhat		Not at all
Influential_____		Influential_____		Influential

22. The United Federation of Teachers

5	4	3	2	1
Very		Somewhat		Not at all
Influential_____		Influential_____		Influential

23. The Community Education Councils

5	4	3	2	1
Very		Somewhat		Not at all
Influential_____		Influential_____		Influential

24. New Visions for Public Schools

5	4	3	2	1
Very		Somewhat		Not at all
Influential_____		Influential_____		Influential

25. Other Community-Based Organizations

5	4	3	2	1
Very		Somewhat		Not at all
Influential_____		Influential_____		Influential

26. Philanthropic Foundations

5	4	3	2	1
Very		Somewhat		Not at all
Influential_____		Influential_____		Influential

27. Charter Schools

5	4	3	2	1
Very		Somewhat		Not at all
Influential_____		Influential_____		Influential

May I contact you for a follow-up interview? _____ YES _____ NO
Preferred method of contact:

_____

Thank you for your contribution to this study.

LOS ANGELES SCHOOL REFORM SURVEY

1. Please list all of your organizational affiliations that are relevant to K-12 education in Los Angeles (i.e., employer, civic, political, and volunteer organizations):

2. Primary affiliation:

3. What is your title or role?

* * *

4. In your opinion, is LAUSD improving, staying about the same, or getting worse? Please circle one:
   A. Improving   B. Staying about the same   C. Getting worse

5. Which of the following aspects of local education are you **most** involved with? Please check all that apply.
   ___ Monitoring and assessing progress of district-level reforms
   ___ Monitoring and assessing progress of school-level reforms
   ___ Setting the policy direction for the district
   ___ Implementing new procedures for the central district administration
   ___ Creating and supporting new public schools
   ___ Creating and supporting new charter schools
   ___ Providing funding to support district reforms
   ___ Recruiting/training new principals and/or district administrators
   ___ Recruiting/training new teachers
   ___ Supporting principal professional development
   ___ Supporting teacher professional development
   ___ Facilitating partnerships between the district and nonprofit organizations
   ___ Analyzing student achievement data

___ Training school- or district-level personnel to use student achievement data

___ Curriculum selection and/or development

___ District support services (facilities maintenance, transportation, etc.)

___ Additional support services for students (i.e., after-school, health, mentoring)

___ Raising funds/development/grant writing

___ Engaging with parents and community organizations about local education

___ Involving business leaders in local education

___ Organizing and mobilizing parents

___ Organizing and mobilizing students

If the aspect of local education that you are **most** involved with is not included in the list, please write it here:

6. What specific roadblocks make it difficult to carry out your objectives for this school district? Please explain.

7. Do you think this school district has too many charter schools, too few charter schools, or just the right number?

　　___ *Too many*

　　___ *Too few*

　　___ *Just right*

8. Which of the following best describes the role of philanthropic foundations in school reform in this district?

　　___ Philanthropies do not have a very important role in school reform here.

　　___ Philanthropies provide an important source of funding, but they do not set the direction for school reform here.

　　___ Philanthropies provide an important source of funding, and they help set the direction for school reform here.

The next question asks you to look at a list of possible reform strategies.

9. Please choose **your three top priorities** from this list.

_____Pay teachers more

_____Recruit more high-quality teachers for high-need schools

_____Reduce the size of classes

_____Reward teachers who improve student achievement with a bonus

_____District administration hold all schools accountable for high academic standards

_____Devolve decisions about the budget for individual schools from the administration to the schools

_____Devolve decisions about hiring for individual schools from the administration to the schools

_____Devolve decisions about curriculum for individual schools from the administration to the schools

_____Schools should better reflect the values of their local community

_____Increase parent role in school site decisions

_____Increase opportunities for parent choice among schools in the district

_____Grant greater autonomy to highly successful "model schools" and encourage diffusion of their innovations

_____Principals must serve as instructional leaders

_____Involve more nonprofit partners in supporting schools

_____Apply for more outside funding from philanthropies

10. Who do you currently regard as a *frequent and reliable collaborator* on local education issues? Please list individuals and their organizational or institutional affiliation.

11. Have any of the following organizations or institutions provided you with **useful data or research**? Please check all that apply.

____ Advancement Project

____ Alliance for a Better Community

____ Alliance for College-Ready Public Schools

____ Annenberg Foundation
____ Asian American Legal Defense Fund
____ Aspen Institute
____ Aspire Public Schools
____ Bill and Melinda Gates Foundation
____ Board of Education (LAUSD)
____ Broad Foundation
____ CADRE (Community Asset Development Re-defining Education)
____ California Charter Schools Association
____ California Institute of Technology
____ California State Department of   Education
____ California State University, Long Beach
____ California State University, L.A.
____ California State University, Northridge
____ Communities for Educational Equity
____ Community Coalition
____ Community Partners
____ Concerned Citizens of South Central LA
____ Education Justice Collaborative
____ ExED
____ Families in Schools
____ Green Dot Public Schools
____ Green Dot Teachers Union (Associacion de Maestros Unidos)
____ Hewlett Foundation
____ Hispanic Clergy Council
____ Inner City Arts
____ InnerCity Struggle
____ Institute for Democracy, Education, and Access at UCLA (IDEA)
____ Johns Hopkins University
____ Just Schools California
____ KIPP
____ LA Voice (PICO)
____ LEARN–Los Angeles Educational Alliance for Restructuring Now
____ Liberty Hill
____ Los Angeles ACORN
____ Los Angeles County Office of Education
____ Los Angeles Metro Strategy (IAF)
____ Los Angeles Parents Union
____ Los Angeles Unified School District
____ Loyola Marymount University
____ Mathematically Correct

____ MDRC

____ Mexican American Legal Defense and Educational Fund (MALDEF)

____ National Council of La Raza

____ Pacific Charter School Development

____ Parents for Unity

____ Parent-U-Turn

____ Partnership for Los Angeles Schools

____ Partnerships to Uplift Communities (PUC)

____ People Organized for Westside Renewal (POWER)

____ Pueblo Nuevo Development

____ Rx for Reading

____ Small Schools Alliance

____ South Central Youth Empowered thru Action (SCYEA)

____ Strategic Concepts in Organizing and Policy Education (SCOPE)

____ The Inner City Education Foundation

____ The New Teacher Project

____ University of California, Los Angeles

____ University of Southern California

____ U.S. Department of Education

____ United Teachers Los Angeles (UTLA)

____ Wonder of Reading

If any organizations or institutions that have provided you with **useful data or research** are **NOT** included in the list, please list them here:

12. Have any of the following organizations or institutions provided you with useful information about **local community needs or preferences**? Please check all that apply.

____ Advancement Project

____ Alliance for a Better Community

____ Alliance for College-Ready Public Schools

____ Annenberg Foundation

____ Asian American Legal Defense Fund

____ Aspen Institute

____ Aspire Public Schools

____ Bill and Melinda Gates Foundation

____ Board of Education (LAUSD)

____ Broad Foundation

____ CADRE (Community Asset Development Re-defining   Education)
____ California Charter Schools Association
____ California Institute of Technology
____ California State Department of   Education
____ California State University, Long Beach
____ California State University, L.A.
____ California State University, Northridge
____ Communities for Educational Equity
____ Community Coalition
____ Community Partners
____ Concerned Citizens of South Central LA
____ Education Justice Collaborative
____ ExED
____ Families in Schools
____ Green Dot Public Schools
____ Green Dot Teachers Union (Associacion de Maestros Unidos)
____ Hewlett Foundation
____ Hispanic Clergy Council
____ Inner City Arts
____ InnerCity Struggle
____ Institute for Democracy, Education, and Access at UCLA (IDEA)
____ Johns Hopkins University
____ Just Schools California
____ KIPP
____ LA Voice (PICO)
____ LEARN–Los Angeles Educational Alliance for Restructuring Now
____ Liberty Hill
____ Los Angeles ACORN
____ Los Angeles County Office of Education
____ Los Angeles Metro Strategy (IAF)
____ Los Angeles Parents Union
____ Los Angeles Unified School District
____ Loyola Marymount University
____ Mathematically Correct
____ MDRC
____ Mexican American Legal Defense and Educational Fund (MALDEF)
____ National Council of La Raza
____ Pacific Charter School Development
____ Parents for Unity
____ Parent-U-Turn
____ Partnership for Los Angeles Schools

____ Partnerships to Uplift Communities (PUC)

____ People Organized for Westside Renewal (POWER)

____ Pueblo Nuevo Development

____ Rx for Reading

____ Small Schools Alliance

____ South Central Youth Empowered thru Action (SCYEA)

____ Strategic Concepts in Organizing and Policy Education (SCOPE)

____ The Inner City Education Foundation

____ The New Teacher Project

____ University of California, Los Angeles

____ University of Southern California

____ U.S. Department of Education

____ United Teachers Los Angeles (UTLA)

____ Wonder of Reading

If any organizations or institutions that have provided you with useful information about **local community needs or preferences** are **NOT** included in the list, please list here:

Leadership: The next set of questions asks you to think of individuals or organizations that are playing important leadership roles in local education.

13. Are there individuals or organizations involved in local education that you regard as change agents? In other words, have any leaders been particularly influential by mobilizing new resources or developing new strategies to improve education?

If so, please list below (please be as specific as possible).

14. Are there individuals or organizations involved in local education that you regard as honest brokers or mediators? In other words, have any leaders played an important role in mediating conflict or building bridges between different groups?

If so, please list below (please be as specific as possible).

15. Are there individuals or organizations involved in local education that you regard as operational leaders? In other words, do any leaders play a key role by operating efficiently in a complex environment?
If so, please list below (please be as specific as possible).

16. Are there individuals or organizations involved in local education that you regard as gatekeepers or veto players? In other words, are there any leaders who must be on board with a decision for change to occur?
If so, please list below (please be as specific as possible).

For the next three questions, please circle the option that most closely reflects your opinion.

17. "Philanthropies are too influential in this district."

Strongly	Somewhat	Neutral	Somewhat	Strongly
disagree_____	disagree_____		agree_____	agree

18. "In this district, the teachers' union obstructs efforts to reform the schools."

Strongly	Somewhat	Neutral	Somewhat	Strongly
disagree_____	disagree_____		agree_____	agree

19. "Community organizations and parent groups are shut out of education politics here."

Strongly	Somewhat	Neutral	Somewhat	Strongly
disagree_____	disagree_____		agree_____	agree

For the following questions, please indicate **the level of influence** (on a scale from 1 to 5) of each individual, organization, or institution on **school district policy**.

20. The Superintendent

5	4	3	2	1
Very		Somewhat		Not at all
Influential_____		Influential_____		Influential

21. The Mayor

5	4	3	2	1
Very		Somewhat		Not at all
Influential_____		Influential_____		Influential

22. United Teachers Los Angeles

5	4	3	2	1
Very		Somewhat		Not at all
Influential_____		Influential_____		Influential

23. The Board of Education

5	4	3	2	1
Very		Somewhat		Not at all
Influential_____		Influential_____		Influential

24. Community-Based Organizations

5	4	3	2	1
Very		Somewhat		Not at all
Influential_____		Influential_____		Influential

25. Philanthropic Foundations

5	4	3	2	1
Very		Somewhat		Not at all
Influential_____		Influential_____		Influential

26. Charter Schools

5	4	3	2	1
Very		Somewhat		Not at all
Influential_____		Influential_____		Influential

May I contact you for a follow-up interview? _____ *YES* _____ *NO*
Preferred method of contact:

_____

Thank you for your contribution to this study.

NOTES

Introduction

1. The use of the term *Progressives* here refers to the group also known as the Administrative Progressives, as opposed to adherents to Dewey's progressive model of schooling. See David B. Tyack, *The One Best System: A History of American Urban Education* (Cambridge, MA: Harvard University Press, 1974).

2. Hess (2010) and Cuban (2006) have also described the similarities between Progressive era reformers and current education reformers and entrepreneurs. See Frederick M. Hess, *The Same Thing Over and Over: How School Reformers Get Stuck in Yesterday's Ideas* (Cambridge, MA: Harvard University Press, 2010); Larry Cuban, "Educational Entrepreneurs Redux," in *Educational Entrepreneurship: Realities, Challenges, Possibilities* (Cambridge, MA: Harvard Education Press, 2006).

3. Tyack, *The One Best System.*

4. Ibid.

5. Hess, *The Same Thing Over and Over*; Charles T. Kerchner, David J. Menefee-Libey, and Laura S. Mulfinger, "Comparing the Progressive Model and Contemporary Formative Ideas and Trends," in *The Transformation of Great American School Districts: How Big Cities Are Reshaping Public Education*, eds. William L. Boyd, Charles T. Kerchner, and Mark Blyth (Cambridge, MA: Harvard Education Press, 2008).

6. Ibid.; Janelle Scott, "The Politics of Venture Philanthropy in Charter School Policy and Advocacy," *Educational Policy* 23, 1(2009): 106–136.

7. Tyack, *The One Best System.*

8. Frederick M. Hess, *The Future of Educational Entrepreneurship: Possibilities for School Reform* (Cambridge, MA: Harvard Education Press, 2008); Michael Mintrom and Sandra Vergari, "Foundation Engagement in Education Policymaking: Assessing Philanthropic Support of School Choice Initiatives." Los Angeles: Center on Philanthropy and Public Policy (2003).

9. Tyack, *The One Best System*; Kerchner et al., "Comparing the Progressive Model."

10. The accountability and market elements of this agenda are not always supported in equal measure by different Boardroom Progressive allies. Some would favor letting 1,000 flowers bloom by opening diverse new schools applying a range of education strategies; others are firmly in favor of holding all schools to a common set of national standards.

11. Jeffrey R. Henig, "Mayors, Governors, and Presidents: The New Education Executives and the End of Educational Exceptionalism," *Peabody Journal of Education* 84, 3(2009): 283–289.

12. Robert Dahl, *Who Governs? Democracy and Power in an American City* (New Haven, CT: Yale University Press, 1961).

13. Frederick M. Hess, "Introduction," in *With the Best Intentions: How Philanthropy Is Reshaping K-12 Education*, ed. Frederick M. Hess (Cambridge, MA: Harvard Education Press, 2005).

14. Ibid.

15. Frederick M. Hess, "Rethinking America's Schools: Frederick M. Hess Responds," *Philanthropy* 23–24 (2005).

16. Hess, "Introduction," 10.

17. Joel L. Fleishman, *The Foundation: How Private Wealth Is Changing the World* (New York: Public Affairs, 2009).

18. Hess, "Introduction," 12.

19. Diane Ravitch, *The Death and Life of the Great American School System: How Testing and Choice Are Undermining Education* (New York: Basic Books, 2010), 201.

20. Theda Skocpol, *Protecting Soldiers and Mothers: The Political Origins of Social Policy in the United States* (Cambridge, MA: Belknap Press of Harvard University Press, 1992); Paul Pierson, "When Effect Becomes Cause: Policy Feedback and Political Change," *World Politics* 45 (1993): 595–628; Suzanne Mettler, "Bringing the State Back in to Civic Engagement: Policy Feedback Effects of the G.I. Bill for World War II Veterans," *American Political Science Review* 96, 2(2002): 351–365; Andrea L. Campbell, *How Policies Make Citizens: Senior Political Activism and the American Welfare State* (Princeton, NJ: Princeton University Press, 2003); Eric M. Patashnik, *Reforms at Risk: What Happens after Major Policy Changes Are Enacted* (Princeton, NJ: Princeton University Press, 2008); Margaret Weir, Jane Rongerude, and Christopher K. Ansell, "Collaboration Is Not Enough: Virtuous Cycles of Reform in Transportation Policy," *Urban Affairs Review* 44, 4(2009): 455–489.

21. Campbell, *How Policies Make Citizens.*

22. Patashnik, *Reforms at Risk.*

23. Ibid., 16.

24. John Portz, Lana Stein, and Robin R. Jones, *City Schools and City Politics: Institutions and Leadership in Pittsburgh, Boston, and St. Louis* (Lawrence: University of Kansas Press, 1999); Clarence N. Stone, "Civic Capacity and Urban Education," *Urban Affairs Review* 36, 5(2001): 595–619; Clarence N. Stone, Jeffrey R. Henig, Bryan D. Jones, and Carol Pierannunzi, *Building Civic Capacity: The Politics of Reforming Urban Schools* (Lawrence: University Press of Kansas, 2001); Jeffrey R. Henig, Richard C. Hula, Marion Orr, and Desiree S. Pedescleaux, *The Color of School Reform: Race, Politics, and the Challenge of Urban Education* (Princeton, NJ: Princeton University Press, 2001); Melissa Marschall and Para Shah, "Keeping Policy Churn off the Agenda: Urban Education and Civic Capacity," *Policy Studies Journal* 33, 2(2005): 161–180; Xavier de Souza Briggs, *Democracy as Problem Solving: Civic Capacity in Communities across the Globe* (Cambridge, MA: MIT Press, 2008); Chris Ansell, Sarah Reckhow, and Andrew Kelly, "How to Reform a Reform Coalition: Outreach, Agenda Expansion, and Brokerage in Urban School Reform," *Policy Studies Journal* 37 (2009): 717–743.

25. Stone, "Civic Capacity and Urban Education"; Marschall and Shah, "Keeping Policy Churn off the Agenda."

26. Patashnik, *Reforms at Risk.*

27. Stone, "Civic Capacity and Urban Education," 614.

28. http://foundationcenter.org/pnd/news/story.jhtml?id=189500032.

Chapter 1

1. Christopher B. Swanson and Janelle Barlage, *Influence: A Study of the Factors Shaping Education Policy* (Bethesda, MD: Editorial Projects in Education Research Center, 2006).

2. Ibid.

3. Elisabeth S. Clemens and Linda C. Lee, "Catalysts for Change: Foundations and School Reform 1950–2005," in *American Foundations: Roles and Contributions,* eds. Helmut Anheier and David C. Hammack (Washington, DC: Brookings Institute Press, 2010); Joel L. Fleishman, *The Foundation: How Private Wealth Is Changing the World* (New York: Public Affairs, 2009); Frederick M. Hess, "Introduction," in *With the Best Intentions: How Philanthropy Is Reshaping K-12 Education,* ed. Frederick M. Hess (Cambridge, MA: Harvard Education Press, 2005).

4. John W. Kingdon, *Agendas, Alternatives, and Public Policies* (Boston: Little, Brown, 1984).

5. Ibid., 189–190.

6. Olivier Zunz, *Philanthropy in America: A History* (Princeton, NJ: Princeton University Press, 2012).

7. Jack L. Walker, *Mobilizing Interest Groups in America: Patrons, Professions, and Social Movements* (Ann Arbor: University of Michigan Press, 1991).

8. Steven M. Teles, *The Rise of the Conservative Legal Movement: The Battle for Control of the Law* (Princeton, NJ: Princeton University Press, 2008); Tim Bartley, "How Foundations Shape Social Movements: The Construction of an Organizational Field and the Rise of Forest Certification," *Social Problems* 54, 3(2007): 229–255.

9. Zunz, *Philanthropy in America*.

10. Chester E. Finn and Kelly Amis, *Making It Count: A Guide to High Impact Education Philanthropy* (Washington, DC: Thomas B. Fordham Foundation, 2001).

11. Peter Marris and Martin Rein, *Dilemmas of Social Reform: Poverty and Community Action in the United States* (Chicago: University of Chicago Press, 1973): 227.

12. Michael B. Berkman and Eric Plutzer, *Ten Thousand Democracies: Politics and Public Opinion in America's School Districts* (Washington, DC: Georgetown University Press, 2005): 1.

13. Robert A. Dahl, *Who Governs? Democracy and Power in an American City* (New Haven, CT: Yale University Press, 1961); John H. Mollenkopf, *The Contested City* (Princeton, NJ: Princeton University Press, 1983); John M. Quigley, "A Decent Home: Housing Policy in Perspective," in *Brookings-Wharton Papers on Urban Affairs* (Washington, DC: Brookings Institution Press, 2000); Thomas J. Sugrue, *The Origins of Urban Crisis: Race and Inequality in Postwar Detroit* (Princeton, NJ: Princeton University Press, 2005).

14. Dahl, *Who Governs?*

15. Wilbur C. Rich, *Black Mayors and School Politics: The Failure of Reform in Detroit, Gary, and Newark* (New York: Garland, 1996): 5.

16. Dorothy Shipps, *School Reform, Corporate Style: Chicago, 1880–2000* (Lawrence: University of Kansas Press, 2006).

17. Marion Orr, *Black Social Capitol: The Politics of School Reform in Baltimore 1986–1998* (Lawrence: University of Kansas Press, 1999).

18. Clarence N. Stone, Jeffrey R. Henig, Bryan D. Jones, and Carol Pierannunzi, *Building Civic Capacity: The Politics of Reforming Urban Schools* (Lawrence: University Press of Kansas, 2001).

19. Jeffrey R. Henig and Clarence Stone, "Rethinking School Reform: The Distractions of Dogma and the Potential for a New Politics of Progressive Pragmatism," *American Journal of Education* 114, 3(2008): 191–218.

20. Ibid.

21. Sean Cavanagh, "U.S. Common-Standards Push Bares Unsettled Issues," *Education Week*, January 14 (2010).

22. Frederick M. Hess, "Weighing the Case for School Boards: Today and Tomorrow," *Phi Delta Kappan* 91, 6(2010): 15–19.

23. Frederick M. Hess, *The Same Thing Over and Over: How School Reformers Get Stuck in Yesterday's Ideas* (Cambridge, MA: Harvard University Press 2010); Larry Cuban, "Foreword," *Between Public and Private*, eds. Katrina E. Bulkey, Jeffrey R. Henig, and Henry M. Levin (Cambridge, MA: Harvard Education Press, 2010).

24. Hess, *The Same Thing Over and Over*, ix.

25. Cuban, "Foreword," ix.

26. Hess, *The Same Thing Over and Over*.

27. Richard F. Fenno and Frank J. Munger, *National Politics and Federal Aid to Education* (Syracuse, NY: Syracuse University Press, 1962).

28. Ibid.

29. John D. Skrentny, *The Minority Rights Revolution* (Cambridge, MA: Belknap Press of Harvard University Press, 2002).

30. David Stephens, "President Carter, the Congress, and NEA: Creating the Department of Education," *Political Science Quarterly* 98, 4(1983–1984): 641–663.

31. Terrel H. Bell, *The Thirteenth Man* (New York: Free Press, 1988): 25.

32. Bell, *The Thirteenth Man*, 115.

33. The National Commission on Excellence in Education, *A Nation at Risk: The Imperative for Educational Reform*, April 26, 1983.

34. Bell, *The Thirteenth Man*, 131.

35. Paul Manna, *School's In: Federalism and the National Education Agenda* (Washington, DC: Georgetown University Press, 2006).

36. Edward B. Fiske, "States Gain Wider Influence on School Policy." *New York Times*, December 2, 1984.

37. Margaret E. Goertz, *State Educational Standards in the 50 States: An Update* (Princeton, NJ: Educational Testing Service, 1988).

38. Henig and Stone, "Rethinking School Reform."

39. Paul Manna, "Leaving No Child Behind," in *Political Education: National Policy Comes of Age* (New York: Teacher's College Press, 2004): 130.

40. Sara Mead, "Restructured Usually Means Little Has Changed," *Education Next*, Winter (2007): 52–56.

41. Ibid.

42. Henig and Stone, "Rethinking School Reform," 207.

43. Gail L. Sunderman and James S. Kim, "The Expansion of Federal Power and the Politics of Implementing the No Child Left Behind Act," *Teachers College Record* 109, 5(2007): 1057–1085.

44. United States Government Accountability Office, *GAO Report on No Child Left Behind* (2007).

45. Ibid.

46. Ibid., 9–10.

47. David K. Cohen and Susan L. Moffitt, *The Ordeal of Equality: Did Federal Regulation Fix the Schools?* (Cambridge, MA: Harvard University Press, 2009): 170.

48. Cohen and Moffitt, *The Ordeal of Equality*, 171.

49. "PDK/Gallup Poll of the Public's Attitudes Toward Public Schools," *Phi Delta Kappan* (2010).

50. "PDK/Gallup Poll of the Public's Attitudes Toward Public Schools," *Phi Delta Kappan* (2002): 45.

51. "PDK/Gallup Poll of the Public's Attitudes Toward Public Schools," *Phi Delta Kappan* (2010).

52. William J. Mathis, "No Child Left Behind Costs and Benefit," *Phi Delta Kappan* (2003), 679–686.

53. Analysis conducted by the author on Lexis-Nexis academic on December 12, 2010; the analysis involved searching for the phrase "failing schools" in the *New York Times* annually from 1990 to 2010.

54. Sam Dillon, "U.S. Effort to Reshape Schools Faces Challenge," *New York Times*, June 2, 2009: A15.

55. Patricia Burch, "Convergence or Collision: Portfolio Districts, Education Markets, and Federal Education Policy," in *Between Public and Private: Politics, Governance, and the New Portfolio Models for Urban School Reform*, eds. Katrina E. Bulkey, Jeffrey R. Henig, and Henry M. Levin (Cambridge, MA: Harvard Education Press, 2010): 256.

56. Michael J. Petrilli, "Testing the Limits of NCLB," *Education Next* (2007); David Hoff, "New Coalition to Lobby for Changes in NCLB's Provisions on Tutoring," *Education Week*, May 23, 2007.

57. Mead, "Restructured Usually Means Little Has Changed."

58. Sunderman and Kim, "The Expansion of Federal Power and the Politics of Implementing the No Child Left Behind Act," 1063.

59. John E. Chubb and Terry M. Moe, *Politics, Markets and America's Schools* (Washington, DC: Brookings Institution Press, 1990).

60. Chubb and Moe, *Politics, Markets, and America's Schools*, 217.

61. Janelle Scott, "The Politics of Venture Philanthropy in Charter School Policy and Advocacy," *Educational Policy* 23, 1(2009): 106–136.

62. Jeffrey R. Henig, *Spin Cycle: How Research Is Used in Policy Debates* (New York: Russell Sage Foundation, 2008): 51.

63. Henig, *Spin Cycle*, 52.

64. "PDK/Gallup Poll of the Public's Attitudes Toward Public Schools," *Phi Delta Kappan* (2010).

65. "PDK/Gallup Poll of the Public's Attitudes Toward Public Schools," *Phi Delta Kappan* (2000).

66. Francis X. Shen, Kenneth K. Wong, and Michael T. Hartney, "The Politics of Mayoral Support for School Choice." Paper presented at the annual meeting of the American Political Science Association,Washington, DC (2010).

67. Robin Lake, Brianna Dusseault, Melissa Bowen, Allison Demerritt, and Paul Hill, *The National Study of Charter Management Organization (CMO) Effectiveness: Report on Interim Findings*, Mathematica Policy Research and the Center on Reinventing Public Education (2010).

68. Lake et al., *The National Study of Charter Management Organization (CMO) Effectiveness*: 3.

69. www.thomastoch.com/wp2009/sweating-the-big-stuff/.

70. Patrick McGuinn, *No Child Left Behind and the Transformation of Federal Education Policy, 1965–2005* (Lawrence: University Press of Kansas, 2006); Burch, "Convergence or Collision."

71. Paul Hill, *Reinventing Public Education* (Santa Monica, CA: RAND Report, Institute on Education and Training, 1995): xi–xii.

72. Jeffrey R. Henig, "Portfolio Management Models and the Political Economy of Contracting Regimes," in *Between Public and Private: Politics, Governance, and the New Portfolio Models for Urban School Reform*, eds. Katrina E. Bulkey, Jeffrey R. Henig, and Henry M. Levin (Cambridge, MA: Harvard Education Press, 2010): 28.

73. Katrina E. Bulkley, "Introduction: Portfolio Management Models in Urban School Reform," in *Between Public and Private: Politics, Governance, and the New Portfolio Models for Urban School Reform*, eds. Katrina E. Bulkey, Jeffrey R. Henig, and Henry M. Levin (Cambridge, MA: Harvard Education Press, 2010).

74. Peter Marris and Martin Rein, *Dilemmas of Social Reform: Poverty and Community Action in the United States* (Chicago: University of Chicago Press, 1973): 211–212.

75. Zunz, *Philanthropy in America*.

76. Ibid., 29.

77. Ibid., 39.

78. Pamela Barnhouse Walters and Emily A. Bowman, "Foundations and the Making of Public Education in the United States: 1867–1950," in *American Foundations: Roles and Contributions*, eds. Helmut K. Anheier and David C. Hammack (Washington, DC: Brookings Institution Press, 2010).

79. Scott, "The Politics of Venture Philanthropy," 111.

80. Richard D. Kahlenberg, "Ocean Hill–Brownsville, 40 Years Later," *Chronicle Review*, April 25, 2008; Jane Anna Gordon, *Why They Couldn't Wait* (New York: RoutledgeFalmer, 2001).

81. Diane Ravitch, *The Great School Wars* (New York: Basic Books, 1974).

82. Janice Petrovich, *A Foundation Returns to School: Strategies for Improving Public Education* (New York: Ford Foundation, 2008): 15.

83. Rich, *Black Mayors and School Politics*, 58.

84. Rich, *Black Mayors and School Politics*, 57.

85. James M. Ferris, *Foundations and Pubic Policymaking: Leveraging Philanthropic Dollars, Knowledge, and Networks* (Los Angeles: Center on Philanthropy and Public Policy, University of Southern California, 2003): 5.

86. James M. Ferris, Guilbert C. Hentschke, and Hilary J. Harmssen, "Philanthropic Strategies for School Reform: An Analysis of Foundation Choices," *Educational Policy* 22, 5(2008): 705–730.

186 Notes

87. Craig J. Jenkins, "Channeling Social Protest: Foundation Patronage of Contemporary Social Movements," in *Private Action and Public Good*, eds. Walter W. Powell and Elisabeth S. Clemens (New Haven, CT: Yale University Press, 1998).

88. Sada Aksartova, "In Search of Legitimacy: Peace Grant Making of U.S. Philanthropic Foundations, 1988–1996," *Nonprofit and Voluntary Sector Quarterly* 32, 1(2003): 25–46.

89. Ellen C. Lagemann, *The Politics of Knowledge: The Carnegie Corporation, Philanthropy, and Public Policy* (Chicago: University of Chicago Press, 1989).

90. Ibid., 262.

91. Steven M. Teles, *The Rise of the Conservative Legal Movement: The Battle for Control of the Law* (Princeton, NJ: Princeton University Press, 2008): 186.

92. www.foundationcenter.org.

93. http://foundationcenter.org/findfunders/statistics/pdf/04_fund_sub/2010/50_found_sub/f_sub_b20_10.pdf.

94. http://foundationcenter.org/findfunders/statistics/pdf/04_fund_sub/2008/50_found_sub/f_sub_b20_08.pdf.

95. Ibid.

96. http://givingpledge.org/.

97. http://blogs.wsj.com/wealth/2010/08/11/europeans-attack-buffett-gates-pledge-as-undemocratic/.

98. Jessica Bearman and Grantmakers for Education, *Benchmarking 2010: Trends in Education Philanthropy* (Portland: Grantmakers for Education, 2010).

99. Erik W. Robelen, "Grantmakers Seeking to Influence Policy," *Education Week*, December 8, 2010.

100. Ibid.

101. Chester E. Finn and Marci Kanstoroom, "Afterword: Lessons from the Annenberg Challenge," in *Can Philanthropy Fix Our Schools? Appraising Walter Annenberg's $500 Million Gift to Public Education* (Washington, DC: Thomas B. Fordham Foundation, 2000); Barbara Cervone, "When Reach Exceeds Grasp: Taking the Annenberg Challenge to Scale," in *Reconnecting Education and Foundations*, eds. Ray Bacchetti and Thomas Ehrlich (San Francisco: Jossey-Bass, 2007).

102. Joel L. Fleishman, *The Foundation: How Private Wealth Is Changing the World* (New York: Public Affairs, 2009): 267.

103. Marc D. Millot, "Leveraging the Market to Scale Up School Improvement Programs: A Fee-for-Service Primer for Foundations and Nonprofits," in *Expanding the Reach of Education Reforms: Perspectives from Leaders in the Scale-Up of Educational Interventions*, eds. Thomas K. Glennan Jr., Susan J. Bodilly, Jolene R. Galegher, and Kerri A. Kerr (Santa Monica, CA: RAND, 2004): 608.

104. http://www.aei.org/article/21345.

105. Scott, "The Politics of Venture Philanthropy"; Peter Frumkin, "Inside Venture Philanthropy," *Society* 40, 4(2003): 7–15. Although Broad, Gates, and Walton are commonly grouped together as "venture philanthropists," the strategies of these foundations differ considerably, particularly regarding politics. Broad's political orientation is fairly explicit, with strong support for charter schools and attracting noneducators to lead school districts. Gates is somewhat more cautious, but the foundation has made major grants to organizations of elected officials and supports advocacy concerning teacher evaluation and accountability. Walton's political involvement is the least visible, and there is not a prominent public figure representing the foundation, as Eli Broad and Bill Gates do for the foundations bearing their names.

106. www.broadeducation.org/asset/1042-dkspeech_at_dems_for_ed%20reform.pdf.

107. I discuss the shift toward "venture philanthropy" in Reckhow, "Disseminating and Legitimating a New Approach: The Role of Foundations," in *Between Public and Private: Politics, Governance, and the New Portfolio Models for Urban School Reform*, eds. Katrina E. Bulkey, Jeffrey R. Henig, and Henry M. Levin (Cambridge, MA: Harvard Education Press, 2010).

108. *The Bridgespan Group: Harvard Business School Case Study* (Boston: Harvard Business School Publishing, 2000).

109. Tammi Chun, Gail Zellman, and Brian Stecher, *An Evaluation Strategy Developed by RAND for the Broad Foundation* (Santa Monica, CA: RAND, 2001).

110. Josh Edelman, "Portfolio Management Models: From the Practitioner's Eyes," in *Between Public and Private: Politics, Governance, and the New Portfolio Models for Urban School Reform*, eds. Katrina E. Bulkey, Jeffrey R. Henig, and Henry M. Levin (Cambridge, MA: Harvard Education Press, 2010).

111. Mollenkopf, *The Contested City*; Mara Sidney, *Unfair Housing* (Lawrence: University of Kansas Press, 2003); Margaret Weir, Jane Rongerude, and Christopher K. Ansell, "Collaboration Is Not Enough: Virtuous Cycles of Reform in Transportation Policy," *Urban Affairs Review* 44, 4(2009): 455–489.

112. Jeffrey R. Henig, Richard C. Hula, Marion Orr, and Desiree S. Pedescleaux, *The Color of School Reform: Race, Politics, and the Challenge of Urban Education* (Princeton, NJ: Princeton University Press, 2001).

Chapter 2

1. Carl Campanile, "Gates' $4 Million Lesson: Aided School Control," *New York Post*, August 18, 2009; Frederick M. Hess, *Assessing the Case for Mayoral Control of Urban Schools* (Washington, DC: American Enterprise Institute, 2008).

2. Nancy Hoffman and Robert Schwartz, "Foundations and School Reform: Bridging the Cultural Divide," in *Reconnecting Education and Foundations*, eds. Ray Bacchetti and Thomas Ehrlich (San Francisco, CA: Jossey-Bass, 2007): 112.

3. Constancia Warren, personal correspondence with author, July 7, 2008.

4. Ibid.

5. Ibid.

6. These indicators are not intended to be direct measures of the existing density of education organizations in a city. Rather, these are indicators of the "underlying professional . . . capacity" (described by Warren) of the city. This professional capacity, combined with an infusion of foundation funds for K-12 education, would lead to an increased density of education organizations in the city or expansion of existing education organizations.

7. Lynn Jenkins and Donald R. McAdams, "Philanthropy and Urban School District Reform: Lessons from Charlotte, Houston, and San Diego," in *With the Best Intentions: How Philanthropy Is Reshaping K-12 Education*, ed. Frederick M. Hess (Cambridge, MA: Harvard Education Press, 2005): 134.

8. Jay P. Greene, "Buckets into the Sea: Why Philanthropy Isn't Changing Schools, and How It Could," in *With the Best of Intentions: How Philanthropy is Reshaping K-12 Education*, ed. Frederick M. Hess (Cambridge, MA: Harvard Education Press 2005): 51.

9. Greene, "Buckets into the Sea."

10. All of the foundations' 990-PF forms were downloaded at www.eri-nonprofit-salaries.com.

11. For one of the top 15 grant makers in 2000, the Ross Family Charitable Foundation, I was unable to locate a tax return (nor could I find any records of the foundation's grants on the Internet). Thus, I was unable to gather data on these grants, and the 2000 database includes 14 of the 15 largest grant makers.

12. I located this information for all but 25 grants in the 2005 data set and for all but 29 grants in the 2000 data set.

13. Nine of the top 15 grant makers are the same for both years. The Broad Foundation is the most significant grant maker in 2005 that was not a top grant maker in 2000. Each of the results reported here was also assessed with data from only the nine grant makers that were the same in both years. These results are nearly identical to the comparisons reported in the text based on the data from all 15 foundations.

14. The research/advocacy nonprofit category includes local, state, and national organizations. Individually, each of the three categories received a smaller share of grants in 2005 compared to 2000.

15. Bill and Melinda Gates Foundation, 990-PF, 2005.

16. Richard L. Colvin, "A New Generation of Philanthropists and Their Great Ambitions," in *With the Best of Intentions: How Philanthropy Is Reshaping K-12 Education*, ed. Frederick M. Hess (Cambridge, MA: Harvard Education Press, 2005).

17. Compared with Carnegie and Ford, Annenberg is a newer foundation, started in 1989. Nonetheless, the grant-making style of Annenberg is much closer to the older foundations.

18. Frederick M. Hess, "Introduction," in *With the Best Intentions: How Philanthropy is Reshaping K-12 Education*, ed. Frederick M. Hess (Cambridge, MA: Harvard Education Press, 2005).

19. Diane Ravitch, *The Death and Life of the Great American School System: How Testing and Choice Are Undermining Education* (New York: Basic Books, 2010): 199.

20. Janice Petrovitch, interview with author on May 16, 2008.

21. Elisabeth S. Clemens and Linda C. Lee, "Catalysts for Change: Foundations and School Reform 1950–2005," in *American Foundations: Roles and Contributions*, eds. Helmut Anheier and David C. Hammack (Washington, DC: Brookings Institute Press, 2010): 67.

22. Frederick M. Hess and Coby Loup, *The Leadership Limbo: Teacher Labor Agreements in America's Fifty Largest School Districts* (Washington, DC: Thomas B. Fordham Institute, 2008).

23. Regression allows us to test each of the competing explanations, while holding all of the others constant. Tobit regression is a censored regression model. Given that the dependent variable—grant dollars per student—is not observed for values less than zero, a standard linear regression model would produce estimators that are biased downward. See Lee Sigelman and Langche Zeng, "Analyzing Censored and Sample-Selected Data with Tobit and Heckit Models," *Political Analysis* 8, 2(1999): 167–182.

24. There are 94 cases in the model because 6 of the 100 largest school districts had to be excluded. One is Hawaii, which is a state district with no local districts. The other five are in the Washington, D.C., metropolitan area; these cases were excluded because accurate data on nonprofit advocacy density was not available for this region. For further explanation, see Appendix C.

25. *Annual Report Eli and Edythe Broad Foundation* (2008), www.broadfoundation.org/asset/101–124–2008tbfsannualreportfinal.pdf.

26. *Annual Report Eli and Edythe Broad Foundation* (2009–2010), www.broadfoundation.org/asset/101–2009.10%20annual%20report.pdf.

27. I discuss the relationship between mayoral or state control of school districts and foundation funding for districts in "Disseminating and Legitimating a New Approach: The Role of Foundations," in *Between Public and Private: Politics, Governance, and the New Portfolio Models for Urban School Reform*, eds. Katrina E. Bulkey, Jeffrey R. Henig and Henry M. Levin (Cambridge, MA: Harvard Education Press, 2010).

28. Michele Cahill, interview with author on February 9, 2009.

29. Joe Williams, *National Model or Temporary Opportunity? The Oakland Education Reform Story* (Washington, DC: Center for Education Reform, 2007): 4.

30. Stefanie Chambers, *Mayors and Schools: Minority Voices and Democratic Tensions in Urban Education* (Philadelphia: Temple University Press, 2006).

31. Mark Hornbeck, "Duncan Challenges Mayor to Fix DPS," *Detroit News*, February 27, 2009.

Chapter 3

1. www.edweek.org/apps/gmap/.

2. Data downloaded from the National Center for Education Statistics: http://nces.ed.gov/.

3. Seymour Fliegel, *Miracle in East Harlem: The Fight for Choice in Public Education* (New York: Times Books, 1993); Pearl R. Kane, "The Difference between Charter Schools and

Charterlike Schools," in *City Schools: Lessons from New York*, eds. Diane Ravitch and Joseph P. Viteritti (Baltimore, MD: Johns Hopkins University Press, 2000); Charles T. Kerchner, David J. Menefee-Libey, Laura S. Mulfinger, and Stephanie E. Clayton, *Learning from L.A.: Institutional Change in American Public Education* (Cambridge, MA: Harvard Education Press, 2008).

4. Kane, "The Difference between Charter Schools and Charterlike Schools."

5. Kerchner et al., *Learning from L.A.*

6. Lydia Segal, "The Pitfalls of Political Decentralization and Proposals for Reform: The Case of New York City Public Schools," *Public Administration Review* 57, 2(1997): 141–149.

7. Ibid.

8. Fliegel, *Miracle in East Harlem*.

9. Ibid.

10. Deborah Meier, *The Power of Their Ideas: Lessons for America from a Small School in Harlem* (Boston: Beacon, 1995).

11. Fliegel, *Miracle in East Harlem*; Paul Teske, Mark Schneider, Christine Roch, and Melissa Marschall, "Public School Choice: A Status Report," in *City Schools: Lessons from New York*, eds. Diane Ravitch and Joseph P. Viteritti (Baltimore, MD: Johns Hopkins University Press, 2000).

12. Kane, "The Difference between Charter Schools and Charterlike Schools."

13. Raymond Domanico, "A Small Footprint on the Nation's Largest School System," in *Can Philanthropy Fix Our Schools? Appraising Walter Annenberg's $500 Million Gift to Public Education* (Washington, DC: Thomas B. Fordham Foundation, 2000).

14. Ibid.

15. Ibid.

16. *Final Report of the Evaluation of New York Networks for School Renewal* (New York: Institute for Education and Social Policy, New York University 2001).

17. http://blogs.edweek.org/edweek/Bridging-Differences/2008/07/.

18. *Final Report of the Evaluation of New York Networks for School Renewal*, 33.

19. Barbara Cervone, "When Reach Exceeds Grasp: Taking the Annenberg Challenge to Scale," in *Reconnecting Education and Foundations*, eds. Ray Bacchetti and Thomas Ehrlich (San Fransisco, CA: Jossey-Bass, 2007): 151.

20. Deborah Meier, *In Schools We Trust: Creating Communities of Learning in an Era of Testing and Standardization* (Boston: Beacon, 2003).

21. http://blogs.edweek.org/edweek/Bridging-Differences/2008/07/.

22. Interview, July 29, 2008.

23. Judith Rosenberg Rafterty, *Land of Fair Promise: Politics and Reform in Los Angeles Schools, 1885–1941* (Palo Alto, CA: Stanford University Press, 1992).

24. Kerchner et al., *Learning from L.A.*, 35.

25. David J. Menefee-Libey, Benjamin Diehl, Keena Lipsitz, and Nadia Rahimtoola, "The Historic Separation of Schools from City Politics," *Education and Urban Society* 29, 4(1997): 453–473.

26. Ibid., 462.

27. Kerchner et al., *Learning from L.A.*

28. Ibid., 99.

29. Marcella R. Dianda and Ronald Corwin, *Vision and Reality: A First-Year Look at California's Charter Schools* (Los Alamitos, CA: Southwest Regional Laboratory, 1994).

30. Kerchner et al., *Learning from L.A.*, 186.

31. Kerchner et al., *Learning from L.A.*

32. Ann Bradley, "Uneasy Alliance Marks Launch of L.A. Plan," *Education Week*, April 11, 1990.

33. Naush Boghossian, "Lessons to LEARN in Reform of LAUSD?" *Los Angeles Daily News*, July 30, 2006.

34. Majorie E. Wechsler and Linda D. Friedrich, "The Role of Mediating Organizations for School Reform: Independent Agents or District Dependents?" *Journal of Education Policy* 12, 5(1997): 382–401.

35. Kerchner et al., *Learning from L.A.*
36. Wechsler and Friedrich, "The Role of Mediating Organizations for School Reform," 390.
37. Kerchner et al., *Learning from L.A.*
38. Ibid.
39. Ibid.
40. Joan L. Herman and Eva L. Baker, *The Los Angeles Annenberg Metropolitan Project: Evaluation Findings* (Los Angeles: Los Angeles Compact for Evaluation, University of California, Los Angeles, 2003).
41. Ibid., 1.
42. Kerchner et al., *Learning from L.A.*
43. Ibid., 155.
44. Herman and Baker, *The Los Angeles Annenberg Metropolitan Project: Evaluation Findings.*
45. David J. Menefee-Libey, "Systemic Reform in a Federated System: Los Angeles at the Turn of the Millennium," *Education Policy Analysis Archives* 12, 60(2004).
46. Kerchner et al., *Learning from L.A.*, 173.
47. www.familiesinschools.org/site/.
48. Kerchner et al., *Learning from L.A.*, 169.
49. New Visions for Public School grant data, http://foundationcenter.org/; Cervone, "When Reach Exceeds Grasp," 148.
50. Stephen P. Borgatti, Martin G. Everett, and Linton C. Freeman, *Ucinet for Windows: Software for Social Network Analysis* (Cambridge, MA: Harvard Analytic, 2002).
51. Stephen P. Borgatti, *NetDraw: Graph Visualization Software* (Cambridge, MA: Harvard Analytic, 2002).
52. The number of foundations giving grants in each city for each year varied. Five foundations are represented in the 2000 network for New York City (figure 3.1), nine foundations are represented in the 2005 network for New York City (figure 3.2), five foundations are represented in the 2000 network for Los Angeles (figure 3.3), and six foundations are represented in the 2005 network for Los Angeles (figure 3.4).
53. *Annual Report Bill & Melinda Gates Foundation* (2000), http://www.gatesfoundation.org/about/Pages/annual-reports.aspx.
54. Ibid., 4.
55. Ibid., 52.
56. Kellogg Foundation. IRS Form 990-PF. 2000.
57. Broad Foundation. IRS Form 990-PF. 2005.
58. Gates Foundation. IRS Form 990-PF. 2005.
59. Michael Klonsky and Susan Klonsky, *Small Schools: Public School Reform Meets the Ownership Society* (New York: Routledge 2008).
60. *Annual Report Bill & Melinda Gates Foundation* (2003), http://www.gatesfoundation.org/about/Pages/annual-reports.aspx: 5.
61. *Annual Report Bill & Melinda Gates Foundation* (2004), http://www.gatesfoundation.org/about/Pages/annual-reports.aspx: 12.
62. Amanda Paulson, "The Schoolhouses That Gates Built," *Christian Science Monitor*, December 7, 2004.
63. www.pacificcharter.org.
64. http://newschools.org.
65. http://pacificcharter.org/about_us/board.htm.
66. "Charter-related organizations" include CMOs, charter school associations, and organizations that develop charter school facilities.
67. Kerchner et al., *Learning from L.A.*, 189.
68. Monica Higgins, Wendy Robbins, Jennie Weiner, and Frederick Hess, "Creating a Corps of Change Agents," *Education Next* 11, 3(2011); Janelle Scott, "The Politics of Venture Philanthropy in Charter School Policy and Advocacy," *Educational Policy* 23, 1(2009): 106–136.

69. www.nlns.org/Locations_NewYorkCity.jsp.

70. http://www.broadcenter.org/residency/.

71. Norm Fructer, "'Plus Ca Change...': Mayoral Control in New York City," in *The Transformation of Great American School Districts: How Big Cities Are Reshaping Public Education*, eds. William L. Boyd, Charles T. Kerchner, and Mark Blyth (Cambridge, MA: Harvard Education Press, 2008).

72. Jennifer Steinhauer, "Los Angeles Mayor Gains Control of the Schools, but Hardly Total Control," *New York Times*, August 31, 2005.

73. Catherine H. Augustine, Diane Epstein, and Mirka Vuollo, *Governing Urban School Districts: Efforts in Los Angeles to Effect Change* (Santa Monica, CA: RAND, 2006).

74. www.partnershipla.org.

75. Duke Helfand and Howard Blume, "Mayor Gets $50 Million for Schools," *Los Angeles Times*, September 27, 2007.

76. www.youtube.com/watch?v=fSSYHj_6dXU.

77. http://gothamschools.org/2009/03/11/eli-broad-describes-close-ties-to-klein-weingarten-duncan/.

78. Tony Castro, "Eli Broad Has Made His Mark on L.A.," *Los Angeles Daily News*, October 20, 2007.

79. Joel Rubin, "L.A. Charter Schools Are Investment Grade to Broad," *Los Angeles Times*, May 24, 2007.

Chapter 4

1. Data available through the National Center for Education Statistics, Common Core of Data.

2. National Association of State Budget Officers, *State Expenditure Report, Fiscal Year 2006* (Washington, DC: NASBO, 2007).

3. Peter Meyer, "New York City's Education Battles," *Education Next* 8, 2(2008): 11–20; Sewell Chan, "Mayor Announces Plan for Teacher Merit Pay," *New York Times*, October 17, 2007; Elissa Gootman, "Teachers Agree to Bonus Pay Tied to Scores," *New York Times*, October 18, 2007; Elissa Gootman, "Mixed Results on Paying City Students to Pass Tests," *New York Times*, August 19, 2008.

4. *Annual Report Bill & Melinda Gates Foundation* (2003), www.gatesfoundation.org/about/Pages/annual-reports.aspx, 6.

5. www.broadeducation.org/investments/current_investments/investments_all.html.

6. Meredith Honig, "'External' Organizations and the Politics of Urban Educational Leadership: The Case of New Small Autonomous School Initiatives," *Peabody Journal of Education* 84, 3(2009): 394–413.

7. Ibid.

8. To group organizations into these four categories, I conducted a Google search for each organization in my foundation grant database and analyzed the organization's Web site to assess each organization's purpose. I verified my categorization based on my survey of key actors in NYC education policy, described later in this chapter. The survey included questions about the primary activities of individuals in each organization (creating and supporting new public schools, analyzing student achievement data, organizing and mobilizing parents, etc.).

9. www.waltonfamilyfoundation.org/2011-education-reform-grants-by-investment-region#list.

10. http://broadeducation.org/asset/0-090408nyccharters.pdf.

11. Bill & Melinda Gates Foundation, IRS Form 990-PF, 2005.

12. Interview with author on July 29, 2008.

13. Interview with author on September 19, 2008.

14. Interview with author on May 16, 2008.

15. Janice Petrovich, *A Foundation Returns to School: Strategies for Improving Public Education* (New York: Ford Foundation, 2008): 28.

16. Personal correspondence with author, February 28, 2009.

17. Clara Hemphill and Kim Nauer (with Thomas Jacobs, Alessandra Raimondi, Sharon McCloskey, and Rajeev Yerneni), "Managing by the Numbers: Empowerment and Accountability in New York City's Schools" (New York: Center for New York City Affairs, The New School, 2010).

18. http://gothamschools.org/2009/03/11/eli-broad-describes-close-ties-to-klein-weingarten-duncan.

19. Abby Goodnough, "Fixing the Schools," *New York Times*, October 4, 2002, B3.

20. Ibid.

21. Joe Williams, "The Stealth Schools CEO," *New York Daily News*, November 24, 2000.

22. www.nychold.com/cf-wgmembers.html.

23. Ibid.

24. Personal correspondence with author, May 6, 2009.

25. Ibid.

26. Jessica Wolff, "Shaking Up the School System," *Gotham Gazette*, February 2003.

27. Interview with author on February 9, 2009.

28. Norm Fruchter, "'Plus Ca Change ...': Mayoral Control in New York City," in *The Transformation of Great American School Districts: How Big Cities are Reshaping Public Education*, eds. William L. Boyd, Charles T. Kerchner, and Mark Blyth (Cambridge, MA: Harvard Education Press, 2008): 98.

29. http://schools.nyc.gov/AboutUs/schools/childrenfirst.htm.

30. Erik W. Robelen, "Gates Learns to Think Big," *Education Week*, October 11, 2006.

31. Howard S. Bloom, Saskia Levy Thompson, and Rebecca Unterman, *Transforming the High School Experience: How New York City's Small Schools Are Boosting Student Achievement and Graduation Rates* (New York: MDRC, 2010).

32. http://mediaresearchhub.ssrc.org/robert-hughes/person_view.

33. www.urbanassembly.org/ourschools.html.

34. www.replications.org; www.studentachievement.org/schools.aspx; www.nycoutwardbound.org/our-schools/index.html.

35. Clara Hemphill (with Pamela Wheaton and Jacqueline Wayans), *New York City's Best Public High Schools: A Parents' Guide* (New York: Teachers College Press, 2003).

36. Diane Ravitch, *The Death and Life of the Great American School System: How Testing and Choice Are Undermining Education* (New York: Basic Books, 2010).

37. Bloom et al., *Transforming the High School Experience*.

38. Clara Hemphill and Kim Nauer (with Helen Zelon and Thomas Jacobs), *The New Marketplace: How Small School Reforms and School Choice Have Reshaped New York City's High Schools* (New York: Center for New York City Affairs, The New School, 2009): 2.

39. Bloom et al., *Transforming the High School Experience*, 10.

40. www.advocatesforchildren.org/Empty%20Promises%20Report%20%206-16-09.pdf.

41. Ibid., 26.

42. Ibid., 4.

43. Ravitch, *The Death and Life of the Great American School System*, 80.

44. http://nyccharterschools.org/index.php.

45. Juan Gonzalez, "Eva Moskowitz Has Special Access to Schools Chancellor Klein—and Support Others Can Only Dream Of," *New York Daily News*, February 25, 2010.

46. http://docs.google.com/viewer?a=v&pid=sites&srcid=ZGVmYXVsdGRvbWFpbnxueWRuZG9j3xneDoyMjFlOTliYmVlNjcUxMmIw.

47. http://docs.google.com/viewer?a=v&pid=sites&srcid=ZGVmYXVsdGRvbWFpbnxueWRuZG9j3xneDoyMjFlOTliYmVlNjcUxMmIw.

48. http://gothamschools.org/2010/01/11/charter-school-philanthropy-2009.

49. Hemphill and Nauer, "Managing by the Numbers," 10.

50. http://www.newvisions.org/network-approach/the-new-visions-partnership-support-organization.

51. Elizabeth Green, "MBA Invasion," *Scholastic Administrator*, January 2009.

52. Fruchter, "'Plus Ca Change,'" 108.

53. Hemphill and Nauer, "Managing by the Numbers," 2.

54. Interview with author on September 19, 2008.

55. Interview with author on September 17, 2008.

56. Elissa Gootman, "Taught to Be Principals, and Now Facing the Test," *New York Times*, September 8, 2004.

57. Andrea Gabor, "Leadership Principles for Public School Principals," *Strategy + Business*, March 23, 2005, 2.

58. Gabor, "Leadership Principle for Public School Principals."

59. Helen Zelon, "A Matter of Principles: On Training School Chiefs," *City Limits* 19, May 2008.

60. http://schools.nyc.gov/Offices/mediarelations/NewsandSpeeches/2007– 2008/20080627_nycla.htm.

61. *Strategy and Implementation Report*, New York City Center for Economic Opportunity, 2007.

62. www.edlabs.harvard.edu/.

63. *Strategy and Implementation Report*, New York City Center for Economic Opportunity.

64. Diane Ravitch, "We Shouldn't Pay Kids to Learn," *Forbes*, October 17, 2008.

65. Javier C. Hernandez, "New Effort Aims to Test Theories of Education," *New York Times*, September 24, 2008, B6.

66. Roland G. Fryer, "Financial Incentives and Student Achievement: Evidence from Randomized Trials" (NBER Working Paper 15898, 2010).

67. Yoav Gonen, "Can't Buy Me Good Grades," *New York Daily News*, April 9, 2010.

68. Fryer, "Financial Incentives and Student Achievement."

69. Elissa Gootman, "Teachers Agree to Bonus Pay Tied to Scores," *New York Times*, October 18, 2007, A1.

70. http://schools.nyc.gov/Offices/mediarelations/NewsandSpeeches/2008– 2009/20080918_performance_bonuses.htm.

71. Sarena Goodman and Lesley Turner, "Teacher Incentive Pay and Educational Outcomes: Evidence from the NYC Bonus Program," Program on Education Policy and Governance Working Paper Series, Harvard Kennedy School of Government, 2010.

72. Sharon Otterman, "Pilot Program of Teacher Bonuses Is Suspended," *New York Times*, January 21, 2011, A23.

73. www.rand.org/news/press/2011/07/18.html.

74. "How Many Billionaires Does It Take to Fix a School System?" *New York Times Magazine*, March 9, 2008.

75. Prospective respondents were contacted in two ways. First, I contacted individuals by e-mail and provided a link to an online survey. Second, for nonrespondents to the online survey, as well as individuals for whom no e-mail address was available, I distributed paper surveys by mail. A copy of the survey is included in Appendix D.

76. The response rates varied slightly across subgroups. Education nonprofits and parent leaders had the lowest response rates at 33 percent. The highest response rate was unions, 44 percent. The response rate for advocacy organizations was 42 percent. I cannot report an exact response rate for NYC DOE officials because I relied on internal contacts to assist with anonymous survey distribution. My approximate calculations indicate that it does not differ substantially from the overall average of 37 percent.

77. Interview with author on March 28, 2008.

78. Interview with author on February 9, 2009.

79. Focus Group at City University of New York, September 18, 2008.

80. Ibid.

81. Ibid.

82. www.edpriorities.org/About/about.html.

83. http://schools.nyc.gov/NR/rdonlyres/B432D059–6BFE-4198–8453– 466FDE2B22D5/69835/PEPBylawsFinal91409.pdf .

84. Fruchter, "'Plus Ca Change.'"

85. Interview with author on September 23, 2008.

86. David Herszenshorn, "Bloomberg Wins on School Tests after Firing Foes," *New York Times*, March 16, 2004, A1.

87. Stephen P. Borgatti, *NetDraw: Graph Visualization Software* (Cambridge, MA: Harvard, 2002); Stephen P. Borgatti, Martin G. Everett, and Linton C. Freeman, *Ucinet for Windows: Software for Social Network Analysis* (Cambridge, MA: Harvard, 2002).

88. The survey asked respondents to identify their organizational affiliations relevant to K-12 education in New York City, as well as their "main affiliation."

89. Broad Foundation, IRS Form 990-PF, 2005.

90. David Krackhardt and Robert N. Stern, "Informal Networks and Organizational Crises: An Experimental Simulation," *Social Psychology Quarterly* 51, 2(1988): 123–140.

91. Ibid., 127.

92. Jeffrey R. Henig, Eva Gold, Marion Orr, Megan Silander, and Elaine Simon, "Parent and Community Engagement in NYC and the Sustainability Challenge for Urban Education Reform" (prepared for the New York City Education Reform Retrospective Project, 2010).

93. http://parentcommission.org/index.html.

94. www.campaignforbetterschools.org/.

95. Jennifer Medina, "Backers of Mayoral School Control Face Resistance," *New York Times*, January 29, 2009, A21.

96. www.campaignforbetterschools.org/.

97. Henig et al., "Parent and Community Engagement in NY and the Sustainability Challenge for Urban Education Reform," 13.

98. www.nydailynews.com/opinions/2009/03/08/2009-03-08_power_to_the_parents_forget_seats_on_pol-2.html.

99. http://gothamschools.org/2009/03/19/mayoral-control-obama-unseen-stars-at-harlem-charter-night/.

100. http://schools.nyc.gov/NR/rdonlyres/02CA7F0A-AD6A-4788-8ADD-A85F57AA099E/0/DollarsandSense_ACloserLookatTheFundforPublicSchools.pdf.

101. http://gothamschools.org/2009/04/20/new-public-school-ads-hit-the-subways-some-in-spanish/.

102. http://nycpublicschoolparents.blogspot.com/2008/12/bill-gates-rather-meaninglessly-opines.html.

103. Medina, "Backers of Mayoral School Control Face Resistance."

104. Carl Campanile, "Gates' $4 Million Lesson: Aided School Control," *New York Post*, August 18, 2009.

105. Ibid.

106. Ravitch, *The Death and Life of the Great American School System*, 80.

107. Ibid.

108. Randi Weingarten, "Mayoral Control 2.0," *New York Post*, May 21, 2009.

109. http://gothamschools.org/2009/05/19/mayoral-control-critics-give-school-board-literal-rubber-stamps/.

110. www.nydailynews.com/blogs/dailypolitics/2009/02/bloomberg-warns-riots-in-the-s.html.

111. Ibid.

112. http://cityroom.blogs.nytimes.com/2009/08/11/paterson-signs-mayoral-control-bill/.

113. Sharon Otterman and Jennifer Medina, "Boos and Personal Attacks as City Panel Prepares to Vote on School Closings," *New York Times*, January 27, 2010, A21.

114. Ibid.

115. Meredith Kolodner, "United Federation of Teachers Sues in Effort to Block Closure of 19 City Schools," *New York Daily News*, February 1, 2010.

116. Sharon Otterman, "Judge Blocks Closing of 19 New York City Schools," *New York Times*, March 26, 2010, A1.

117. http://gothamschools.org/2011/05/18/teachers-union-lawsuit-takes-aim-at-22-school-closures/.

118. Jeremy Peters, "Schools Chief Has Much in Common with Boss," *New York Times*, November 10, 2010, A28; Michael Barbaro, Sharon Otterman, and Javier Hernandez, "After 3 Months, Mayor Replaces Schools Leader," *New York Times*, April 8, 2011, A1.

119. http://maristpoll.marist.edu/44-tutorial-needed-for-schools-chancellor-cathie-black/.

120. Chris Ansell, Sarah Reckhow, and Andrew Kelly, "How to Reform a Reform Coalition: Outreach, Agenda Expansion, and Brokerage in Urban School Reform," *Policy Studies Journal* 37 (2009): 717–743.

121. Eric M. Patashnik, *Reforms at Risk: What Happens after Major Policy Changes Are Enacted* (Princeton, NJ: Princeton University Press, 2008).

122. Ibid.

123. Henig et al., "Parent and Community Engagement in NY and the Sustainability Challenge for Urban Education Reform," 18.

124. http://nycpublicschoolparents.blogspot.com/2009/02/testimony-on-mayoral-control-for.html.

125. Robert Dahl, *Who Governs? Democracy and Power in an American City* (New Haven, CT: Yale University Press, 1961): 152.

126. Dahl, *Who Governs?* 102.

Chapter 5

1. Charles T. Kerchner, David J. Menefee-Libey, Laura S. Mulfinger, and Stephanie E. Clayton, *Learning from L.A.: Institutional Change in American Public Education* (Cambridge, MA: Harvard Education Press, 2008).

2. David J. Menefee-Libey, Benjamin Diehl, Keena Lipsitz, and Nadia Rahimtoola, "The Historic Separation of Schools from City Politics," *Education and Urban Society* 29, 4(1997): 453–473; Caroline Hendrie, "Plan to Lop Off 200,000 Students from L.A. Unveiled," *Education Week*, April 16, 1997.

3. Kerchner et al., *Learning from L.A.*

4. http://notebook.lausd.net/pls/ptl/docs/PAGE/CA_LAUSD/LAUSDNET/OFFICES/COMMUNICATIONS/11–12FINGERTIPFACTSREVISED.PDF.

5. Robin Lake, Brianna Dusseault, Melissa Bowen, Allison Demerritt, and Paul Hill, *The National Study of Charter Management Organization (CMO) Effectiveness: Report on Interim Findings* (Princeton, NJ: Mathematica Policy Research and the Center on Reinventing Public Education, 2010).

6. Beth Barrett, "Insiders vs. Charters at LAUSD," *LA Weekly*, March 11, 2010.

7. http://dontholdusback.org/wp-content/uploads/2011/10/UTLA_proposal.pdf.

8. Eric M. Patashnik, *Reforms at Risk: What Happens after Major Policy Changes Are Enacted* (Princeton, NJ: Princeton University Press, 2008): 155

9. Interview with author on March 11, 2009.

10. Lake et al., *The National Study of Charter Management Organization (CMO) Effectiveness*, 54.

11. www.gatesfoundation.org/united-states/Pages/the-college-ready-promise-fact-sheet.aspx.

12. Interview with author on March 9, 2009.

13. www.partnershipla.org/About.

14. www.partnershipla.org/system/storage/3/e4/3/54/0809_taxreturn.pdf.

15. www.icefla.org/.

16. www.pucschools.org/about/.

17. Interview with author on March 10, 2009.

18. www.joannejacobs.com/2007/09/locke-liberated/.

19. *Annual Report Bill & Melinda Gates Foundation*, 2007, www.gatesfoundation.org/nr/public/media/annualreports/annualreport07/AR2007US3.html.

20. www.cde.ca.gov/ls/fa/sf/prop39.asp.

21. Thomas Fields-Meyer, "Black vs. Brown at L.A. School," *Time*, May 15, 2008.
22. "Locke High School's Progress," *Los Angeles Times*, December 1, 2008.
23. Ibid.
24. www.annenberginstitute.org/pdf/EKF08_GreenDot.pdf, 3.
25. Steve Lopez, "Seniority, Not Quality, Counts Most at United Teachers Los Angeles," *Los Angeles Times*, March 25, 2009.
26. Interview with author on March 12, 2009.
27. Howard Blume, "Parents Are Urged to Demand More from L.A. Schools," *Los Angeles Times*, May 11, 2009.
28. http://ndn.org/blog/2010/01/californias-educational-earthquake.
29. Bruce Fuller, "Palace Revolt in Los Angeles?" *Education Next* (2010): 20–28.
30. As charter schools in Los Angeles have expanded, the political organizing around charter schools has also grown. In addition to Parent Revolution, other parent advocacy organizations have developed to promote charters and school choice. An umbrella organization affiliated with the California Charter Schools Association—Families That Can—has been mobilizing Los Angeles parents around issues affecting charter schools, such as funding for facilities.
31. Interview with author on March 10, 2009.
32. Ibid.
33. Ibid.
34. Kerchner et al., *Learning from L.A.*, 192.
35. Interview with author on February 24, 2012.
36. Personal correspondence with author, April 6, 2009.
37. Ibid.
38. http://beta.laschoolboard.org/files/Tab6.SternRenew.pdf.
39. Personal correspondence with author, April 6, 2009.
40. Connie Llanos, "Charters, LAUSD in Special Ed Tug of War," *Los Angeles Daily News*, January 6, 2010.
41. Interview with author on March 9, 2009.
42. www.laalliance.org/pdf/2010–11%20Alliance%20Academic%20Performance%20Index-API-Graphs.pdf.
43. www.greendot.org/page.cfm?p=2129.
44. Joan L. Herman, Jordan Rickles, Mark Hansen, Larry Thomas, Alice Gualpa, and Jia Wang, *Evaluation of Green Dot's Locke Transformation Project: Findings from the 2007–08, 2008–09, and 2009–10 School Years* (Los Angeles: National Center for Research on Evaluation, Standards, and Student Testing, University of California, Los Angeles, 2011.)
45. Ibid., iii.
46. Ibid., 50.
47. Interview with author on March 11, 2009.
48. Interview with author on March 9, 2009.
49. Interview with author on March 11, 2009.
50. Tamar Galatzan, "Making Charters Measure Up," *Los Angeles Times*, November 14, 2008.
51. Interview with author on July 27, 2010.
52. http://notebook.lausd.net/pls/ptl/docs/PAGE/CA_LAUSD/FLDR_ORGANIZATIONS/FLDR_INSTRUCTIONAL_SVCS/CHARTER_SCHOOLS_DIVISION/SCHOOL_DIRECTORY/CHARTER_SCHOOL_DISTRICT_POLICY/POLICY%20ON%20CHARTER%20SCHOOL%20AUTHORIZING%20_LAUSD_%20-%20REVISED%2002-07-12.PDF, 2.
53. www.crpe.org/cs/crpe/download/csr_files/res_portf_district-charter_compact_la_dec10.pdf.
54. Initially, a third operator—the Alliance—was also involved in the transformation plan, but the Alliance was not included in the final plan: www.jordanbulldogs.org/; www.partnershipla.org/system/storage/3/c3/7/441/2011.04.27_-_board_meeting_-_attach_b._ii._-_jordan_hs.pdf.

55. Alexander Russo, *Stray Dogs, Saints, and Saviors: Fighting for the Soul of America's Toughest High School* (San Francisco, CA: Jossey-Bass, 2011).

56. Prospective respondents were contacted in two ways. First, I contacted individuals by e-mail and provided a link to an online survey. Second, for nonrespondents to the online survey, as well as individuals for whom no e-mail address was available, I distributed paper surveys by mail. A copy of the survey is included in Appendix D.

57. Advocacy organizations claim to represent a broader group in the community, such as a neighborhood, a racial or ethnic group, or a particular issue position, such as improving the quality of the high school curriculum. Nonprofits primarily offer a service, such as professional development.

58. Compared with New York, the response rates by subgroup varied more widely in Los Angeles. The highest response rate was nonprofit service providers at 62 percent. Other groups with relatively high response rates included LAUSD officials, 54 percent; advocacy organizations, 53 percent; and charter management organizations, 50 percent. Two groups had a considerably lower response rate, 25 percent for both unions and the board of education.

59. Stephen P. Borgatti, Martin G. Everett, and Linton C. Freeman, *Ucinet for Windows: Software for Social Network Analysis* (Cambridge, MA: Harvard, 2002); Stephen P. Borgatti, *NetDraw: Graph Visualization Software* (Cambridge, MA: Harvard, 2002).

60. The survey asked respondents to identify their organizational affiliations relevant to K-12 education in Los Angeles, as well as their "main affiliation."

61. *Outdegree centrality* is a measure of the number of paths from one node to other nodes in the network.

62. Stephen P. Borgatti and Martin G. Everett, "Models of Core/Periphery Structures," *Social Networks* 21, 4(2000): 375–395.

63. Interview with author on March 11, 2009.

64. Howard Blume, "Once-Mighty UTLA Loses Political Muscle," *Los Angeles Times*, February 18, 2011.

65. Ibid.

66. Stephen Ceasar, "L.A. Unified Board Games," *Los Angeles Times*, March 9, 2012.

67. Respondents who answered "no opinion" were excluded from the analysis.

68. Density, the ratio of observed ties over possible ties in a network, provides additional basis for comparison. The density of the New York City community network is 0.021; the density of the Los Angeles community network is 0.034.

69. Though there have been occasional reversals of decentralization, particularly under Superintendent Roy Romer in the early 2000s.

70. www.huffingtonpost.com/charles-kerchner/ray-cortines-birthday-pre_b_664394.html.

71. Douglas D. Ready, Valerie E. Lee, and Kevin G. Welner, "Educational Equity and School Structure: School Size, Overcrowding, and Schools-within-Schools," *Teachers College Record* 106, 10(2004): 1989–2014.

72. Ryan Vaillancourt, "Power Play Erupts at $232 Million Arts School," *Los Angeles Downtown News*, March 27, 2009; Fuller, "Palace Revolt in Los Angeles?"

73. Fuller, "Palace Revolt in Los Angeles?"

74. David Zahniser and Joel Rubin. "Mayor Spent Millions on School Board Races," *Los Angeles Times*, August 1, 2007.

75. Interview with author on July 27, 2010.

76. Interview with author on July 27, 2010.

77. http://notebook.lausd.net/pls/ptl/docs/PAGE/CA_LAUSD/LAUSDNET/RESOURCES/VOLUNTEER_PAGE/SCHOOL_OF_CHOICE/PUBLIC%20SCHOOL%20CHOICE%20MOTION%208-25-09.PDF.

78. Fuller, "Palace Revolt in Los Angeles?"

79. Interview with author on July 27, 2010.

80. Connie Llanos, "Charter Schools Win Out in Latest Round of Reform Effort," *Los Angeles Daily News*, March 15, 2011.

81. www.data.ed.gov/grants/investing-in-innovation/applicant/14645.
82. http://4teachingexcellence.org/.
83. Howard Blume, "L.A. Unified Hires Gates Foundation Official as Deputy Superintendent," *Los Angeles Times*, June 23, 2010.
84. www.broadacademy.org/.
85. http://publicschoolchoice.lausd.net/sites/default/files/PCS1%203.0%20CHANGE.PDF.
86. www.scpr.org/programs/airtalk/2011/10/27/21141/lausd-contract.
87. http://publicschoolchoice.lausd.net/sites/default/files/UTLA-LAUSD%20TA.pdf.
88. Ibid.
89. Interview with the author on February 24, 2012.
90. http://scholasticadministrator.typepad.com/thisweekineducation/2011/12/lausd-utla-reach-agreement-granting-wider-autonomy-to-all-schools-on-teacher-placement-and-budgets-893-kpccthe-los-angel.html.
91. www.huffingtonpost.com/ama-nyamekye/la-teachers-contract_b_1200380.html.
92. Howard Blume, "New Teacher Contract Could Shut Down School Choice Program," *Los Angeles Times*, December 11, 2011.
93. Albert O. Hirschman, *Exit, Voice, and Loyalty: Responses to Decline in Firms, Organizations, and States* (Cambridge, MA: Harvard University Press 1970).
94. http://dontholdusback.org/.
95. Patashnik, *Reforms at Risk*.
96. Ibid., 168.
97. Interview with author on March 11, 2009.
98. www.cocosouthla.org/node/387.
99. Interview with author on March 11, 2009.
100. http://innercitystruggle.org/section/view/new_schools.
101. www.laprogressive.com/innercity-school/.
102. www.utla.net/node/2687.
103. Fuller, "Palace Revolt in Los Angeles?" 28.
104. www.newtla.com/index.html.
105. http://blogs.laweekly.com/informer/2011/03/warren_fletcher_wins_utla_elec.php.
106. www.newtla.com/index.html.
107. Howard Blume, "Whistle Blowing Teachers to Open a Charter School," *Los Angeles Times*, January 18, 2012.
108. Steve Lopez, "Will the Real A. J. Duffy Please Speak Up?" *Los Angeles Times*, September 7, 2011.
109. www.nctq.org/tr3/consulting/docs/nctq_lausd_06–07–2011.pdf.
110. Hillel Aron, "Progressives Find Religion on LAUSD Reform," *LA Weekly*, October 27, 2011.
111. Interview with author, March 23, 2012.
112. www.huffingtonpost.com/charles-kerchner/bringing-a-third-chair-to_b_1018083.html.
113. http://dontholdusback.org/wp-content/uploads/board-letter-10–18–11.pdf;   www.huffingtonpost.com/charles-kerchner/bringing-a-third-chair-to_b_1018083.html.
114. Personal correspondence with author, March 20, 2012.
115. Maria Brenes, personal correspondence with author, March 20, 2012.
116. Interview with author, March 23, 2012.
117. www.huffingtonpost.com/charles-kerchner/bringing-a-third-chair-to_b_1018083.html.
118. Mark Blythe, "Studying Educational Systems with the Tools of Institutional Theory," in *The Transformation of Great American School Districts: How Big Cities Are Reshaping Public Education*, eds. William L. Boyd, Charles T. Kerchner, and Mark Blyth (Cambridge, MA: Harvard Education Press, 2008).

Chapter 6

1. Chris Ansell, Sarah Reckhow, and Andrew Kelly, "How to Reform a Reform Coalition: Outreach, Agenda Expansion, and Brokerage in Urban School Reform," *Policy Studies Journal*

37 (2009): 717–743; Sarah Reckhow, "Disseminating and Legitimating a New Approach: The Role of Foundations," in *Between Public and Private: Politics, Governance, and the New Portfolio Models for Urban School Reform*, eds. Katrina E. Bulkey, Jeffrey R. Henig, and Henry M. Levin (Cambridge, MA: Harvard Education Press, 2010).

2. Joanne Barkan, "Got Dough? How Billionaires Rule Our Schools," *Dissent*, Winter (2011); Sam Dillon, "Behind Grass-Roots Advocacy, Bill Gates," *New York Times*, May 21, 2011; Ann Doss Helms, "Who's the Power behind CMS?" *Charlotte Observer*, May 11, 2011; Thomas Goldsmith and Hui T. Keung, "L.A. Billionaire's Money and Ideas May Leave Mark in Wake," [Raleigh, NC] *News & Observer*, April 3, 2011.

3. Jeffrey R. Henig and Clarence Stone, "Rethinking School Reform: The Distractions of Dogma and the Potential for a New Politics of Progressive Pragmatism," *American Journal of Education* 114, 3(2008): 206.

4. Andrea L. Campbell, *How Policies Make Citizens: Senior Political Activism and the American Welfare State* (Princeton, NJ: Princeton University Press, 2003); Eric M. Patashnik, *Reforms at Risk: What Happens after Major Policy Changes Are Enacted* (Princeton, NJ: Princeton University Press, 2008).

5. Patashnik, *Reforms at Risk.*

6. Elaine Sharp, *Does Local Government Matter? How Urban Policies Shape Civic Engagement* (Minneapolis: University of Minnesota Press, 2012); Elaine Sharp, "Local Government, Social Programs, and Political Participation: A Test of Policy-Centered Theory," *State & Local Government Review* 41, 3(2009): 182–192; Margaret Weir, Jane Rongerude, and Christopher K. Ansell, "Collaboration Is Not Enough: Virtuous Cycles of Reform in Transportation Policy," *Urban Affairs Review* 44, 4(2009): 455–489.

7. Nick Anderson, "Gates Foundation Gives $335 Million for Teacher Effectiveness," *Washington Post*, November 20, 2009.

8. Steven M. Teles and Mark Schmitt, "The Elusive Craft of Evaluating Advocacy," *Stanford Social Innovation Review*, Summer (2011).

9. Anne Schneider and Helen Ingram, *Policy Design for Democracy* (Lawrence: University of Kansas Press, 1997); Campbell, *How Policies Make Citizens*; Suzanne Mettler and Joe Soss, "The Consequences of Public Policy for Democratic Citizenship: Bridging Policy Studies and Mass Politics," *Perspectives on Politics* 2, 1(2004): 55–73.

10. David Nakamura, "Fenty Gets School Reform Tips from Bloomberg," *Washington Post*, October 17, 2006, B4.

11. Mike Debonis, "Fund and Games," *Washington City Paper*, March 4, 2009.

12. Ibid.

13. www.saveourschoolsdc.org/coalitionstatement.html.

14. Bill Turque, "Poll: Polarizing D.C. Schools Chief Rhee Helps, Hurts Fenty among Democrats," *Washington Post*, September 1, 2010.

15. Bill Turque, "Rhee Feeling 'Guilt' over Fenty Loss," *Washington Post*, September 15, 2010; Nikita Stewart and Paul Schwartzman, "How Adrian Fenty Lost His Reelection Bid for D.C. Mayor," *Washington Post*, September 16, 2010.

16. Ansell et al., "How to Reform a Reform Coalition."

17. Joe Williams, *National Model or Temporary Opportunity? The Oakland Education Reform Story* (Washington, DC: Center for Education Reform, 2007): 3–4.

18. Ansell et al., "How to Reform a Reform Coalition."

19. Ibid.," 736.

20. Katy Murphy, "Oakland School District: Is It Better Off after the State Takeover?" *Oakland Tribune*, March 26, 2010.

21. Katy Murphy, "Oakland's Small Schools Movement, 10 Years Later," *Oakland Tribune*, May 5, 2009.

22. www.gopublicschools.org/.

23. Annie E. Casey Foundation, *The Path of Most Resistance: Reflections on Lessons Learned from New Futures* (Baltimore, MD: Annie E. Casey Foundation, 1993), 15.

24. Reckhow, "Disseminating and Legitimating a New Approach."

25. *Annual Report Eli and Edythe Broad Foundation*, 2009–2010, www.broadfoundation.org/asset/101–2009.10%20annual%20report.pdf (September 30, 2009), 5.

26. http://blogs.edweek.org/edweek/campaign-k-12/2009/03/do_all_ed_dept_roads_lead_to_g.html.

27. www.ed.gov/news/pressreleases/2009/05/05192009c.html.

28. http://blogs.edweek.org/edweek/campaign-k-12/2009/03/arne_duncan_advocates_mayoral.html.

29. http://dashboard.publiccharters.org/node/742.

30. www.educationgadfly.net/flypaper/2009/03/oii-lives/.

31. Patrick McGuinn, "Creating Cover and Constructing Capacity: Assessing the Origins, Evolution, and Impact of Race to the Top," in *Education Stimulus Watch, Special Report 6* (Washington, DC: American Enterprise Institute, 2010): 3.

32. Sam Dillon, "After Complaints, Gates Foundation Opens Education Aid Offer to All States," *New York Times*, October 28, 2009, A19.

33. Ibid.

34. www.gatesfoundation.org/press-releases/Pages/investing-in-innovation-i3-fund-launch-100429.aspx.

35. Dillon, "Behind Grass-Roots Advocacy"; Erik W. Robelen, "Gates Learns to Think Big," *Education Week* 11, 2006.

36. I discuss the growing convergence between the philanthropic agenda and federal education policy in "Disseminating and Legitimating a New Approach: The Role of Foundations."

37. Data downloaded from the National Center for Education Statistics, http://nces.ed.gov/.

38. Frederick M. Hess, *Spinning Wheels: The Politics of Urban School Reform* (Washington, DC: Brookings Institution Press, 1998): 5.

39. Howard Blume, "Los Angeles Unified Board Hires Five Key Administrators at Deasy's Request," *Los Angeles Times*, April 27, 2011; Jennifer Mrozowski, "DPS Manager to Earn $344K," *Detroit News*, March 3, 2009.

40. Joel L. Fleishman, *The Foundation: How Private Wealth Is Changing the World* (New York: Public Affairs, 2009).

Appendix A

1. *Source*: Data downloaded from the Foundation Center.

2. I was unable to locate a tax return for this foundation.

Appendix C

1. www.edweek.org/apps/maps/.

2. Jeffrey R. Henig and Wilbur C. Rich, "Mayor-Centrism in Context," in *Mayors in the Middle: Politics, Race, and Mayoral Control of Urban Schools*, eds. Jeffrey R. Henig and Wilbur C. Rich (Princeton, NJ: Princeton University Press, 2004); Kenneth K. Wong and Francis X. Shen, "When Mayors Lead Urban Schools: Toward Developing a Framework to Assess the Effects of Mayoral Takeover of Urban Districts" (Paper presented at the annual meeting of the American Political Science Association, Philadelphia, August 27, 2003); Kenneth K. Wong, Francis X. Shen, Dorothea Anagnostopoulos, and Stacey Rutledge, *The Education Mayor: Improving America's Schools* (Washington, DC: Georgetown University Press, 2007).

3. Frederick M. Hess and Coby Loup, *The Leadership Limbo: Teacher Labor Agreements in America's Fifty Largest School Districts* (Washington, DC: Thomas B. Fordham Institute, 2008).

4. Peter K. Eisinger and Richard C. Hula, "Gunslinger School Administrators: Nontraditional Leadership in Urban School Systems in the United States," *Urban Education* 39, 6(2004): 621–637.

REFERENCES

Aksartova, Sada. "In Search of Legitimacy: Peace Grant Making of U.S. Philanthropic Foundations, 1988–1996." *Nonprofit and Voluntary Sector Quarterly* 32, 1 (2003): 25–46.

Anderson, Nick. "Gates Foundation Gives $335 Million for Teacher Effectiveness." *Washington Post*, November 20, 2009.

Annie E. Casey Foundation. *The Path of Most Resistance: Reflections on Lessons Learned from New Futures*. Baltimore: Annie E. Casey Foundation, 1993.

Annual Report Bill & Melinda Gates Foundation. 2000. www.gatesfoundation.org/annualreport/Pages/annual-reports.aspx.

Annual Report Bill & Melinda Gates Foundation. 2003. www.gatesfoundation.org/annualreport/Pages/annual-reports.aspx.

Annual Report Bill & Melinda Gates Foundation. 2004. www.gatesfoundation.org/annualreport/Pages/annual-reports.aspx.

Annual Report Bill & Melinda Gates Foundation. 2007. www.gatesfoundation.org/annualreport/Pages/annual-reports.aspx.

Annual Report Eli and Edythe Broad Foundation. 2008. www.broadfoundation.org/asset/101–124--2008tbfsannualreportfinal.pdf.

Annual Report Eli and Edythe Broad Foundation. 2009–2010. www.broadfoundation.org/asset/101–2009.10%20annual%20report.pdf.

Ansell, Chris, Sarah Reckhow, and Andrew Kelly. "How to Reform a Reform Coalition: Outreach, Agenda Expansion, and Brokerage in Urban School Reform." *Policy Studies Journal* 37 (2009): 717–743.

Aron, Hillel. "Progressives Find Religion on LAUSD Reform." *LA Weekly*, October 27, 2011.

Augustine, Catherine H., Diane Epstein, and Mirka Vuollo. *Governing Urban School Districts: Efforts in Los Angeles to Effect Change*. Santa Monica, CA: RAND, 2006.

Barbaro, Michael, Sharon Otterman, and Javier Hernandez. "After 3 Months, Mayor Replaces Schools Leader." *New York Times*, April 8, 2011, A1.

Barkan, Joanne. "Got Dough? How Billionaires Rule Our Schools." *Dissent*, Winter (2011).

Barrett, Beth. "Insiders vs. Charters at LAUSD." *LA Weekly*, March 11, 2010.

Bartley, Tim. "How Foundations Shape Social Movements: The Construction of an Organizational Field and the Rise of Forest Certification." *Social Problems* 54, 3(2007): 229–255.

Bell, Terrel H. *The Thirteenth Man*. New York: Free Press, 1988.

Berkman, Michael B., and Eric Plutzer. *Ten Thousand Democracies: Politics and Public Opinion in America's School Districts*. Washington, DC: Georgetown University Press, 2005.

Bloom, Howard S., Saskia Levy Thompson, and Rebecca Unterman. *Transforming the High School Experience: How New York City's Small Schools Are Boosting Student Achievement and Graduation Rates*. New York: MDRC, 2010.

Blume, Howard. "L.A. Unified Hires Gates Foundation Official as Deputy Superintendent." *Los Angeles Times*, June 23, 2010.

Blume, Howard. "Los Angeles Unified Board Hires Five Key Administrators at Deasy's Request." *Los Angeles Times*, April 27, 2011.

Blume, Howard. "New Teacher Contract Could Shut Down School Choice Program." *Los Angeles Times*, December 11, 2011.

Blume, Howard. "Once-Mighty UTLA Loses Political Muscle." *Los Angeles Times*, February 18, 2011.

Blume, Howard. "Parents Are Urged to Demand More from L.A. Schools." *Los Angeles Times*, May 11, 2009.

Blume, Howard. "Whistle Blowing Teachers to Open a Charter School." *Los Angeles Times*, January 18, 2012.

Blyth, Mark. "Studying Educational Systems with the Tools of Institutional Theory." In *The Transformation of Great American School Districts: How Big Cities Are Reshaping Public Education*, eds. William L. Boyd, Charles T. Kerchner, and Mark Blyth. Cambridge, MA: Harvard Education Press, 2008.

Boghossian, Naush. "Lessons to LEARN in Reform of LAUSD?" *Los Angeles Daily News*, July 30, 2006.

Borgatti, Stephen P. *NetDraw: Graph Visualization Software*. Cambridge, MA: Harvard, 2002.

Borgatti, Stephen P., and Martin G. Everett. "Models of Core/Periphery Structures." *Social Networks* 21, 4(2000): 375–395.

Borgatti, Stephen P., Martin G. Everett, and Linton C. Freeman. *Ucinet for Windows: Software for Social Network Analysis*. Cambridge, MA: Harvard, 2002.

Bradley, Ann. "Uneasy Alliance Marks Launch of L.A. Plan." *Education Week*, April 11, 1990.

Briggs, Xavier de Souza. *Democracy as Problem Solving: Civic Capacity in Communities across the Globe*. Cambridge, MA: MIT Press, 2008.

Bulkley, Katrina E. "Introduction: Portfolio Management Models in Urban School Reform." In *Between Public and Private: Politics, Governance, and the New Portfolio Models for Urban School Reform*, eds. Katrina E. Bulkey, Jeffrey R. Henig, and Henry M. Levin. Cambridge, MA: Harvard Education Press, 2010.

Burch, Patricia. "Convergence or Collision: Portfolio Districts, Education Markets, and Federal Education Policy." In *Between Public and Private: Politics, Governance, and the New Portfolio Models for Urban School Reform*, eds. Katrina E. Bulkey, Jeffrey R. Henig, and Henry M. Levin. Cambridge, MA: Harvard Education Press, 2010.

Campanile, Carl. "Gates' $4 Million Lesson: Aided School Control." *New York Post*, August 18, 2009.

Campbell, Andrea L. *How Policies Make Citizens: Senior Political Activism and the American Welfare State*. Princeton, NJ: Princeton University Press, 2003.

Castro, Tony. "Eli Broad Has Made His Mark on L.A." *Los Angeles Daily News*, October 20, 2007.

Cavanagh, Sean. "U.S. Common-Standards Push Bares Unsettled Issues." *Education Week*, January 14, 2010.

Ceasar, Stephen. "L.A. Unified Board Games." *Los Angeles Times*, March 9, 2012.

Cervone, Barbara. "When Reach Exceeds Grasp: Taking the Annenberg Challenge to Scale." In *Reconnecting Education and Foundations*, eds. Ray Bacchetti and Thomas Ehrlich. San Francisco, CA: Jossey-Bass, 2007.

Chambers, Stefanie. *Mayors and Schools: Minority Voices and Democratic Tensions in Urban Education*. Philadelphia: Temple University Press, 2006.

Chan, Sewell. "Mayor Announces Plan for Teacher Merit Pay." *New York Times*, October 17, 2007.

Chubb, John E., and Terry M. Moe. *Politics, Markets and America's Schools*. Washington, DC: Brookings Institution Press, 1990.

Chun, Tammi, Gail Zellman, and Brian Stecher. *An Evaluation Strategy Developed by RAND for the Broad Foundation*. Santa Monica, CA: RAND, 2001.

Clemens, Elisabeth S., and Linda C. Lee. "Catalysts for Change: Foundations and School Reform 1950–2005." In *American Foundations: Roles and Contributions*, eds. Helmut Anheier and David C. Hammack. Washington, DC: Brookings Institution Press, 2010.

Cohen, David K., and Susan L. Moffitt. *The Ordeal of Equality: Did Federal Regulation Fix the Schools?* Cambridge, MA: Harvard University Press, 2009.

Colvin, Richard L. "A New Generation of Philanthropists and Their Great Ambitions." In *With the Best of Intentions: How Philanthropy Is Reshaping K-12 Education*, ed. Frederick M. Hess. Cambridge, MA: Harvard Education Press, 2005.

Larry Cuban, "Educational Entrepreneurs Redux." In *Educational Entrepreneurship: Realities, Challenges, Possibilities*. Cambridge, MA: Harvard Education Press, 2006.

Cuban, Larry. "Foreward." In *Between Public and Private: Politics, Governance, and the New Portfolio Models for Urban School Reform*, eds. Katrina E. Bulkey, Jeffrey R. Henig, and Henry M. Levin. Cambridge, MA: Harvard Education Press, 2010.

Dahl, Robert A. *Who Governs? Democracy and Power in an American City*. New Haven, CT: Yale University Press, 1961.

DeBonis, Mike. "Fund and Games." *Washington City Paper*, March 4, 2009.

Dianda, Marcella R., and Ronald Corwin. *Vision and Reality: A First-Year Look at California's Charter Schools*. Los Alamitos, CA: Southwest Regional Laboratory, 1994.

Dillon, Sam. "After Complaints, Gates Foundation Opens Education Aid Offer to All States." *New York Times*, October 28, 2009, A19.

Dillon, Sam. "Behind Grass-Roots Advocacy, Bill Gates." *New York Times*, May 21, 2011.

Dillon, Sam. "U.S. Effort to Reshape Schools Faces Challange." *New York Times*, June 2, 2009, A15.

Domanico, Raymond. "A Small Footprint on the Nation's Largest School System." In *Can Philanthropy Fix Our Schools? Appraising Walter Annenberg's $500 Million Dollar Gift to Public Education*. Washington, DC: Thomas B. Fordham Foundation, 2000.

Edelman, Josh. "Portfolio Management Models: From the Practitioner's Eyes." In *Between Public and Private: Politics, Governance, and the New Portfolio Models for Urban School Reform*, eds. Katrina E. Bulkey, Jeffrey R. Henig, and Henry M. Levin. Cambridge, MA: Harvard Education Press, 2010.

Eisinger, Peter K., and Richard C. Hula. "Gunslinger School Administrators: Nontraditional Leadership in Urban School Systems in the United States." *Urban Education* 39, 6(2004): 621–637.

Empty Promises: A Case Study of Restructuring and the Exclusion of English Language Learners in Two Brooklyn High Schools. New York: Advocates for Children of New York and the Asian American Legal Defense and Education Fund, 2009.

Fenno, Richard F., and Frank J. Munger. *National Politics and Federal Aid to Education*. Syracuse, NY: Syracuse University Press, 1962.

Ferris, James M. "Foundations and Pubic Policymaking: Leveraging Philanthropic Dollars, Knowledge, and Networks." Los Angeles: University of Southern California Center on Philanthropy and Public Policy, 2003.

Ferris, James M., Guilbert C. Hentschke, and Hilary J. Harmssen. Philanthropic Strategies for School Reform: An Analysis of Foundation Choices. *Educational Policy* 22, 5(2008): 705–730.

Fields-Meyer, Thomas. "Black vs. Brown at L.A. School." *Time*, May 15, 2008.

Final Report of the Evaluation of New York Networks for School Renewal. New York: New York University Institute for Education and Social Policy, 2001.

Finn, Chester E., and Kelly Amis. *Making It Count: A Guide to High Impact Education Philanthropy*. Washington, DC: Thomas B. Fordham Foundation, 2001.

Finn, Chester E., and Marci Kanstoroom. "Afterword: Lessons from the Annenberg Challenge." In *Can Philanthropy Fix Our Schools?: Appraising Walter Annenberg's $500 Million Gift to Public Education*. Washington, DC: Thomas B. Fordham Foundation, 2000.

Fiske, Edward B. "States Gain Wider Influence on School Policy." *New York Times*, December 2, 1984.

Fleishman, Joel L. *The Foundation: How Private Wealth Is Changing the World*. New York: Public Affairs, 2009.

Fliegel, Seymour. *Miracle in East Harlem: The Fight for Choice in Public Education*. New York: Times Books, 1993.

Fruchter, Norm. "'Plus Ca Change . . .': Mayoral Control in New York City." In *The Transformation of Great American School Districts: How Big Cities Are Reshaping Public Education*, eds. William L. Boyd, Charles T. Kerchner, and Mark Blyth. Cambridge, MA: Harvard Education Press, 2008.

Frumkin, Peter. "Inside Venture Philanthropy." *Society* 40, 4(2003): 7–15.

Fryer, Roland G. "Financial Incentives and Student Achievement: Evidence from Randomized Trials." NBER Working Paper 15898, 2010.

Fuller, Bruce. "Palace Revolt in Los Angeles?" *Education Next* (2010): 20–28.

Gabor, Andrea. "Leadership Principles for Public School Principals." *Strategy + Business*, March 23, 2005.

Galatzan, Tamar. "Making Charters Measure Up." *Los Angeles Times*, November 14, 2008.

Goertz, Margaret E. *State Educational Standards in the 50 States: An Update*. Princeton, NJ: Princeton Educational Testing Service, 1988.

Goldsmith, Thomas, and Hui T. Keung. "L.A. Billionaire's Money and Ideas May Leave Mark in Wake." [Raleigh, NC] *News & Observer*, April 3, 2011.

Gonen, Yoav. "Can't Buy Me Good Grades." *New York Daily News*, April 9, 2010.

Gonzalez, Juan. "Eva Moskowitz Has Special Access to Schools Chancellor Klein—and Support Others Can Only Dream Of." *New York Daily News*, February 25, 2010.

Goodman, Sarena, and Lesley Turner. "Teacher Incentive Pay and Educational Outcomes: Evidence from the NYC Bonus Program." Cambridge, MA: Harvard Kennedy School of Government Program on Education Policy and Governance Working Paper Series, 2010.

Goodnough, Abby. "Fixing the Schools." *New York Times*, October 4, 2002, B3.

Gootman, Elissa. "Mixed Results on Paying City Students to Pass Tests." *New York Times*, August 19, 2008.

Gootman, Elissa. "Taught to Be Principals, and Now Facing the Test." *New York Times*, September 8, 2004.

Gootman, Elissa. "Teachers Agree to Bonus Pay Tied to Scores." *New York Times*, October 18, 2007, A1.

Gordon, Jane Anna. *Why They Couldn't Wait*. New York: RoutledgeFalmer, 2001.

Grantmakers for Education. *Benchmarking 2010: Trends in Education Philanthropy*. Portland, OR: Grantmakers for Education, 2010.

Green, Elizabeth. "MBA Invasion." *Scholastic Administrator*, January 2009.

Greene, Jay P. "Buckets into the Sea: Why Philanthropy Isn't Changing Schools, and How It Could." In *With the Best of Intentions: How Philanthropy is Reshaping K-12 Education*, ed. Frederick M. Hess. Cambridge, MA: Harvard Education Press, 2005.

Helfand, Duke, and Howard Blume. "Mayor Gets $50 Million for Schools." *Los Angeles Times*, September 27, 2007.

Helms, Ann Doss. "Who's the Power behind CMS?" *Charlotte Observer*, May 11, 2011.

Hemphill, Clara (with Pamela Wheaton and Jacquelyn Wayans). *New York City's Best Public High Schools: A Parents' Guide*. New York: Teachers College Press, 2003.

Hemphill, Clara, and Kim Nauer (with Helen Zelon and Thomas Jacobs). *The New Marketplace: How Small School Reforms and School Choice Have Reshaped New York City's High Schools*. New York: The New School Center for New York City Affairs, 2009.

Hemphill, Clara, and Kim Nauer (with Thomas Jacobs, Alessandra Raimondi, Sharon McCloskey, and Rajeev Yerneni). *Managing by the Numbers: Empowerment and Accountability in New York City's Schools*. New York: The New School Center for New York City Affairs, 2010.

Hendrie, Caroline. "Plan to Lop Off 200,000 Students from L.A. Unveiled." *Education Week*, April 16, 1997.

Henig, Jeffrey R. "Mayors, Governors, and Presidents: The New Education Executives and the End of Educational Exceptionalism." *Peabody Journal of Education* 84, 3(2009): 283–289.

Henig, Jeffrey R. "Portfolio Management Models and the Political Economy of Contracting Regimes." In *Between Public and Private: Politics, Governance, and the New Portfolio Models for Urban School Reform*, eds. Katrina E. Bulkey, Jeffrey R. Henig, and Henry M. Levin. Cambridge, MA: Harvard Education Press, 2010.

Henig, Jeffrey R. *Spin Cycle: How Research Is Used in Policy Debates*. New York: Russell Sage Foundation, 2008.

Henig, Jeffrey R., Eva Gold, Marion Orr, Megan Silander, and Elaine Simon. "Parent and Community Engagement in NYC and the Sustainability Challenge for Urban Education Reform." Prepared for the New York City Education Reform Retrospective Project, 2010.

Henig, Jeffrey R., Richard C. Hula, Marion Orr, and Desiree S. Pedescleaux. *The Color of School Reform: Race, Politics, and the Challenge of Urban Education.* Princeton, NJ: Princeton University Press, 2001.

Henig, Jeffrey R., and Wilbur C. Rich. "Mayor-Centrism in Context." In *Mayors in the Middle: Politics, Race, and Mayoral Control of Urban Schools,* eds. Jeffrey R. Henig and Wilbur C. Rich. Princeton, NJ: Princeton University Press, 2004.

Henig, Jeffrey R., and Clarence Stone. "Rethinking School Reform: The Distractions of Dogma and the Potential for a New Politics of Progressive Pragmatism." *American Journal of Education* 114, 3(2008): 191–218.

Herman, Joan L., and Eva L. Baker. *The Los Angeles Annenberg Metropolitan Project: Evaluation Findings.* Los Angeles: Los Angeles Compact for Evaluation, University of California, Los Angeles, 2003.

Herman, Joan L., Jordan Rickles, Mark Hansen, Larry Thomas, Alice Gualpa, and Jia Wang. *Evaluation of Green Dot's Locke Transformation Project: Findings from the 2007–08, 2008–09, and 2009–10 School Years.* Los Angeles: National Center for Research on Evaluation, Standards, and Student Testing, University of California, Los Angeles, 2011.

Hernandez, Javier C. "New Effort Aims to Test Theories of Education." *New York Times,* September 24, 2008, B6.

Herszenshorn, David. "Bloomberg Wins on School Tests after Firing Foes." *New York Times,* March 16, 2004, A1.

Hess, Frederick M. *Assessing the Case for Mayoral Control of Urban Schools.* Washington, DC: American Enterprise Institute, 2008.

Hess, Frederick M. *The Future of Educational Entrepreneurship: Possibilities for School Reform.* Cambridge, MA: Harvard Education Press, 2008.

Hess, Frederick M. "Introduction." In *With the Best Intentions: How Philanthropy Is Reshaping K-12 Education,* ed. Frederick M. Hess. Cambridge, MA: Harvard Education Press, 2005.

Hess, Frederick M. "Rethinking America's Schools: Frederick M. Hess Responds." *Philanthropy* 23/24 (2005).

Hess, Frederick M. *The Same Thing Over and Over: How School Reformers Get Stuck in Yesterday's Ideas.* Cambridge, MA: Harvard University Press, 2010.

Hess, Frederick M. *Spinning Wheels: The Politics of Urban School Reform.* Washington, DC: Brookings Institution Press, 1998.

Hess, Frederick M. "Weighing the Case for School Boards: Today and Tomorrow." *Phi Delta Kappan* 91, 6(2010): 15–19.

Hess, Frederick M., and Coby Loup. *The Leadership Limbo: Teacher Labor Agreements in America's Fifty Largest School Districts.* Washington, DC: Thomas B. Fordham Institute, 2008.

Higgins, Monica, Wendy Robbins, Jennie Weiner, and Frederick Hess. "Creating a Corps of Change Agents." *Education Next* 11, 3(2011).

Hill, Paul. *Reinventing Public Education.* Santa Monica, CA: RAND Institute on Education and Training, 1995.

Hirschman, Albert O. *Exit, Voice, and Loyalty: Responses to Decline in Firms, Organizations, and States.* Cambridge, MA: Harvard University Press, 1970.

Hoff, David. "New Coalition to Lobby for Changes in NCLB's Provisions on Tutoring." *Education Week,* May 23, 2007.

Hoffman, Nancy, and Robert Schwartz. "Foundations and School Reform: Bridging the Cultural Divide." In *Reconnecting Education and Foundations,* eds. Ray Bacchetti and Thomas Ehrlich. San Fransisco, CA: Jossey-Bass, 2007.

Honig, Meredith. "'External' Organizations and the Politics of Urban Educational Leadership: The Case of New Small Autonomous School Initiatives." *Peabody Journal of Education* 84, 3(2009): 394–413.

Hornbeck, Mark. "Duncan Challenges Mayor to Fix DPS." *Detroit News*, February 27, 2009.

"How Many Billionaires Does It Take to Fix a School System?" *New York Times Magazine*, March 9, 2008.

Jenkins, Craig J. "Channeling Social Protest: Foundation Patronage of Contemporary Social Movements." In *Private Action and Public Good*, eds. Walter W. Powell and Elisabeth S. Clemens. New Haven, CT: Yale University Press, 1998.

Jenkins, Lynn, and Donald R. McAdams. "Philanthropy and Urban School District Reform: Lessons from Charlotte, Houston, and San Diego." In *With the Best Intentions: How Philanthropy Is Reshaping K-12 Education*, ed. Frederick M. Hess. Cambridge, MA: Harvard Education Press, 2005.

Kahlenberg, Richard D. "Ocean Hill–Brownsville, 40 Years Later." *Chronicle Review*, April 25, 2008.

Kane, Pearl R. "The Difference between Charter Schools and Charterlike Schools." In *City Schools: Lessons from New York*, eds. Diane Ravitch and Joseph P. Viteritti. Baltimore, MD: Johns Hopkins University Press, 2000.

Kerchner, Charles T., David J. Menefee-Libey, and Laura S. Mulfinger. "Comparing the Progressive Model and Contemporary Formative Ideas and Trends." In *The Transformation of Great American School Districts: How Big Cities Are Reshaping Public Education*, eds. William L. Boyd, Charles T. Kerchner, and Mark Blyth. Cambridge, MA: Harvard Education Press, 2008.

Kerchner, Charles T., David J. Menefee-Libey, Laura S. Mulfinger, and Stephanie E. Clayton. *Learning from L.A.: Institutional Change in American Public Education*. Cambridge, MA: Harvard Education Press, 2008.

Kingdon, John W. *Agendas, Alternatives, and Public Policies*. Boston: Little, Brown, 1984.

Klonsky, Michael, and Susan Klonsky. *Small Schools: Public School Reform Meets the Ownership Society*. New York: Routledge, 2008.

Kolodner, Meredith. "United Federation of Teachers Sues in Effort to Block Closure of 19 City Schools." *New York Daily News*, February 1, 2010.

Krackhardt, David, and Robert N. Stern. "Informal Networks and Organizational Crises: An Experimental Simulation." *Social Psychology Quarterly* 51, 2(1988): 123–140.

Lagemann, Ellen C. *The Politics of Knowledge: The Carnegie Corporation, Philanthropy, and Public Policy*. Chicago: University of Chicago Press, 1989.

Lake, Robin, Brianna Dusseault, Melissa Bowen, Allison Demerritt, and Paul Hill. *The National Study of Charter Management Organization (CMO) Effectiveness: Report on Interim Findings*. Princeton, NJ: Mathematica Policy Research and the Center on Reinventing Public Education, 2010.

Llanos, Connie. "Charter Schools Win Out in Latest Round of Reform Effort." *Los Angeles Daily News*, March 15, 2011.

Llanos, Connie. "Charters, LAUSD in Special Ed Tug of War." *Los Angeles Daily News*, January 6, 2010.

"Locke High School's Progress." *Los Angeles Times*, December 1, 2008.

Lopez, Steve. "Seniority, Not Quality, Counts Most at United Teachers Los Angeles." *Los Angeles Times*, March 25, 2009.

Lopez, Steve. "Will the Real A. J. Duffy Please Speak Up?" *Los Angeles Times*, September 7, 2011.

Manna, Paul. "Leaving No Child Behind." In *Political Education: National Policy Comes of Age*. New York: Teacher's College Press, 2004.

Manna, Paul. *School's In: Federalism and the National Education Agenda*. Washington, DC: Georgetown University Press, 2006.

Marris, Peter, and Martin Rein. *Dilemmas of Social Reform: Poverty and Community Action in the United States*. Chicago: University of Chicago Press, 1973.

Marschall, Melissa, and Para Shah. "Keeping Policy Churn off the Agenda: Urban Education and Civic Capacity." *Policy Studies Journal* 33, 2(2005): 161–180.

Mathis, William J. "No Child Left Behind Costs and Benefit." *Phi Delta Kappan* (2003): 679–686.

McGuinn, Patrick. *Creating Cover and Constructing Capacity: Assessing the Origins, Evolution, and Impact of Race to the Top*. Education Stimulus Watch, Special Report 6. Washington, DC: American Enterprise Institute, 2010.

McGuinn, Patrick. *No Child Left Behind and the Transformation of Federal Education Policy, 1965–2005*. Lawrence: University Press of Kansas, 2006.

Mead, Sara. "Restructured Usually Means Little Has Changed." *Education Next*, Winter (2007): 52–56.

Medina, Jennifer. "Backers of Mayoral School Control Face Resistance." *New York Times*, January 29, 2009, A21.

Meier, Deborah. *In Schools We Trust: Creating Communities of Learning in an Era of Testing and Standardization*. Boston: Beacon, 2003.

Meier, Deborah. *The Power of Their Ideas: Lessons for America from a Small School in Harlem*. Boston: Beacon, 1995.

Menefee-Libey, David J. "Systemic Reform in a Federated System: Los Angeles at the Turn of the Millennium." *Education Policy Analysis Archives* 12, 60(2004).

Menefee-Libey, David J., Benjamin Diehl, Keena Lipsitz, and Nadia Rahimtoola. "The Historic Separation of Schools from City Politics." *Education and Urban Society* 29, 4(1997): 453–473.

Mettler, Suzanne. "Bringing the State Back in to Civic Engagement: Policy Feedback Effects of the G.I. Bill for World War II Veterans." *American Political Science Review* 96, 2(2002): 351–365.

Mettler, Suzanne, and Joe Soss. "The Consequences of Public Policy for Democratic Citizenship: Bridging Policy Studies and Mass Politics." *Perspectives on Politics* 2, 1(2004): 55–73.

Meyer, Peter. "New York City's Education Battles." *Education Next* 8, 2(2008): 11–20.

Millot, Marc D. "Leveraging the Market to Scale Up School Improvement Programs: A Fee-for-Service Primer for Foundations and Nonprofits." In *Expanding the Reach of Education Reforms: Perspectives from Leaders in the Scale-Up of Educational Interventions*, eds. Thomas K. Glennan Jr., Susan J. Bodilly, Jolene R. Galegher, and Kerri A. Kerr. Santa Monica, CA: RAND, 2004.

Mintrom, Michael, and Sandra Vergari. "Foundation Engagement in Education Policymaking: Assessing Philanthropic Support of School Choice Initiatives." Los Angeles: Center on Philanthropy and Public Policy, 2003.

Mollenkopf, John H. *The Contested City*. Princeton, NJ: Princeton University Press, 1983.

Mrozowski, Jennifer. "DPS Manager to Earn $344K." *Detroit News*, March 3, 2009.

Murphy, Katy. "Oakland School District: Is It Better Off after the State Takeover?" *Oakland Tribune*, March 26, 2010.

Murphy, Katy. "Oakland's Small Schools Movement, 10 Years Later." *Oakland Tribune*, May 5, 2009.

Nakamura, David. "Fenty Gets School Reform Tips from Bloomberg." *Washington Post*, October 17, 2006, B4.

National Association of State Budget Officers. *State Expenditure Report, Fiscal Year 2006*. Washington, DC: NASBO, 2007.

The National Commission on Excellence in Education. *A Nation at Risk: The Imperative for Educational Reform*. April 26, 1983.

Orr, Marion. *Black Social Capitol: The Politics of School Reform in Baltimore 1986–1998*. Lawrence: University of Kansas Press, 1999.

Otterman, Sharon. "Judge Blocks Closing of 19 New York City Schools." *New York Times*, March 26, 2010, A1.

Otterman, Sharon. "Pilot Program of Teacher Bonuses Is Suspended." *New York Times*, January 21, 2011, A23.

Otterman, Sharon, and Jennifer Medina. "Boos and Personal Attacks as City Panel Prepares to Vote on School Closings." *New York Times*, January 27, 2010, A21.

Patashnik, Eric M. *Reforms at Risk: What Happens after Major Policy Changes Are Enacted*. Princeton, NJ: Princeton University Press, 2008.

Paulson, Amanda. "The Schoolhouses That Gates Built." *Christian Science Monitor*, December 7, 2004.

"PDK/Gallup Poll of the Public's Attitudes Toward Public Schools." *Phi Delta Kappan* (2010).

"PDK/Gallup Poll of the Public's Attitudes Toward Public Schools." *Phi Delta Kappan* (2002).

"PDK/Gallup Poll of the Public's Attitudes Toward Public Schools." *Phi Delta Kappan* (2000).

Peters, Jeremy. "Schools Chief Has Much in Common with Boss." *New York Times*, November 10, 2010, A28.

Petrilli, Michael J. "Testing the Limits of NCLB." *Education Next* (2007).

Petrovich, Janice. *A Foundation Returns to School: Strategies for Improving Public Education*. New York: Ford Foundation, 2008.

Pierson, Paul. When Effect Becomes Cause: Policy Feedback and Political Change. *World Politics* 45 (1993): 595–628.

Portz, John, Lana Stein, and Robin R. Jones. *City Schools and City Politics: Institutions and Leadership in Pittsburgh, Boston, and St. Louis*. Lawrence: University of Kansas Press, 1999.

Quigley, John M. *A Decent Home: Housing Policy in Perspective*. Brookings-Wharton Papers on Urban Affairs. Washington, DC: Brookings Institution Press, 2000.

Raftery, Judith Rosenberg. *Land of Fair Promise: Politics and Reform in Los Angeles Schools, 1885–1941*. Palo Alto, CA: Stanford University Press, 1992.

Ravitch, Diane. *The Death and Life of the Great American School System: How Testing and Choice Are Undermining Education*. New York: Basic Books, 2010.

Ravitch, Diane. *The Great School Wars*. New York: Basic Books, 1974.

Ravitch, Diane. "We Shouldn't Pay Kids To Learn." *Forbes*, October 17, 2008.

Ready, Douglas D., Valerie E. Lee, and Kevin G. Welner. "Educational Equity and School Structure: School Size, Overcrowding, and Schools-within-Schools." *Teachers College Record* 106, 10(2004): 1989–2014.

Reckhow, Sarah. "Disseminating and Legitimating a New Approach: The Role of Foundations." In *Between Public and Private: Politics, Governance, and the New Portfolio Models for Urban School Reform*, eds. Katrina E. Bulkey, Jeffrey R. Henig, and Henry M. Levin. Cambridge, MA: Harvard Education Press, 2010.

Rich, Wilbur C. *Black Mayors and School Politics: The Failure of Reform in Detroit, Gary, and Newark*. New York: Garland, 1996.

Robelen, Erik W. "Gates Learns to Think Big." *Education Week*, October 11, 2006.

Robelen, Erik W. "Grantmakers Seeking to Influence Policy." *Education Week*, December 8, 2010.

Rubin, Joel. "L.A. Charter Schools Are Investment Grade to Broad." *Los Angeles Times*, May 24, 2007.

Russo, Alexander. *Stray Dogs, Saints, and Saviors: Fighting for the Soul of America's Toughest High School*. San Francisco, CA: Jossey-Bass, 2011.

Schneider, Anne, and Helen Ingram. *Policy Design for Democracy*. Lawrence: University of Kansas Press, 1997.

Scott, Janelle. "The Politics of Venture Philanthropy in Charter School Policy and Advocacy." *Educational Policy* 23, 1(2009): 106–136.

Segal, Lydia. "The Pitfalls of Political Decentralization and Proposals for Reform: The Case of New York City Public Schools." *Public Administration Review* 57, 2(1997): 141–149.

Sharp, Elaine. *Does Local Government Matter? How Urban Policies Shape Civic Engagement*. Minneapolis: University of Minnesota Press, 2012.

Sharp, Elaine. "Local Government, Social Programs, and Political Participation: A Test of Policy-Centered Theory." *State & Local Government Review*, 41, 3(2009): 182–192.

Shen, Francis X., Kenneth K. Wong, and Michael T. Hartney. "The Politics of Mayoral Support for School Choice." Paper presented at the annual meeting of the American Political Science Association, Washington, DC, 2010.

Shipps, Dorothy. *School Reform, Corporate Style: Chicago, 1880–2000*. Lawrence: University of Kansas Press, 2006.

Sidney, Mara. *Unfair Housing*. Lawrence: University of Kansas Press, 2003.

Sigelman, Lee, and Langche Zeng. "Analyzing Censored and Sample-Selected Data with Tobit and Heckit Models." *Political Analysis* 8, 2(1999): 167–182.

Skocpol, Theda. *Protecting Soldiers and Mothers: The Political Origins of Social Policy in United States.* Cambridge, MA: Belknap Press of Harvard University Press, 1992.

Skrentny, John D. *The Minority Rights Revolution.* Cambridge, MA: Belknap Press of Harvard University Press, 2002.

Steinhauer, Jennifer. "Los Angeles Mayor Gains Control of the Schools, but Hardly Total Control." *New York Times,* August 31, 2005.

Stephens, David. "President Carter, the Congress, and NEA: Creating the Department of Education." *Political Science Quarterly* 98, 4(1983–1984): 641–663.

Stewart, Nikita, and Paul Schwartzman. "How Adrian Fenty Lost His Reelection Bid for D.C. Mayor." *Washington Post,* September 16, 2010.

Stone, Clarence N. "Civic Capacity and Urban Education." *Urban Affairs Review* 36, 5(2001): 595–619.

Stone, Clarence N., Jeffrey R. Henig, Bryan D. Jones, and Carol Pierannunzi. *Building Civic Capacity: The Politics of Reforming Urban Schools.* Lawrence: University Press of Kansas, 2001.

Strategy and Implementation Report. New York City Center for Economic Opportunity, 2007.

Sugrue, Thomas J. *The Origins of Urban Crisis: Race and Inequality in Postwar Detroit.* Princeton, NJ: Princeton University Press, 2005.

Sunderman, Gail L., and James S. Kim. "The Expansion of Federal Power and the Politics of Implementing the No Child Left Behind Act." *Teachers College Record* 109, 5(2007): 1057–1085.

Swanson, Christopher B., and Janelle Barlage. *Influence: A Study of the Factors Shaping Education Policy.* Bethesda, MD: Editorial Projects in Education Research Center, 2006.

Teles, Steven M. *The Rise of the Conservative Legal Movement: The Battle for Control of the Law.* Princeton, NJ: Princeton University Press, 2008.

Teles, Steven M., and Mark Schmitt. "The Elusive Craft of Evaluating Advocacy." *Stanford Social Innovation Review,* Summer (2011).

Teske, Paul, Mark Schneider, Christine Roch, and Melissa Marschall. "Public School Choice: A Status Report." In *City Schools: Lessons from New York,* eds. Diane Ravitch and Joseph P. Viteritti. Baltimore, MD: Johns Hopkins University Press, 2000.

"The Bridgespan Group." Harvard Business School Case Study. Boston, MA: Harvard Business School Publishing, 2000.

Toch, Thomas. "Sweating the Big Stuff: A Progress Report on the Movement to Scale Up the Nation's Best Charter Schools." 2009. www.thomastoch.com/wp/2009/sweating-the-big-stuff/.

Turque, Bill. "Poll: Polarizing D.C. Schools Chief Rhee Helps, Hurts Fenty among Democrats." *Washington Post,* September 1, 2010.

Turque, Bill. "Rhee Feeling 'Guilt' over Fenty Loss." *Washington Post,* September 15, 2010.

Tyack, David B. *The One Best System: A History of American Urban Education.* Cambridge, MA: Harvard University Press, 1974.

United States Census Bureau. *Census 2000 Gateway.* 2000. www.census.gov/main/www/cen2000.html.

United States Government Accountability Office. *GAO Report on No Child Left Behind.* 2007.

Vaillancourt, Ryan. "Power Play Erupts at $232 Million Arts School." *Los Angeles Downtown News,* March 27, 2009.

Walker, Jack L. *Mobilizing Interest Groups in America: Patrons, Professions, and Social Movements.* Ann Arbor: University of Michigan Press, 1991.

Walters, Pamela Barnhouse, and Emily A. Bowman. "Foundations and the Making of Public Education in the United States: 1867–1950." In *American Foundations: Roles and Contributions,* eds: Helmut K. Anheier and David C. Hammack. Washington, DC: Brookings Institution Press, 2010.

Wechsler, Majorie E., and Linda D. Friedrich. "The Role of Mediating Organizations for School Reform: Independent Agents or District Dependents?" *Journal of Education Policy* 12, 5(1997): 382–401.

Weingarten, Randi. "Mayoral Control 2.0." *New York Post*, May 21, 2009.

Weir, Margaret, Jane Rongerude, and Christopher K. Ansell. "Collaboration Is Not Enough: Virtuous Cycles of Reform in Transportation Policy." *Urban Affairs Review* 44, 4(2009): 455–489.

Williams, Joe. *National Model or Temporary Opportunity? The Oakland Education Reform Story*. Washington, DC: Center for Education Reform, 2007.

Williams, Joe. "The Stealth Schools CEO." *New York Daily News*, November 24, 2002.

Wolff, Jessica. "Shaking Up the School System." *Gotham Gazette*, February 2003.

Wong, Kenneth K., and Francis X. Shen. "When Mayors Lead Urban Schools: Toward Developing a Framework to Assess the Effects of Mayoral Takeover of Urban Districts." Paper presented at the 99th annual meeting of the American Political Science Association, 2003.

Wong, Kenneth K., Francis X. Shen, Dorothea Anagnostopoulos, and Stacey Rutledge. *The Education Mayor: Improving America's Schools*. Washington, DC: Georgetown University Press, 2007.

Zahniser, David, and Joel Rubin. "Mayor Spent Millions on School Board Races." *Los Angeles Times*, August 1, 2007.

Zelon, Helen. "A Matter of Principles: On Training School Chiefs." *City Limits*, May 18, 2008.

Zunz, Olivier. *Philanthropy in America: A History*. Princeton, NJ: Princeton University Press, 2012.

INDEX

Note: Material in tables is indicated by italic page numbers. Endnotes are indicated by n. after the page number.

CPSIA information can be obtained at www.ICGtesting.com
Printed in the USA
BVOW08s0753131115

426913BV00005B/16/P